IMAGES
of America

COLERAIN TOWNSHIP

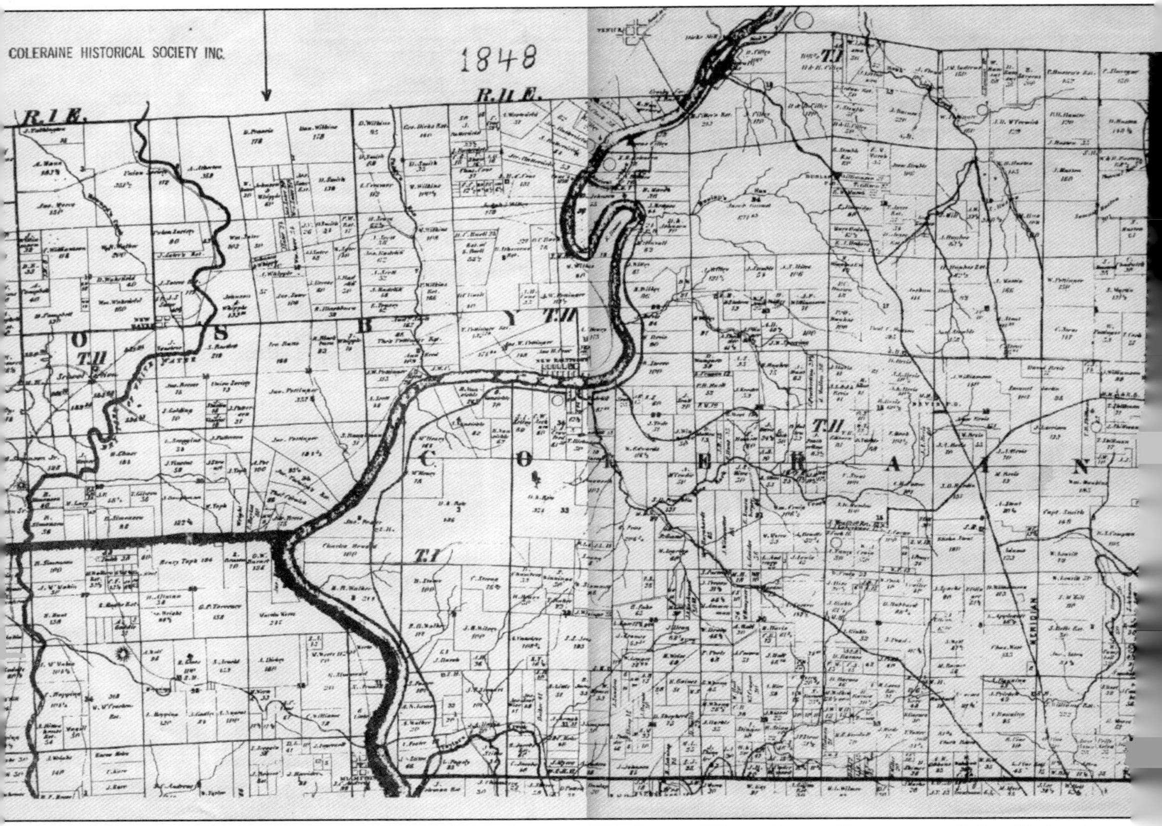

This map from 1848 shows the boundaries of Colerain Township. (Courtesy of the Coleraine Historical Society.)

On the Cover: This is the Hornung Meat Market. This business had a store in Dunlap and also in Hamilton. It is believed this is the Dunlap store. The butchers are very well dressed and ready for customers. (Courtesy of Doug Bevis.)

IMAGES
of America

COLERAIN TOWNSHIP

Frank Scholle and Don Linz

ARCADIA
PUBLISHING

ISBN 978-0-7385-8433-1

Published by Arcadia Publishing
Charleston, South Carolina

Printed in the United States of America

Library of Congress Control Number: 2009940859

For all general information contact Arcadia Publishing at:
Telephone 843-853-2070
Fax 843-853-0044
E-mail sales@arcadiapublishing.com
For customer service and orders:
Toll-Free 1-888-313-2665

Visit us on the Internet at www.arcadiapublishing.com

To Colerain Township, Betty Scholle, and Rose Linz with heartfelt thanks.

CONTENTS

ACKNOWLEDGMENTS

We would like to thank all the Colerain Township residents and former residents who have been so forthcoming with photographs, information, and stories about Colerain. Without their help, this book would not be possible.

We would like to thank the Coleraine Historical Society, especially Mary Burdette, president; Dennis Haskamp, archivist; and John Torok, trustee. Mel Blust, Bob Muehlenhard, and district chief Darrell Brown of the Colerain Township Fire Department; Jerry Koch of Keystone Printing; photo specialist Fawn Thomas, and so many other people contributed in so many ways to make everything fall into place. All reasonable efforts were made to name contributing sources.

We want to thank Ruth J. Wells, the first president of the Coleraine Historical Society, Colerain historian, and editor of the *Coleraine Pageant*, the monthly publication of the society. Her book, *Colerain Township Revisited*, which was published in 1994, the bicentennial of the township, provided invaluable historic information about Colerain.

Gravestone Inscriptions and Cemetery Records of Colerain Township, Ohio, 1794–1994 was recorded and compiled by Bailey Stewart Rogers and arranged and edited by Linda Ruedenauer Ebersole. This book provided immense information for our book.

A thank-you to our wives, Betty Scholle and Rose Linz, for their understanding during the long process of producing this book. In endeavors like this, support from all sides is an important factor. Without it, we could not have accomplished our goal.

A huge thank-you to the Coleraine Historical Society, which was founded in 1964. It is a nonprofit organization whose purpose is to acquire and preserve the historical materials, knowledge, and artifacts of Colerain Township, the largest township and one of the oldest (1794) in the State of Ohio.

The society hosts meetings for members and guests on the third Wednesday of each month at 7:30 p.m. at the Colerain Senior Center at 4300 Springdale Road. They have guest speakers every other month on historical topics, some of whom dress in period costumes. The society encourages interested individuals to attend meetings and visit their Web site (colerainehistorical.org), or you can contact the webmaster at CHSinfo@fuse.net or write to them at: The Coleraine Historical Society, P.O. Box 53726, Colerain Township, Ohio, 45253.

Introduction

Colerain Township predated our state government. The size and shape of the township was determined by the congressional acts establishing the various land grants. As the Ohio territory became populated, it was only natural that the surveyed townships should become the basic unit of local government. In 1803, the elected officials of a township consisted of three trustees, a clerk, two overseers of the poor, and a sufficient number of supervisors of highways, in addition to two justices of the peace; these officials registered brands and fulfilled the needs of local government.

Colerain Township, one of the largest and oldest townships in the state, was created in 1794 by the court of general quarter sessions of the peace. In 1803, Ohio became a state, and the township boundaries were defined to include the western tier of sections in the Springfield Township, the northwestern section of the Mill Creek Township, and the three easternmost sections of the northern tier of the Green Township. To illustrate, Mount Healthy, west of Hamilton Pike, was a part of Colerain Township at this time. This boundary remained for 25 or more years.

The earliest settlement was Fort Coleraine (this is the source of the township's name) established by John Dunlap in 1790 and was commonly known as Dunlap's Station. Dunlap was one of John Cleves Symmes's surveyors and a native of Coleraine, Ireland. Another station was established by John Campbell around 1795, probably opposite Miamitown on the east bank of the Great Miami River. There is not much information known on this establishment. All traces of the first Village of Coleraine have disappeared. It was situated on the bend of the Miami, several miles below the bridge to Ross.

A second Colerain was started just above the (Venice) Ross Bridge. In 1819, David Stone of New Hampshire built a cotton mill in Colerain where Toad Creek enters the Great Miami (on River Road, just east of its intersection with Colerain Avenue). In 1821, this was sold to Giles Richards and Timothy Goodman. A gristmill and a sawmill were built. A tavern and dye house were also added, and a thriving town grew here. The cotton mill later became Matson's Woolen Mill. This village virtually vanished by 1875, and nothing remains to mark its location today.

The Village of Bevis was established by Jesse Bevis on the early Colerain Avenue around 1816. When the new turnpike was built, leaving the line of the old road, he relocated it about a quarter of a mile or so west of its original site. In 1835, Bevis was given a post office and Jesse Bevis was named postmaster; he was replaced by James A. Bevis in 1861.

Groesbeck was founded as West Union sometime later. It was named for Charles West, a Methodist lay preacher who gave land for a church named for him, and the union of the Olive Branch and Asbury Methodist congregations. The name was changed to Groesbeck in 1857 with the advent of the postal service. There was already a West Union in Ohio, making a name change necessary.

Georgetown (Dunlap) was laid out in 1829 at the junction of Colerain Avenue and Kemper Road (an early road connecting Springfield Pike and Colerain Avenue). A post office was established in 1837 with David Wallace as postmaster.

Pleasant Run was named for the nearby stream and was located on the east line of the township, about a half mile south of the Butler County line. James Huston was the postmaster in 1846, and Paul Huston took over in 1856. An early hotel, Farmer's Rest, was located here on the Hamilton Turnpike.

Taylor's Creek is a small community east of Miamitown and the Great Miami River. It is located on the Harrison Turnpike. John A. Davis became its first postmaster in 1857. Later the post office was moved into the Althaus store.

Barnesburg is a village that straggled along the Blue Rock turnpike. It was named for early settlers in the area—the Barnes family—who came from Kentucky in the early 1800s. The post office was located in the tavern and store of Alois Jutzi in 1874. Only its name remains today because of highway construction, which moved the old road and created a new road.

Another little village on the Blue Rock turnpike was Creedville, located in the area where Blue Rock turnpike and Cheviot Roads came together. A tollhouse for the Blue Rock turnpike was located at the point where Hanley Road joins it. The tollhouse also housed a store and post office.

It is very noticeable that all the villages were found on the turnpikes. There were three in the township. The earliest turnpike (Colerain) bisected the township from north to south. The Harrison turnpike skirted along the southern edge, while the other turnpike (Hamilton) was found on parts of the eastern line of the township.

Colerain Township has experienced phenomenal growth since World War II. In 1910, Colerain had a population of just over 3,800 residents, not enough residents to have its own post office. The township was primarily a farming community. By 1950, the population had almost doubled to 7,500. From 1960 to 1980, the population grew to almost 57,000. This growth also prompted the building of many subdivisions and the selling of many farms that had been in families for years. Colerain now has about 63,000 residents, more than many cities in the State of Ohio.

The earlier settlers would not even recognize the area, which is now home to several shopping centers, major businesses, and modern highways, which have replaced the old mud and gravel roads where very few, if any, curbs and sidewalks would have been found. Today interstate highways cross the township, making travel to almost anywhere easy for the motorist.

Many of the old roads were named for early settlers and carry with them the bond of the township's historic past. Many of the old villages are still identified by their location even though the old buildings are gone and perhaps their roads relocated. The pioneering sprit that was evident in 1794 is still present today in an updated fashion.

One

Pioneering the Future

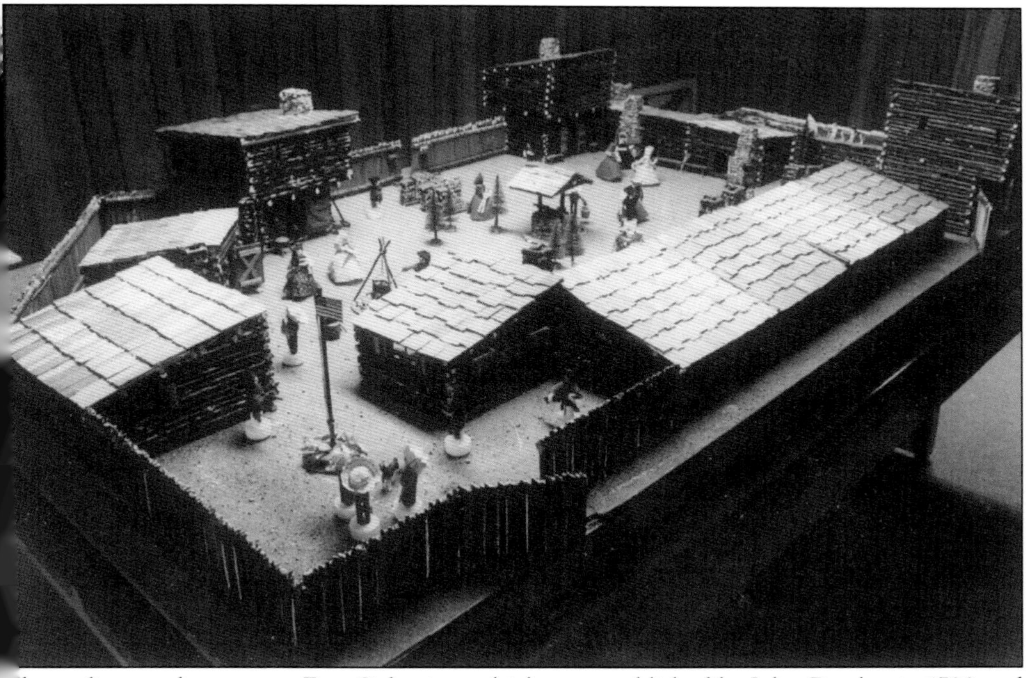

'he earliest settlement was Fort Coleraine, which was established by John Dunlap in 1790 and ›mmonly called Dunlap's Station. The source of the township's name came from this area. It as located on the bend of the Great Miami River, several miles below the present bridge to oss, Ohio. Dunlap was the farthest settlement from any militia assistance at Fort Washington Hamilton County. John Dunlap, along with 11 families, built a remote frontier defense ;ainst Native American attack. The fort, or Dunlap's Station, sustained a brutal attack by ative Americans in 1791. The model pictured was made by Bob Muehlenhard. The model took 'er two years to complete and has been shown at various schools and museums. (Courtesy of ›b Muehlenhard.)

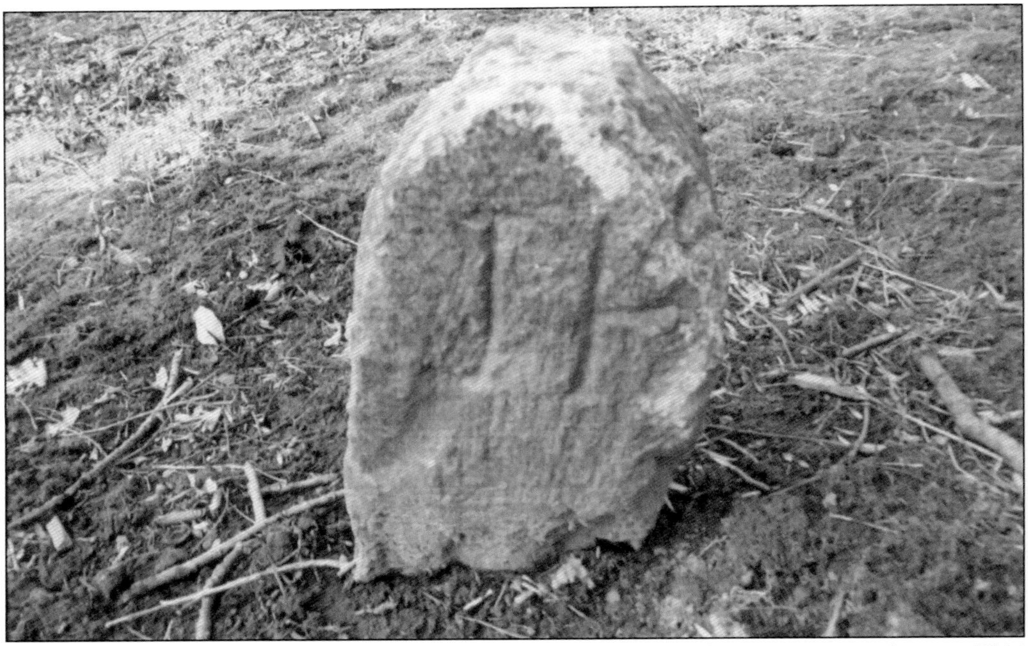

This is part of a tiny plot of land on the east side of Harrison Pike, up a private drive at 7544 Harrison Pike. Off to the right is the site of a pioneer cemetery. It is the Foster Cemetery where the graves of early settlers of the Colerain Township are found. A crude, homemade tombstone marked only with the initials I. P. marks the grave of Issac Polk, a revolutionary soldier and early schoolteacher who died on December 23, 1831. (Courtesy of Don Linz.)

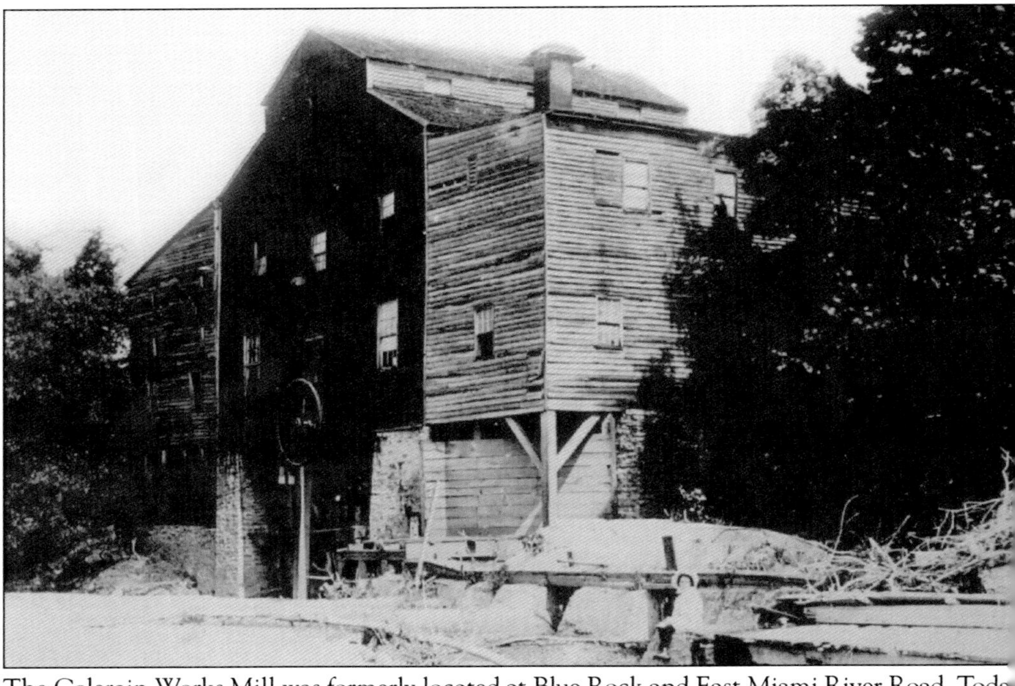

The Colerain Works Mill was formerly located at Blue Rock and East Miami River Road. Toda this is the site of the new Blue Rock bridge. (Courtesy of the Coleraine Historical Society.)

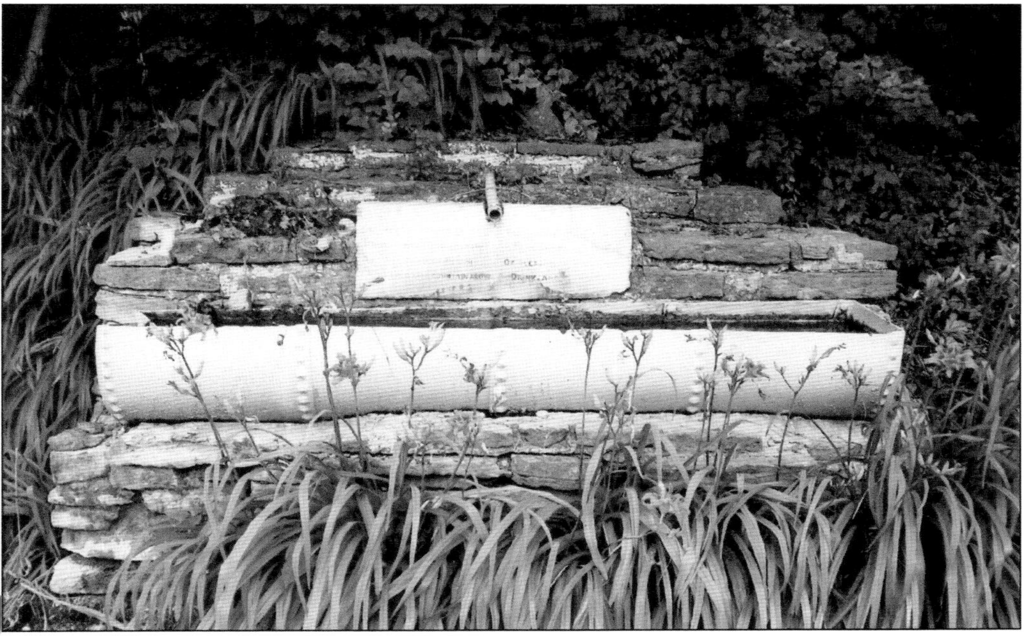

A unique watering trough given to the township by Giles Richards can be seen on old Colerain Avenue. The trough is a half of the old iron rollers that were used to build the Colerain turnpike. "A. D. 1867" is engraved on the face of the two marble slabs just above the trough with an inscription from the John Greenleaf Whittier poem, "On a Fountain: For Dorothea L. Dix."

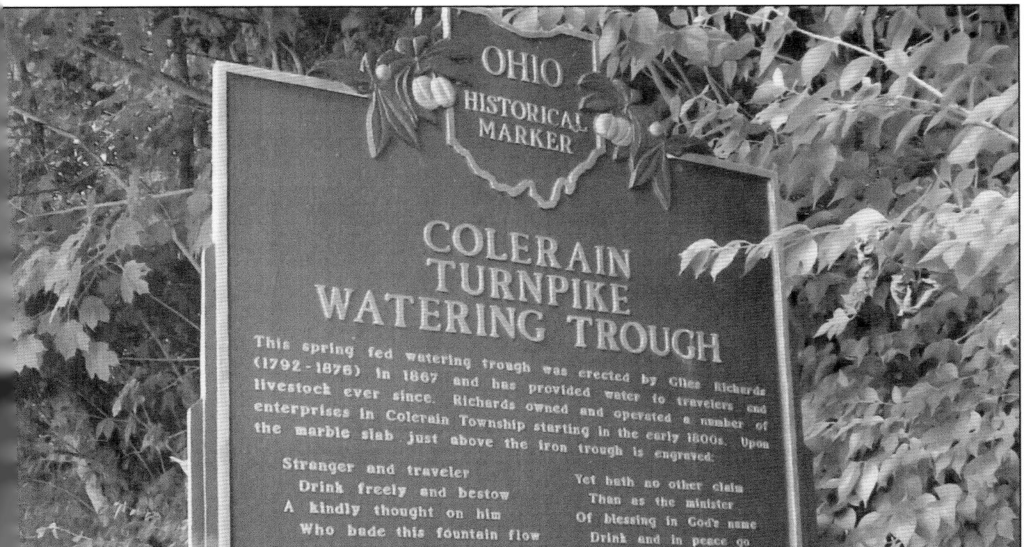

ere is the Ohio marker at the site. Whittier's poem reads, "*Stranger and Traveler / Drink freely* *d bestow / A kindly thought on him / Who bade this fountain flow. / Yet hath no other claim / Than* *the minister / Of blessing in God's name / Drink and in peace go.*" (Courtesy of Don Linz.)

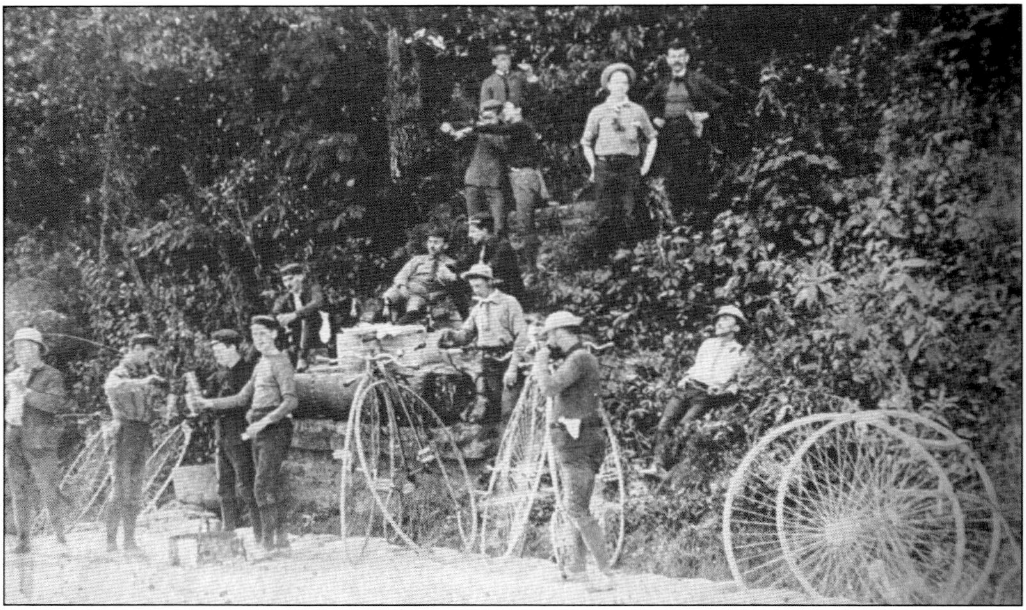

This is an undated photograph of a Brighton Cycling Club outing. It was probably taken in the late 1870s or early 1880s when these high-wheel or ordinary bicycles enjoyed a brief popularity. The ordinary bicycle was introduced to America at the Philadelphia Bicentennial Exposition in 1876 but quickly became obsolete when the safety bicycle was introduced in the mid–1880s. (Courtesy of the Coleraine Historical Society.)

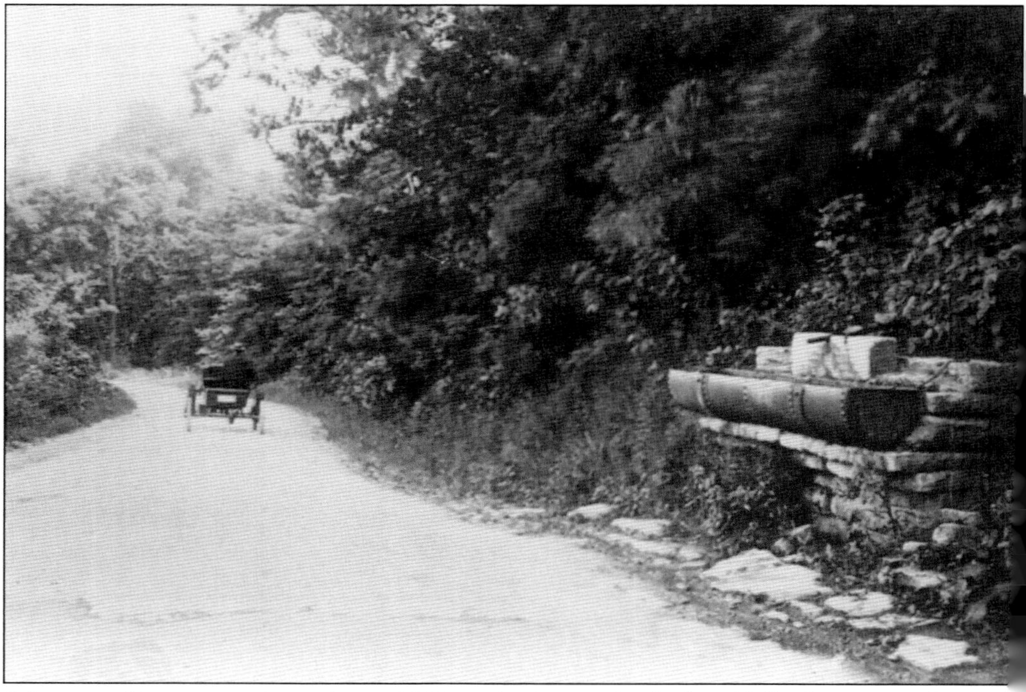

A horse and buggy travels south on old Colerain Avenue in the late 1800s. It is pictured passin the Giles Richards water trough. (Courtesy of Dan Kinne.)

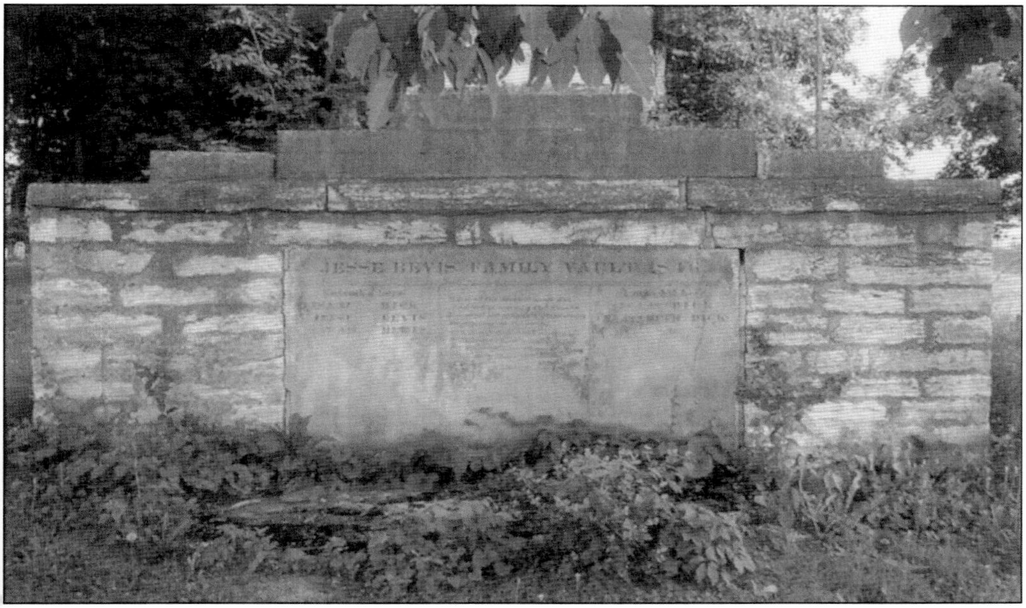

The Bevis Cedar Grove Cemetery was first opened in 1870 and is the largest old cemetery in the township. Jesse Bevis and many members of his family are buried here. Bevis, for whom the cemetery was named, was an early postmaster in the township, and a post office was located in the large frame building he built in 1818 that also housed a general store, tavern, and hotel. (Courtesy of Don Linz.)

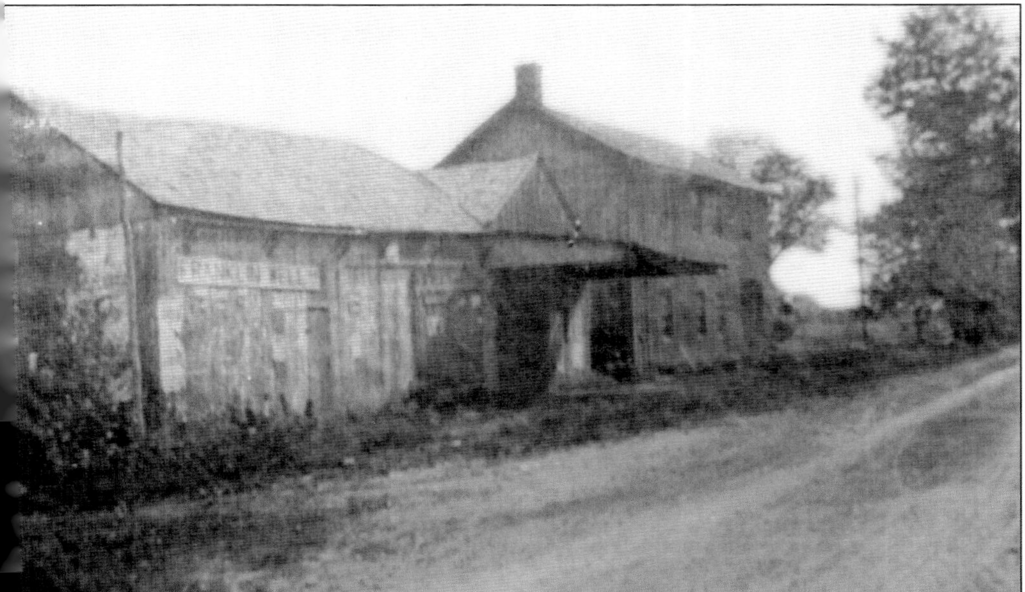

'ater was a major concern for early township residents. Jesse Bevis, one of the early settlers of olerain, and his sons dug a well next to an old blacksmith shop. The well was 20 feet across and some) feet deep. It was located at the southeast corner of Colerain Avenue and Bevis Lane. The well as named in honor of Benjamin Franklin. (Courtesy of the Coleraine Historical Society.)

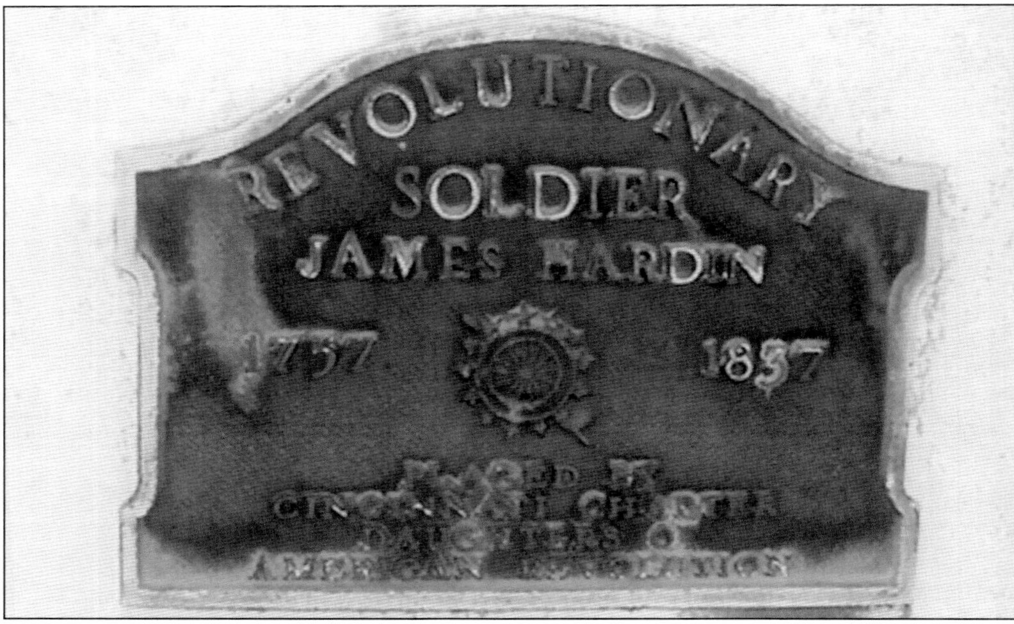

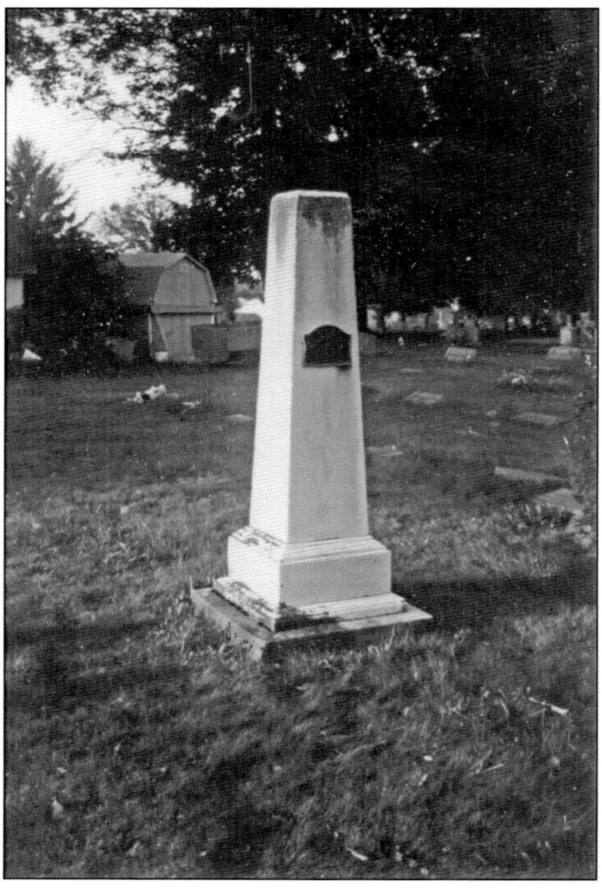

Revolutionary War soldier James Hardin was a Colerain Township pioneer. In the early 1800s, he built a home from hewn logs on Springdale Road. His home was used as a voting station during the presidential election of Thomas Jefferson. (Courtesy of Don Linz.)

James Hardin was buried in the Hardin family cemetery located on his Springdale Road property. In 1937, his body was moved to the Bevis Cemetery on Colerain Avenue. At one time, Hardin served as treasurer of Colerain Township. (Courtesy of Don Linz.)

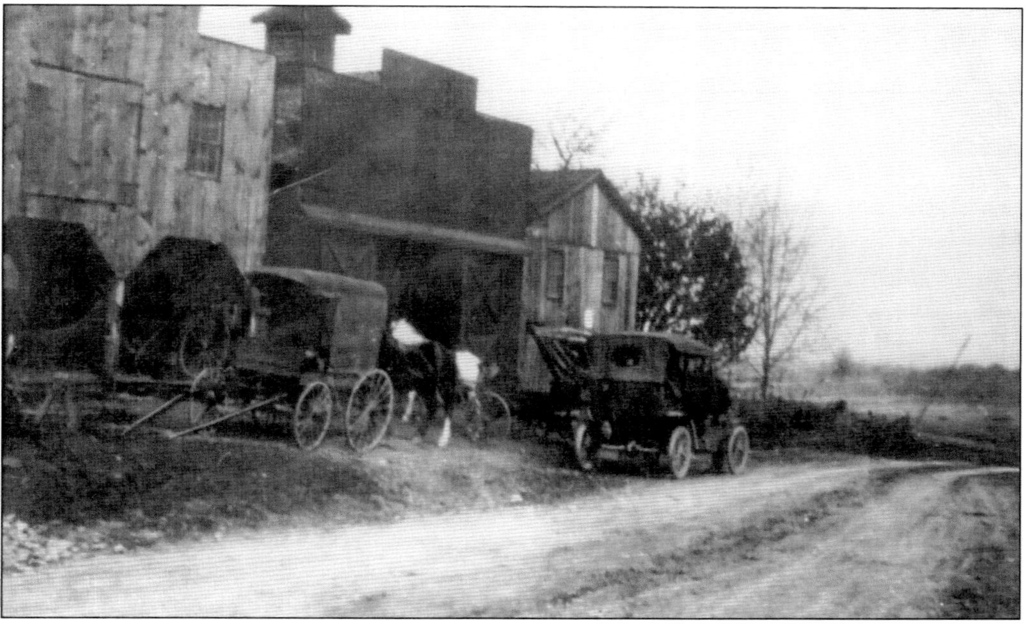

The Frey Wagon Works was one of the many wagon and blacksmith shops throughout Colerain Township. The shop was located on Springdale Road opposite the Gaines Road intersection. During the Civil War, Morgan's Raiders passed through the area and, at gunpoint, forced the Freys to shoe their horses. With the advent of the automobile, there was a marked decline in business. Recognizing the changing times, William Frey, the eldest son of Elias Frey, opened a garage just a few miles away in White Oak. (Courtesy of the Coleraine Historical Society.)

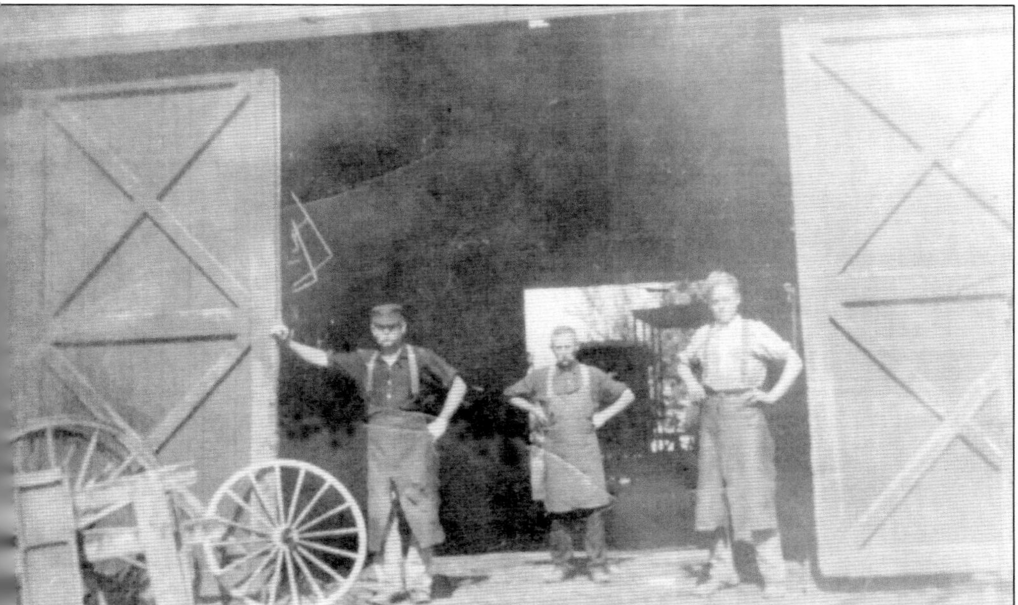

ctured here are the workers of the Frey Wagon Works blacksmith shop. From left to right e Elias Frey, his brother Louis, and Elias's son William Frey. (Courtesy of the Coleraine istorical Society.)

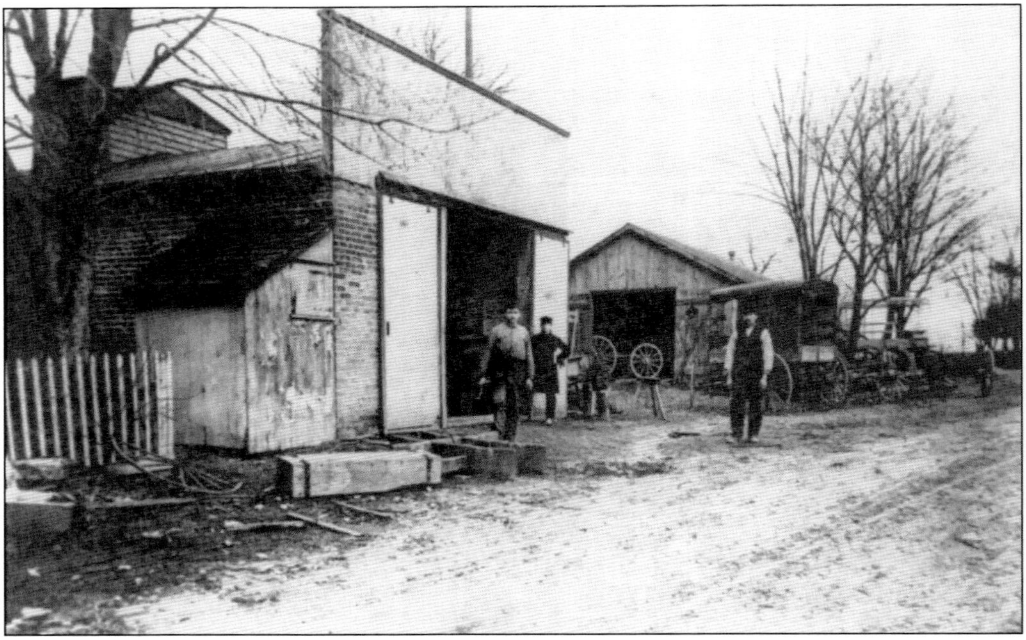

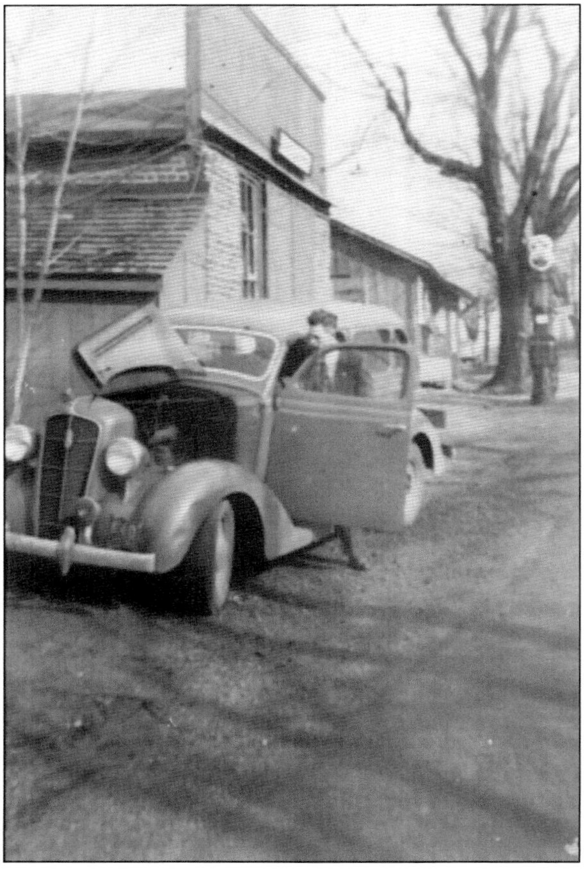

Here is a picture of George Gaiser's Pioneer Blacksmith Shop. It was located on the east side of Blue Rock Road, just north of Livingston Road, next to his home. The building still stands but has been modified through the years. His half brother, John Gaiser, had his shop on Colerain Avenue where the Red Carpet Motel is located. He was in business in the late 1800s and early 1900s. (Courtesy of the Coleraine Historical Society.)

This car apparently needed help, so it stopped in front of Gaiser's old blacksmith shop on Blue Rock Road, north of Livingston. This garage serviced automobiles when horses were no longer used as they once were. Notice the old gas pumps. (Courtesy of Mel Blust.)

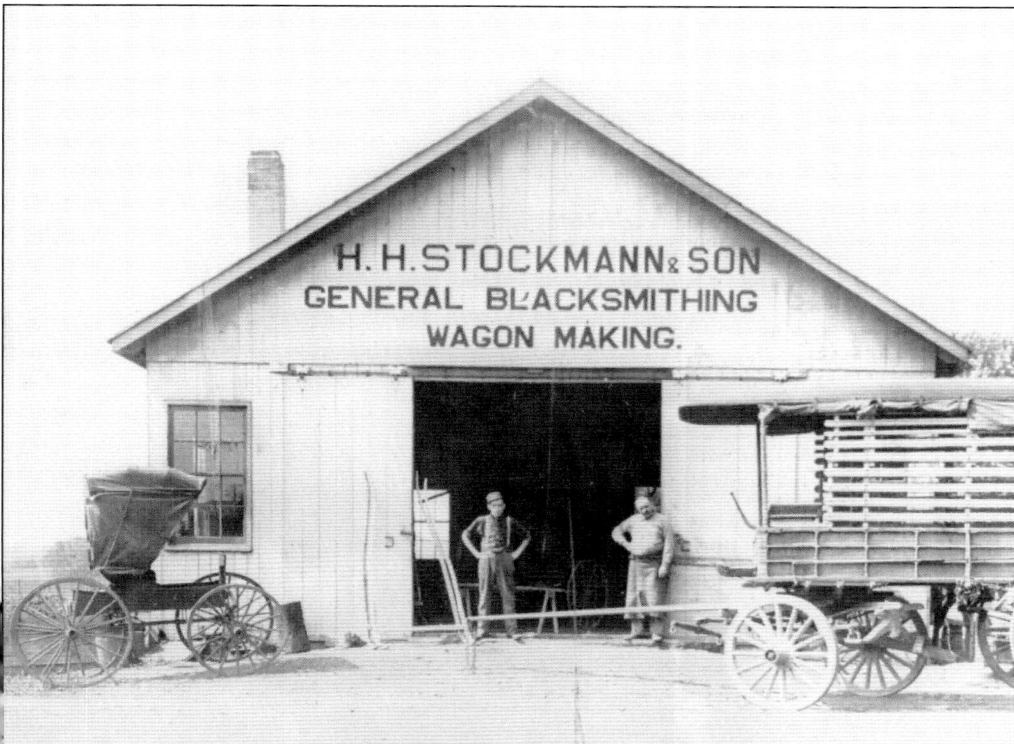

H. H. Stockmann & Son General Blacksmithing and Wagon Making was located on the southwest :orner of Colerain Avenue and Galbraith Road in the late 1800s. The charge for shoeing a horse was $1 for four shoes. (Courtesy of the Coleraine Historical Society.)

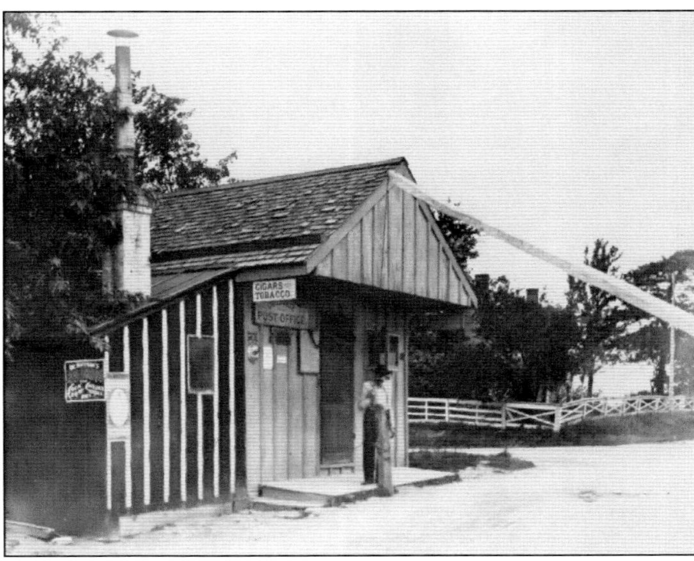

'his old building was ›cated at the corner of ›lue Rock and Hanley ›oads and has an ıteresting history. It was ›sed as a tollhouse, and mil Gutzwiller operated general store in the uilding. Believed to have ›een built in 1840, it was so used as the Creedville ›st Office until 1905. ;ourtesy of the Coleraine istorical Society.)

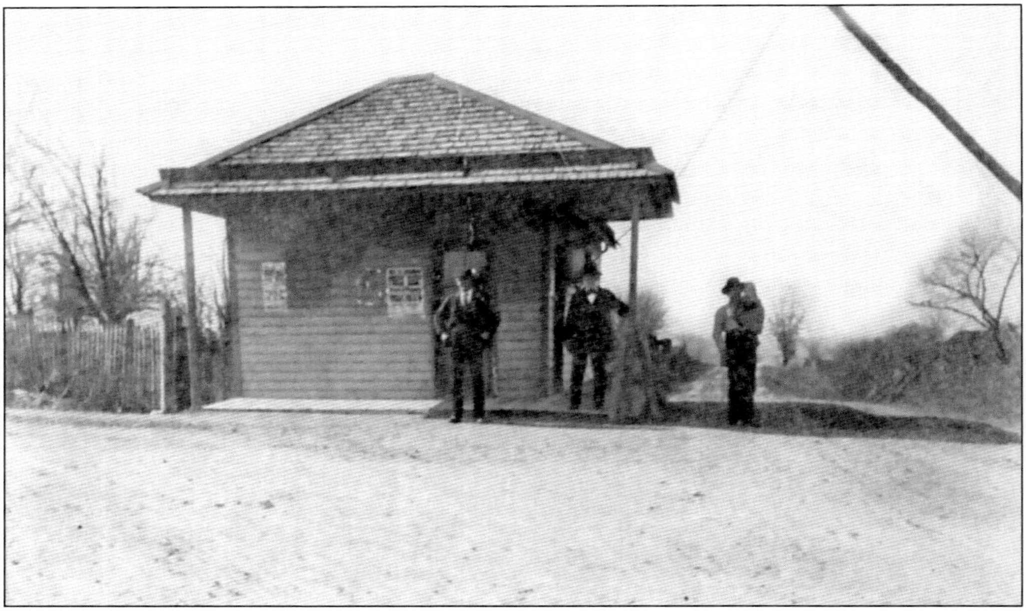

This old tollhouse was located on the northwest corner of Springdale and Blue Rock Roads. Many roads were owned by private individuals or companies, and a fee was charged to use these roads. The money was used to maintain the roads and to pay workers. The tollhouse was a small building with a bar or tollgate that was raised so motorists could travel the road to the next tollhouse. The tollhouses were normally about 5 miles apart. (Courtesy of the Coleraine Historical Society.)

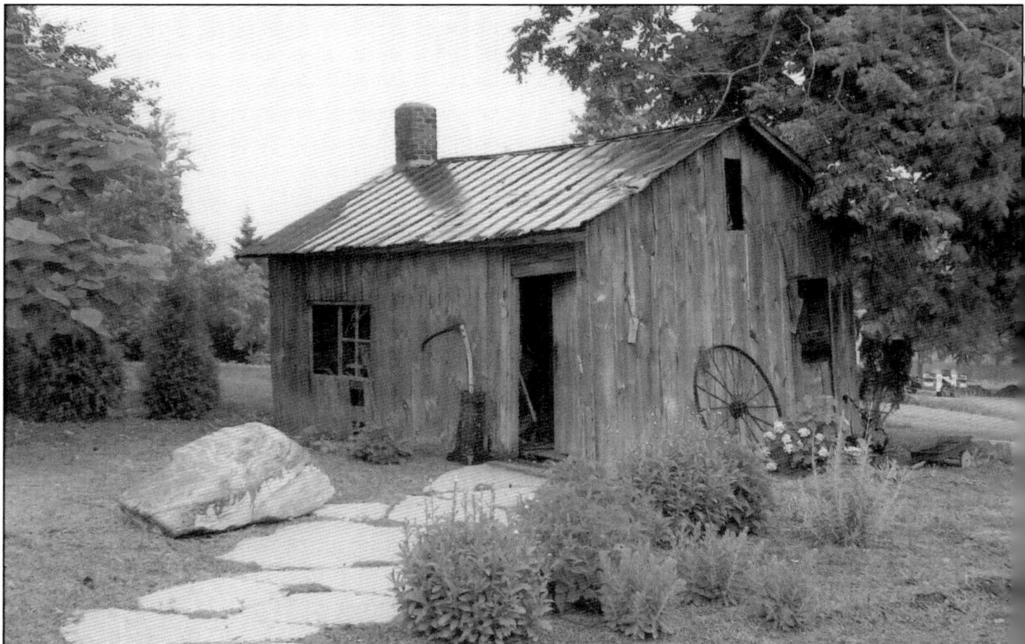

This weather-beaten frame building on the east side of Cheviot Road near the United Dair Farmers store is rumored to have been used as a recruiting station for the North during the Civ War. (Courtesy of Don Linz.)

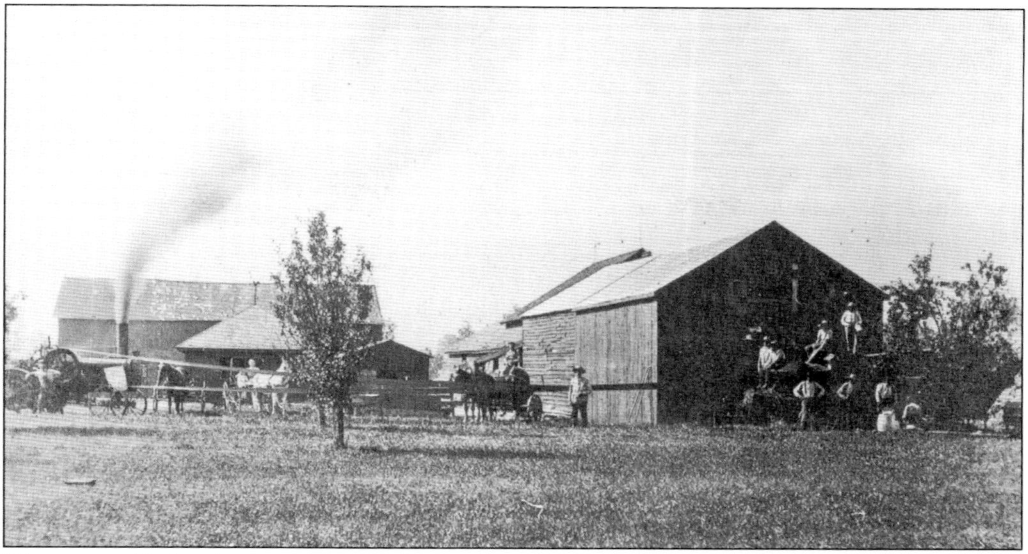

This is an old threshing machine that was used on the sheaves of wheat on farms in Colerain Township. Note that the steam engine is placed upwind from the thresher. The steam engine required water, and a water wagon was a necessary part of threshing. The water wagon can be seen in the center of the picture. It took about 10 men for this kind of operation. The ladies always prepared food for the hungry workers. (Courtesy of Bob Muehlenhard.)

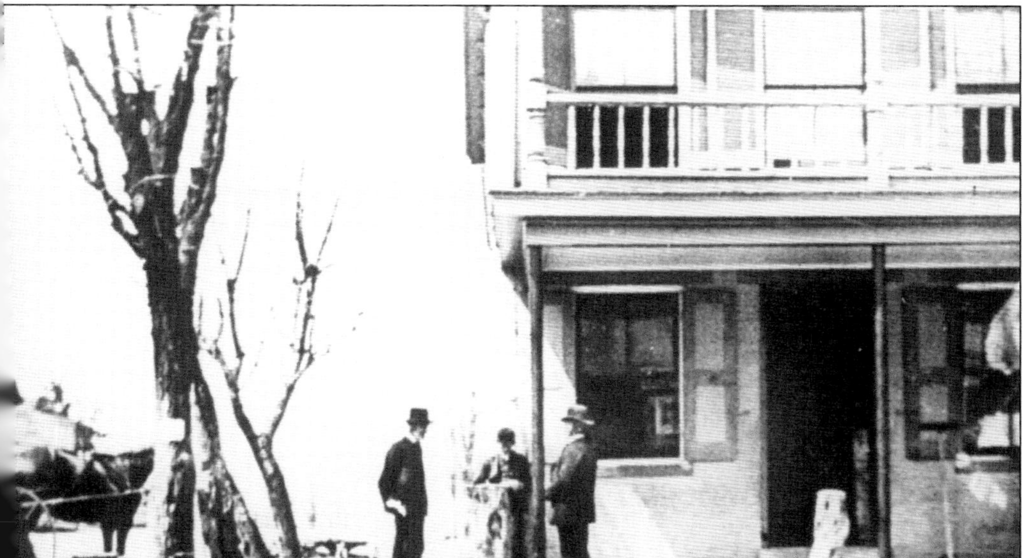

ne of the earliest doctors in Colerain Township was Dr. Alexander B. Luce. He lived at 3218 ompton Road. His home was a station along the Underground Railroad. Gen. John Hunt Morgan d his Morgan's Raiders are also said to have stopped at Luce's home to get water for the men d their horses. That is the good doctor in the top hat on the left, standing on Compton Road Mount Healthy. (Courtesy of the Coleraine Historical Society.)

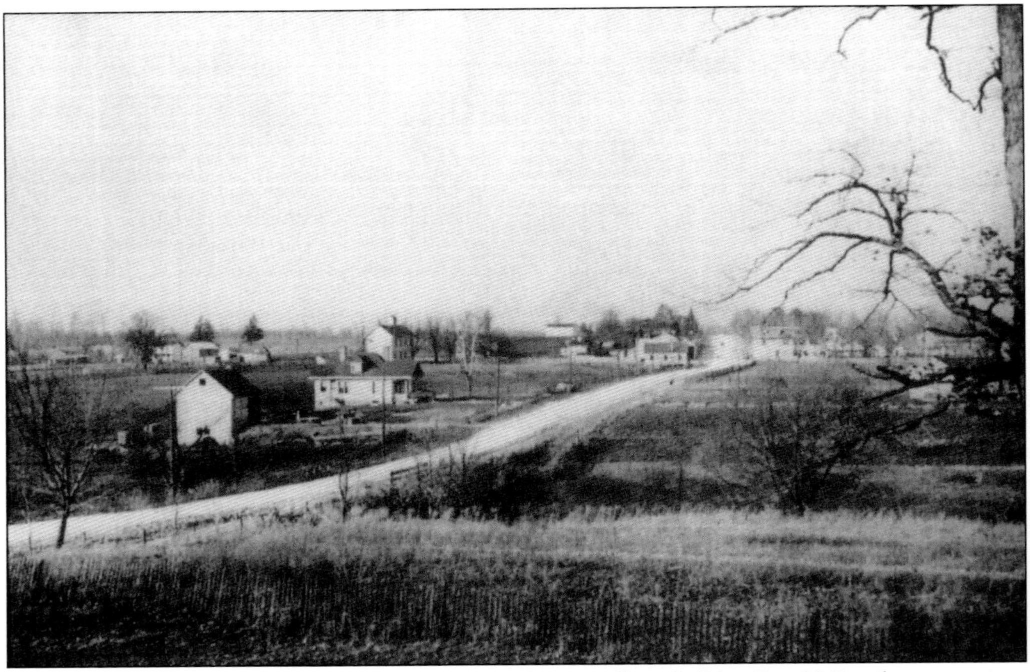

This is looking north on Colerain Avenue toward the Galbraith (Van Zandt) Road intersection. In the lower left center is a barn, which is presently the Wedge Inn. In the middle left is the old Groesbeck School. (Courtesy of Richard Huber.)

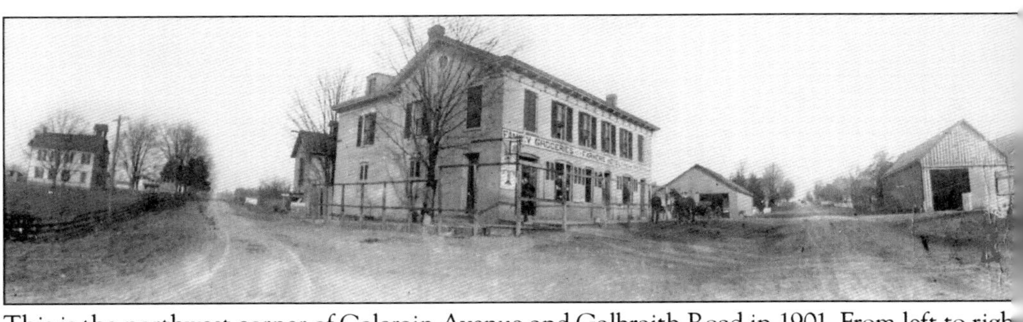

This is the northwest corner of Colerain Avenue and Galbraith Road in 1901. From left to righ are the old Groesbeck school, Galbraith Road (then known as Van Zandt Road); Wiesenhahn hotel, grocery, and holding barn; Colerain Avenue; Luichinger's hotel and holding barn. (Courtes of Ray Finke.)

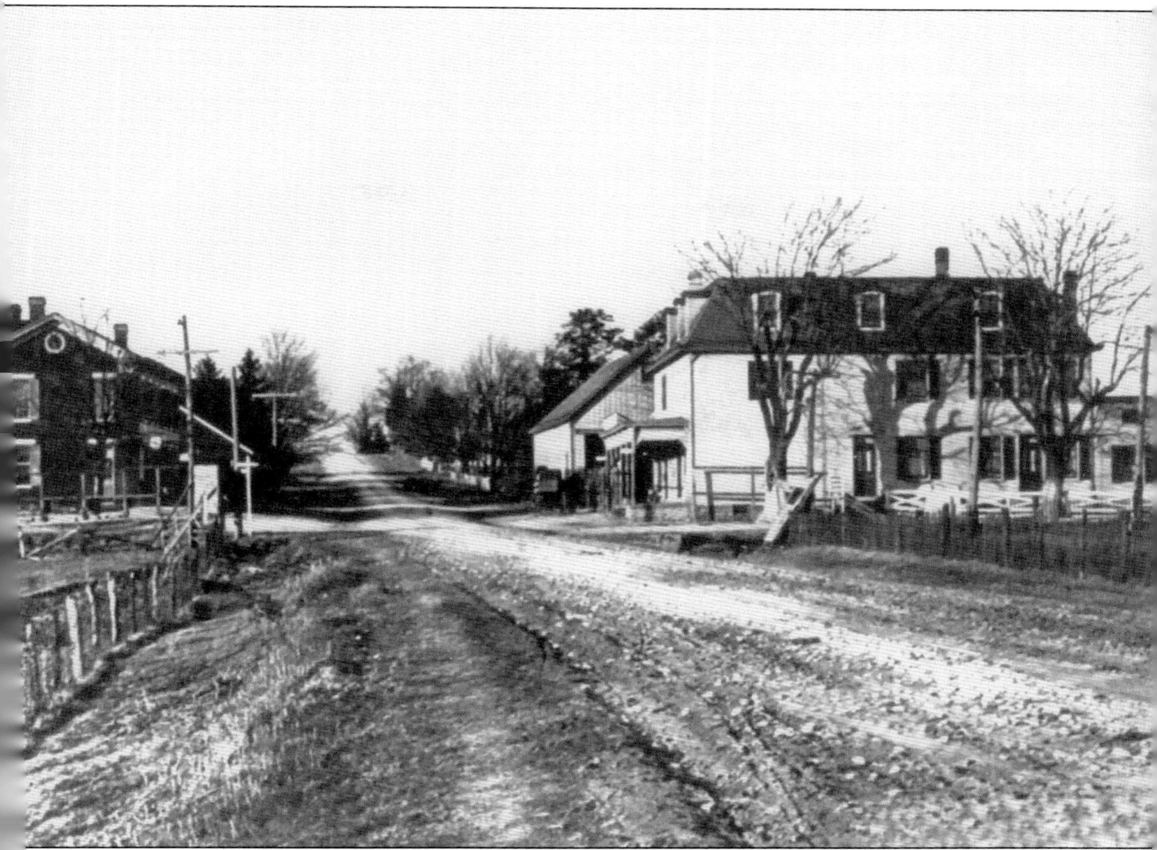

Pictured is a view of Colerain Avenue looking north of Galbraith (Van Zandt) Road. In the early days, this intersection was the heart of Colerain Township. There were two hotels, Wiesenhahn's on the northwest corner and Luichinger's on the northeast corner. Just north of the hotels were holding barns to hold the animals that the drovers were taking to market, as this area was a regular stop along the way. There were also holding pens for the animals on the southeast and southwest corners of the intersection and a blacksmith shop nearby if needed. The two inns mentioned were the scenes of many political gatherings and rallies over the years. (Coutersy of the Cincinnati Historical Society.)

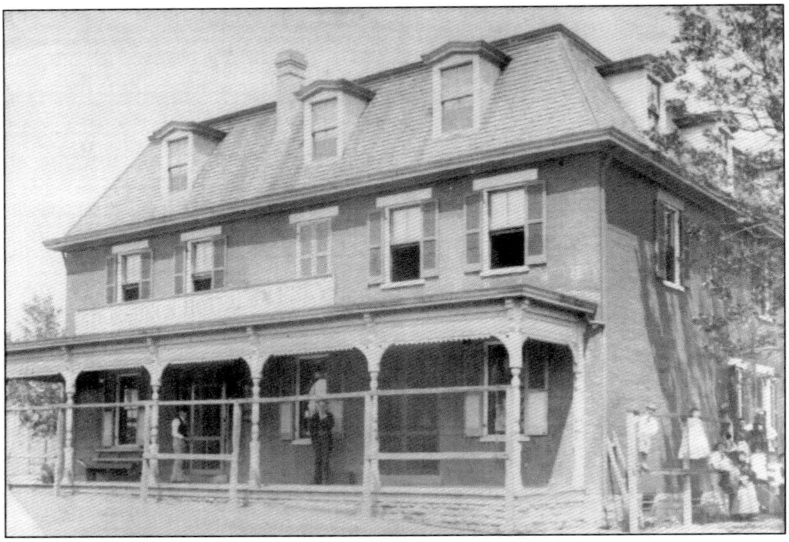

This is the Frey Building, formerly Luichinger's Hotel, at the northeast corner of Colerain Avenue and Galbraith Road. Frey's carried coal, feed, flour, hardware, woodenware, groceries, dry goods, notions, boots, shoes, and school supplies. (Courtesy of the Coleraine Historical Society.)

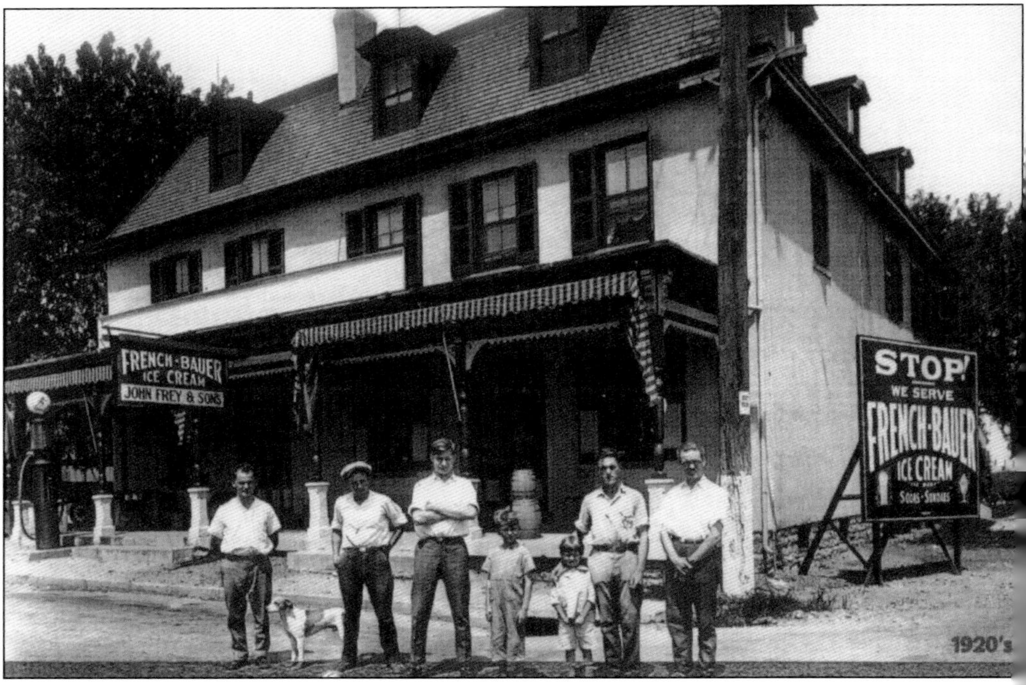

This is the Frey's grocery store as it appeared in the 1920s. Upstairs was the Groesbeck Hote Pictured from left to right are Alban Frey, Blinken (the dog), Bob Foster, three unidentified, Chi Moore, and Ed Frey. John Frey was very helpful when the Colerain Township School centralize in 1924. Benches were placed in Frey's truck, and students were picked up and taken to schoo When school was over, the reverse took place. (Courtesy of the Coleraine Historical Society.)

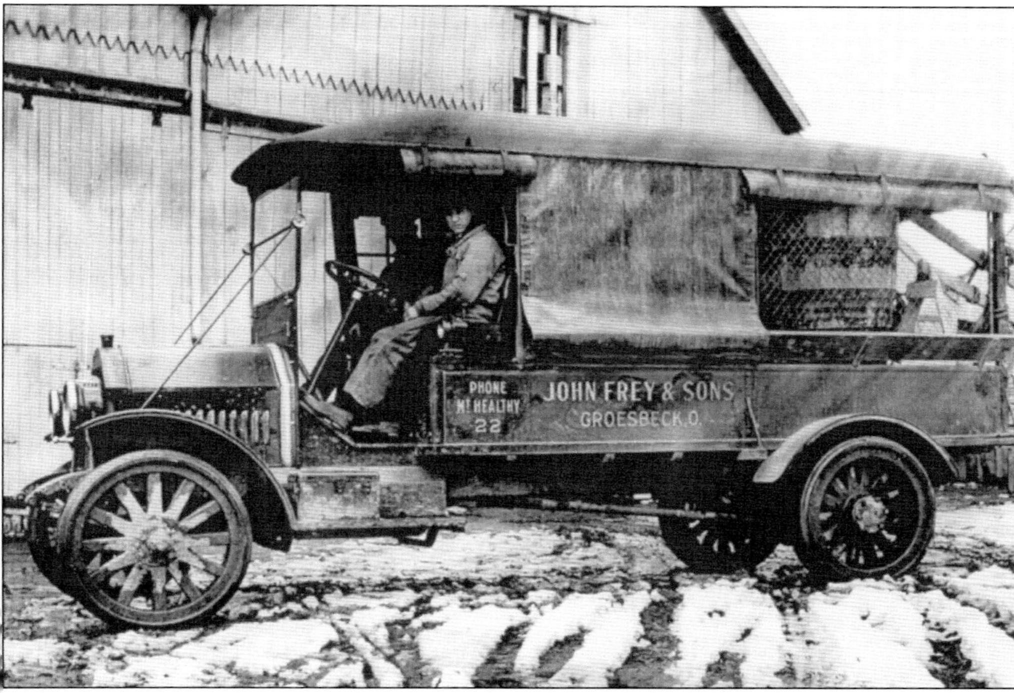

Here is John Frey's grocery truck, which doubled as a school bus. That is John Frey in the driver's seat. Notice the telephone number. (Courtesy of the Coleraine Historical Society.)

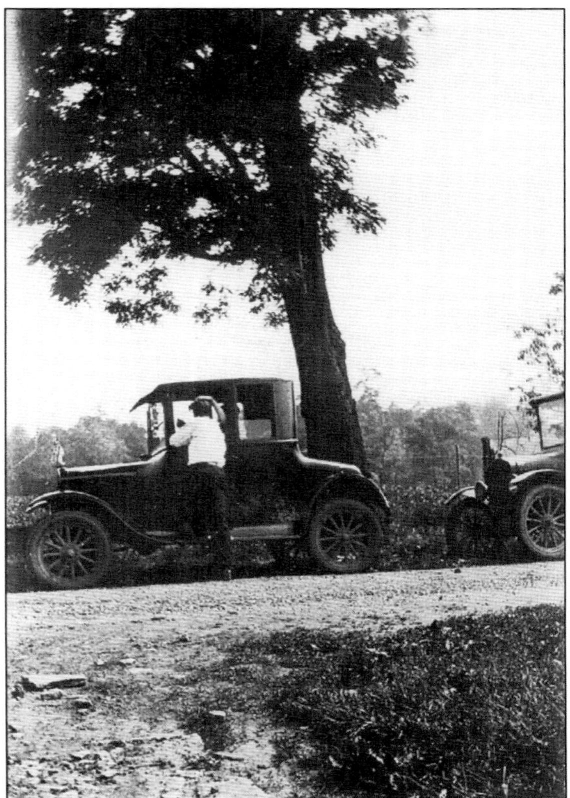

Colerain Township was a sleepy ırm community when this picture 'as taken. Back in those days, there ere few paved roads and even fewer ıtomobiles. Cars needed constant :pairing and regular upkeep. ıctured are not one but two cars ıt for a ride on the uncluttered ads of Colerain Township. Courtesy of Bob Muehlenhard.)

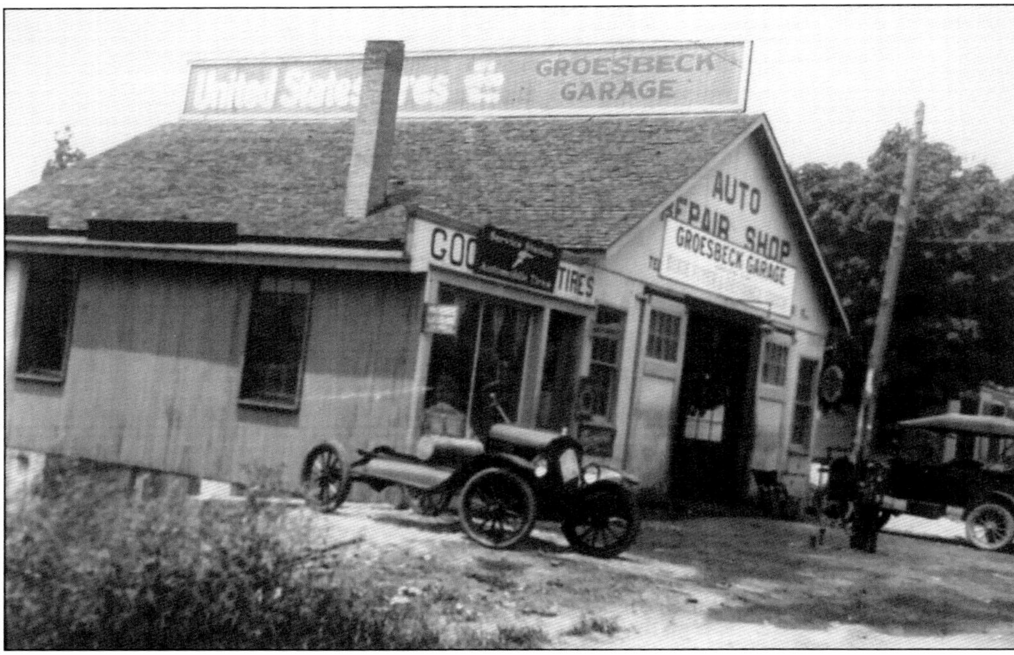

This is the Groesbeck Garage, formerly the H.H. Stockmann & Son blacksmith shop on the southwest corner of Colerain Avenue and Galbraith Road in the 1900s. (Courtesy of Ray Finke.)

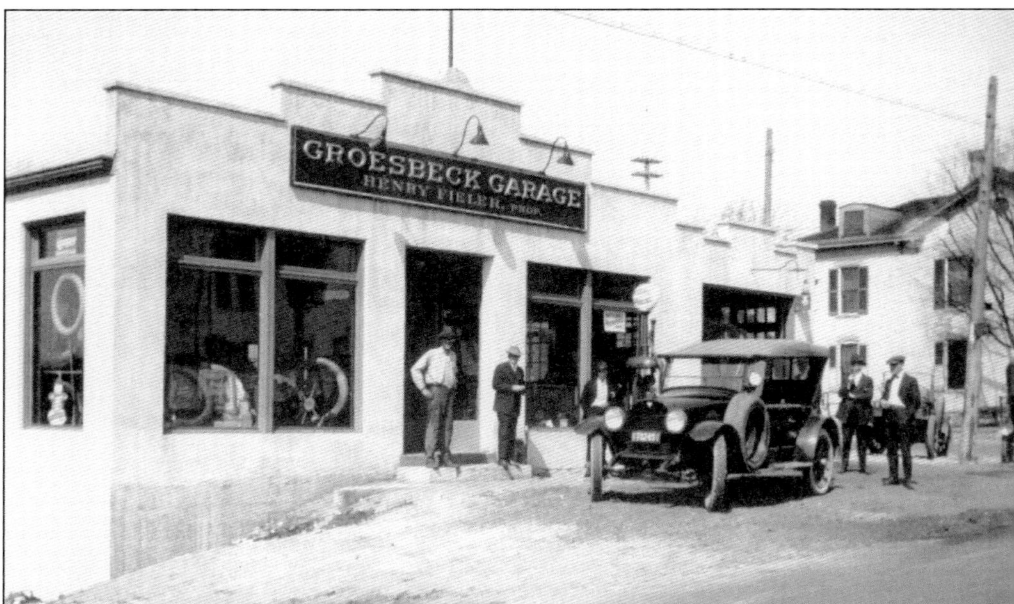

Here is an updated version of Groesbeck Garage operated by Henry Fieler. It too was located o the southwest corner of Colerain Avenue and Galbraith Road. At the time, this was the hea of the township. Fieler's Garage was later the home of the Groesbeck fire department. (Courtes of Richard Huber.)

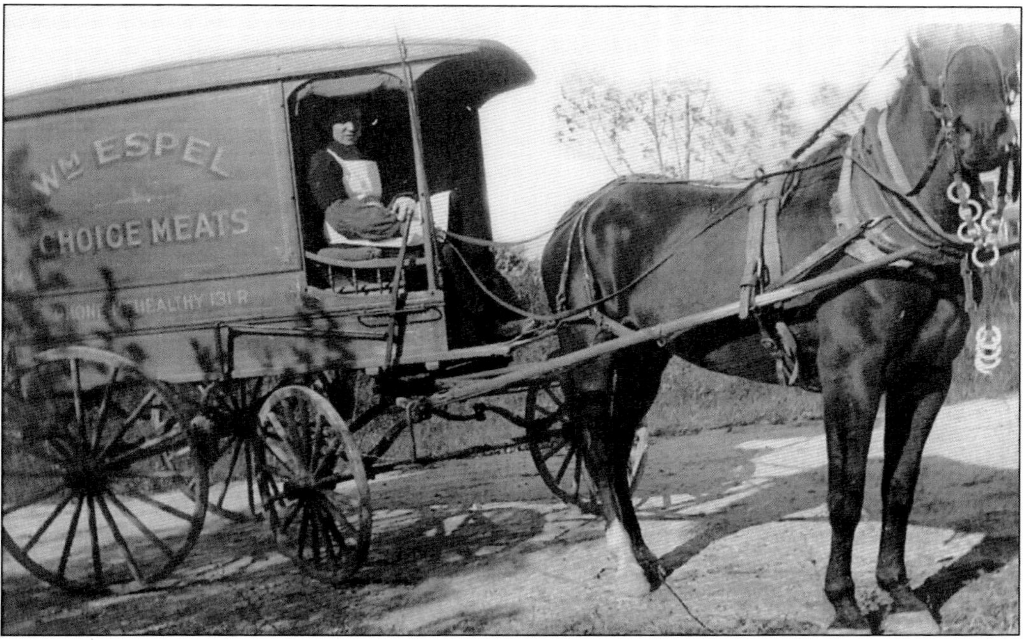

William Espel was a butcher who literally took his show on the road. In his butcher shop on wheels, he sold custom-cut beef, pork, and lamb. The meat was preserved by ice. He also carried a few groceries. Many residents in the township relied on him to make regular rounds and supply them with their groceries. (Courtesy of Joe and Rita Benz.)

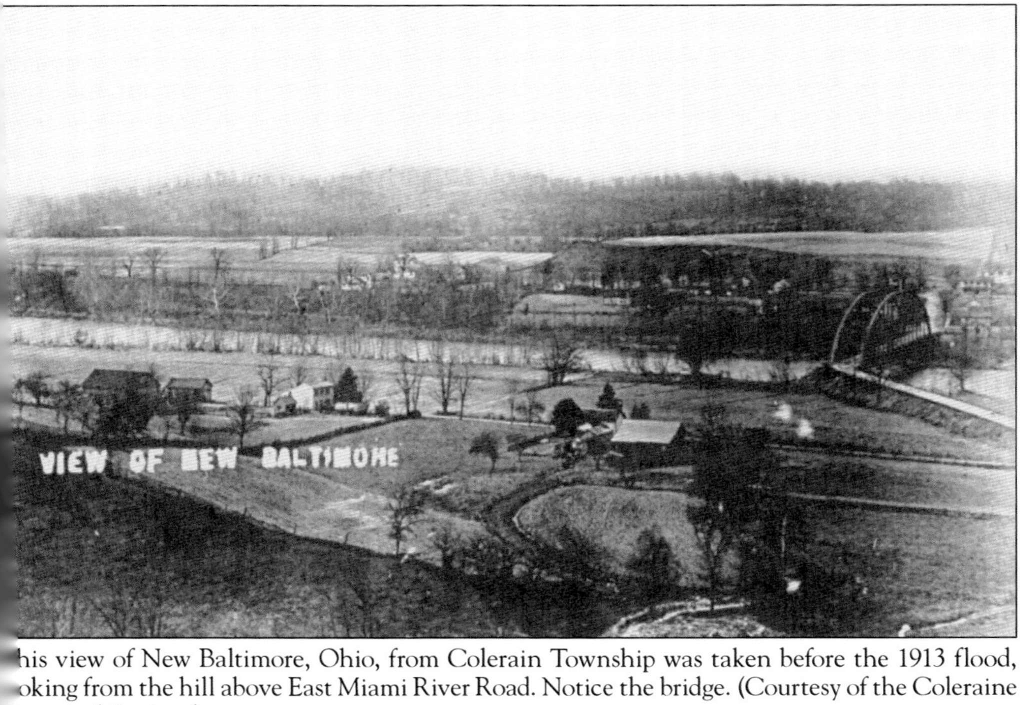

his view of New Baltimore, Ohio, from Colerain Township was taken before the 1913 flood, oking from the hill above East Miami River Road. Notice the bridge. (Courtesy of the Coleraine istorical Society.)

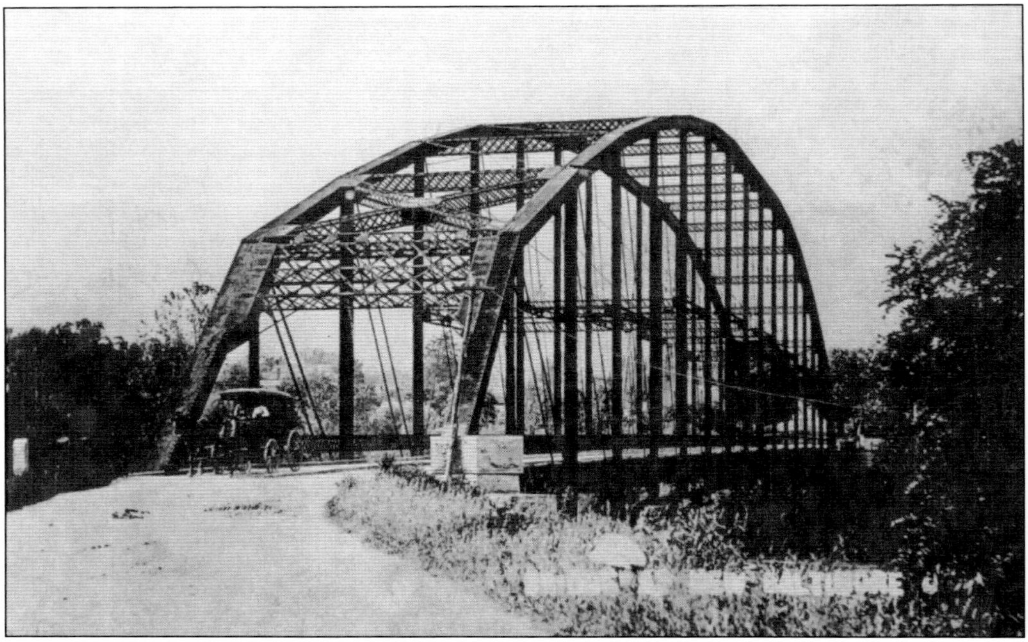

This is the bridge in New Baltimore before the 1913 flood. (Courtesy of the Coleraine Historical Society.)

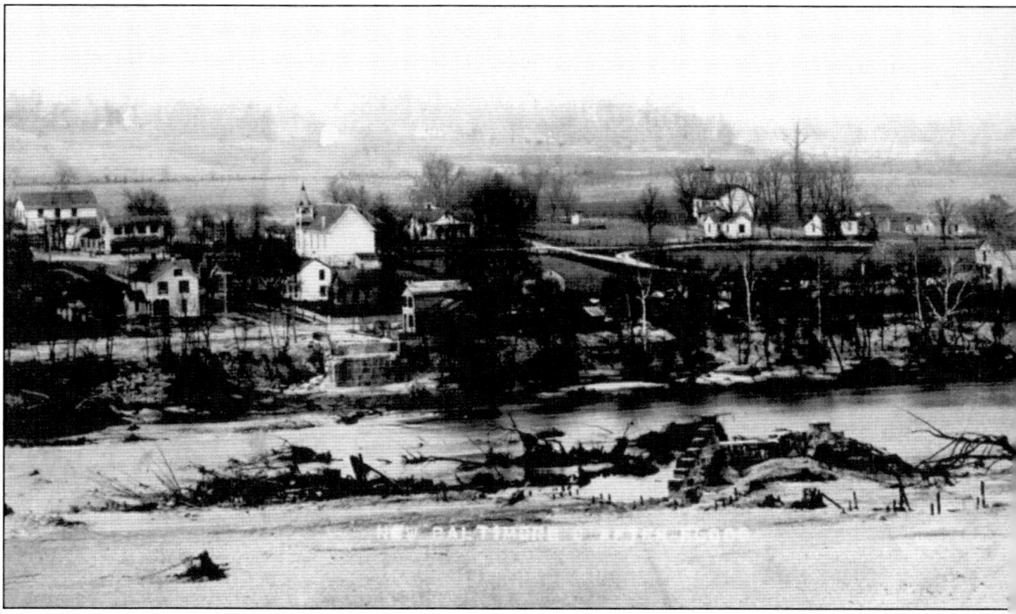

Here is a photograph of New Baltimore, Ohio, after the 1913 flood. The bridge is gone, but th piers are in place. (Courtesy of the Coleraine Historical Society.)

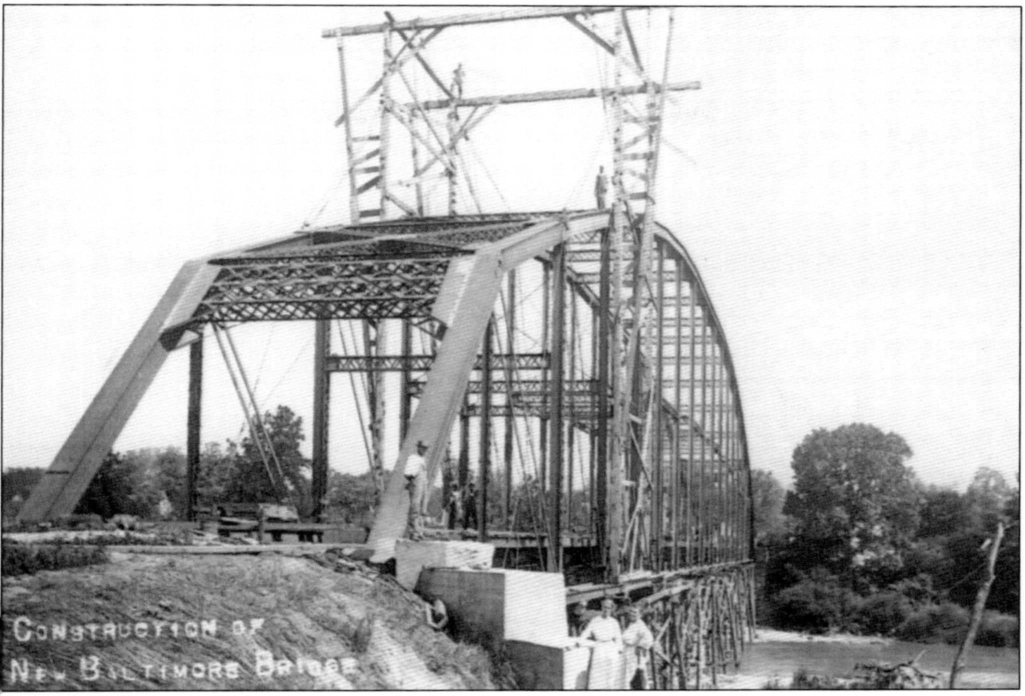

The New Baltimore bridge is under construction after the 1913 flood. (Courtesy of the Coleraine Historical Society.)

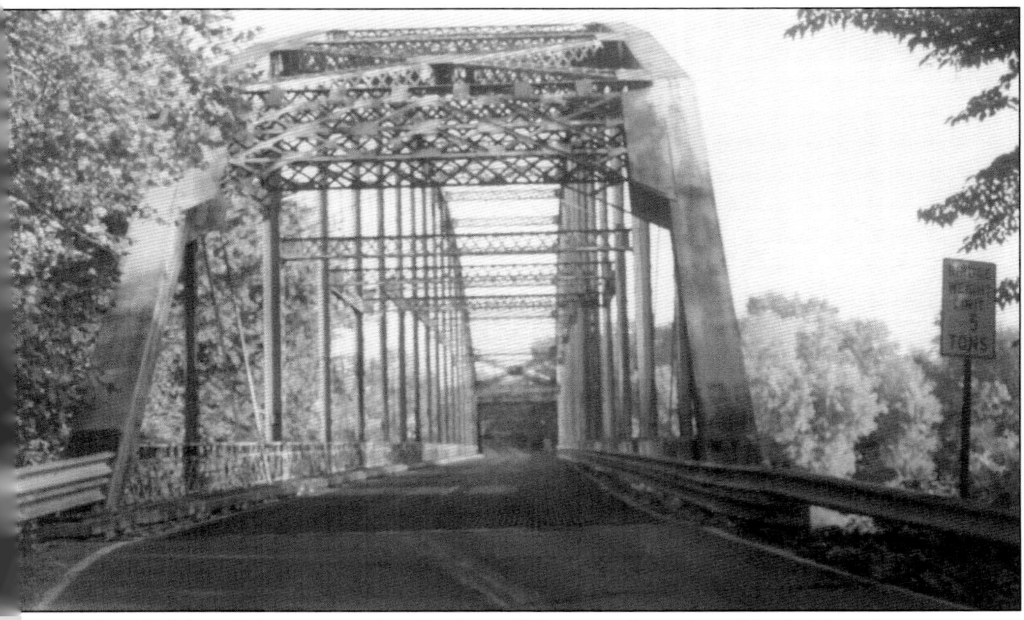

ere is the old New Baltimore bridge, built in 1914 to replace the older bridge that was swept vay by the 1913 flood. This bridge was declared unsafe for vehicular traffic in 2003 and was ter used as a pedestrian bridge. The Hamilton County Engineers office said it would cost over million to replace it and the bridge was demolished in 2004 and replaced with a new bridge the east. (Courtesy of Doug Bevis.)

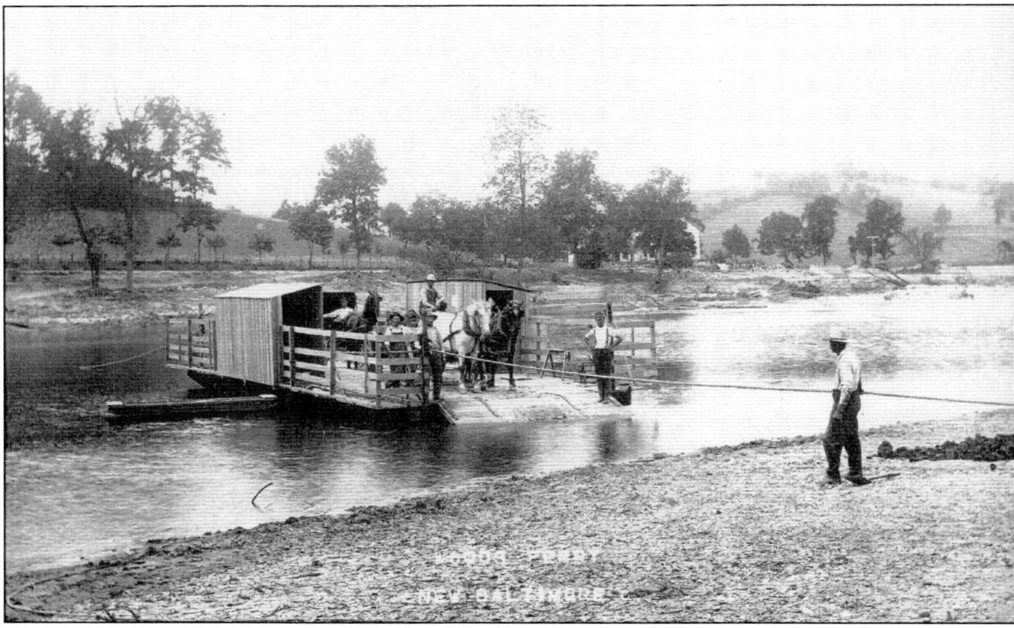

Wood's Ferry replaced the New Baltimore Bridge. Frank Engel is seen with the white and black team. John Flick is with the horse and buggy while Henry McCredie, in bib overalls, ropes the ferry across. (Courtesy of the Coleraine Historical Society.)

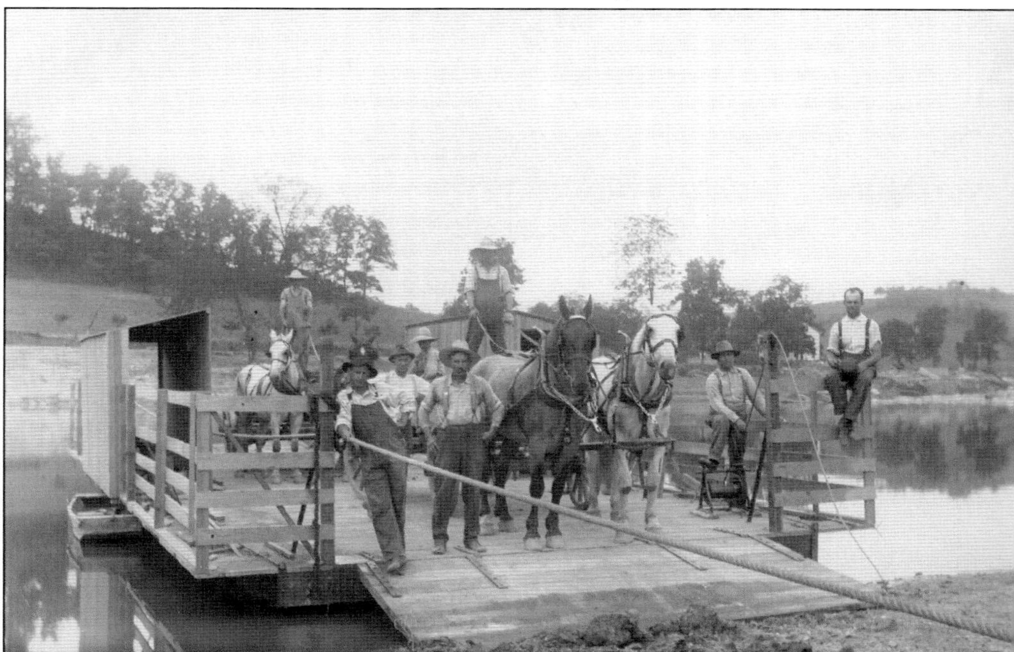

For a time, the Wood's Ferry served residents after the New Baltimore bridge was swept away i the 1913 flood. As in the photograph above, Frank Engel has the reins of the front black an white team, John Flick is with the other black and white team, and Henry McCredie is in th bib overalls. (Courtesy of Doug Bevis.)

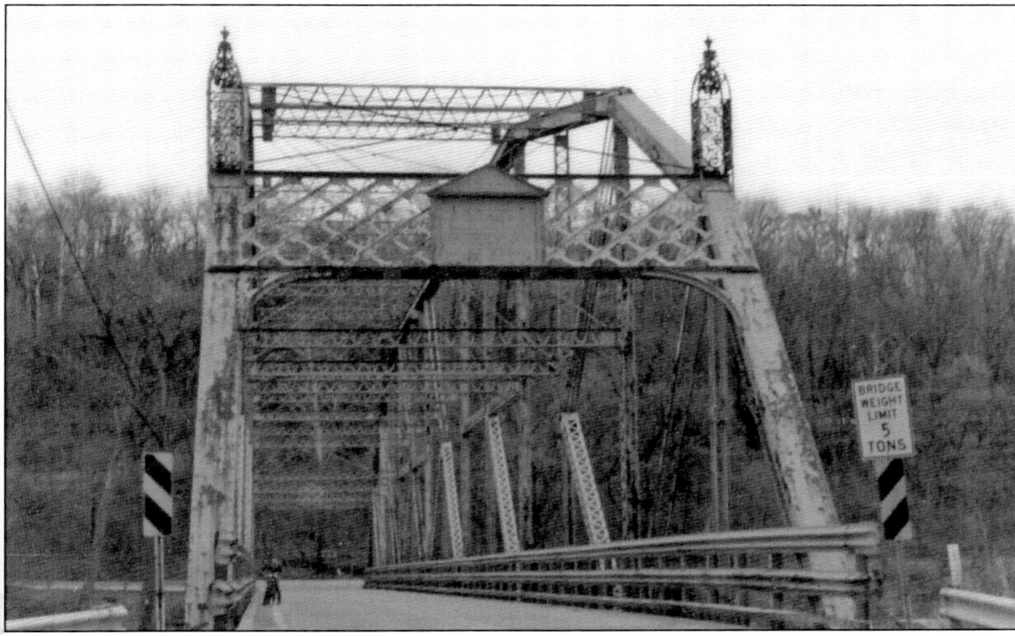

The old Colerain Venice bridge, seen here and built in 1895, was removed in 1990 and replaced with new a bridge. The finials from this bridge are located in the Colerain Heritage Memorial Park on Springdale Road in front of the administration building. (Courtesy of the Hamilton County Engineers office.)

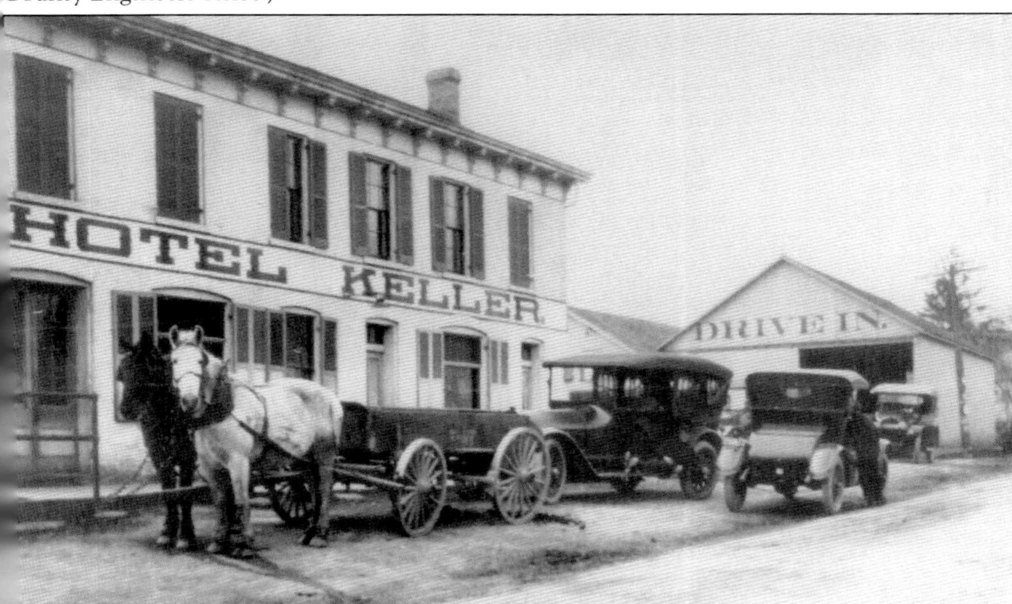

ere is a contrast between the horse and buggy and the automobile, which was coming into its vn. The Hotel Keller, formerly Wiesenhahn's Hotel, is in the background with a large barn that as previously used to house animals being driven to market and is now being used to repair itomobiles. These buildings were located at the northwest corner of Colerain Avenue and albraith Road. (Courtesy of the Coleraine Historical Society.)

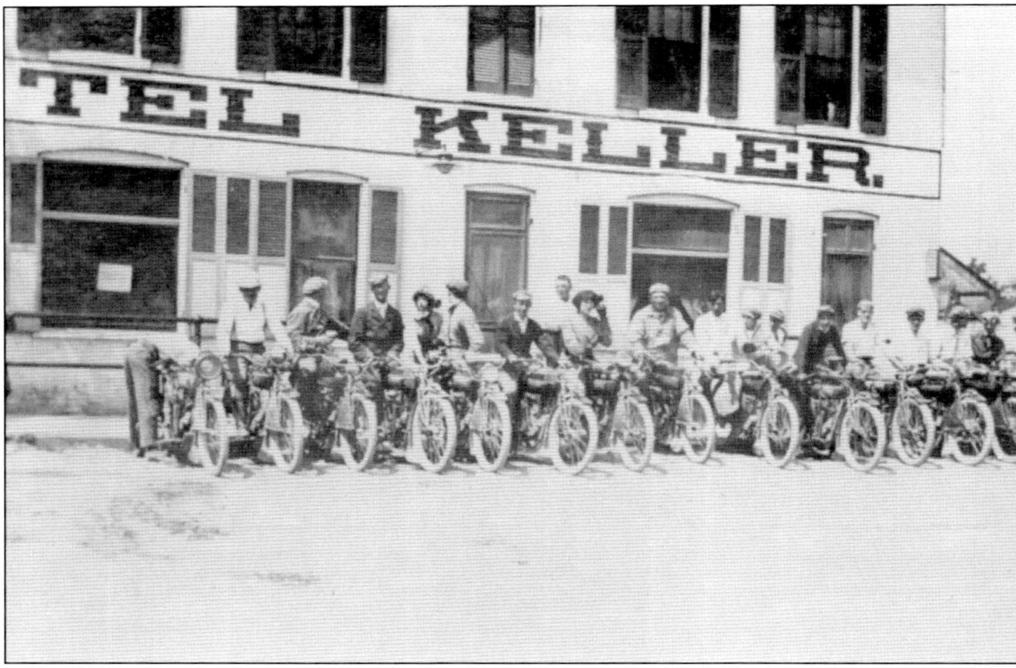

A motorcycle club lines up in front of the Hotel Keller at the northwest corner of Colerain Avenue and Galbraith Road in the early 1900s. (Courtesy of the Coleraine Historical Society.)

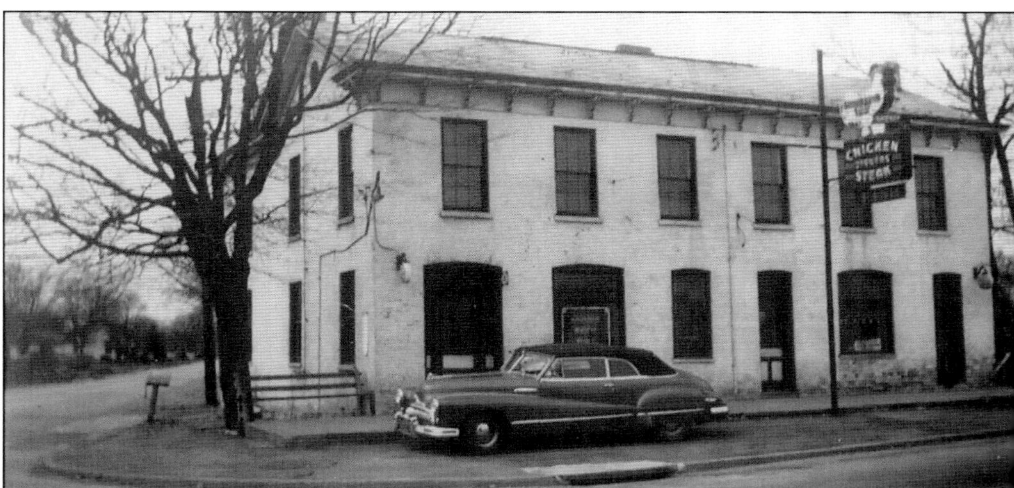

A 1937 Buick convertible is parked in front of the Groesbeck Inn, formerly the Hotel Keller, a the northwest corner of Colerain Avenue and Galbraith Road. (Courtesy of Earl Frey.)

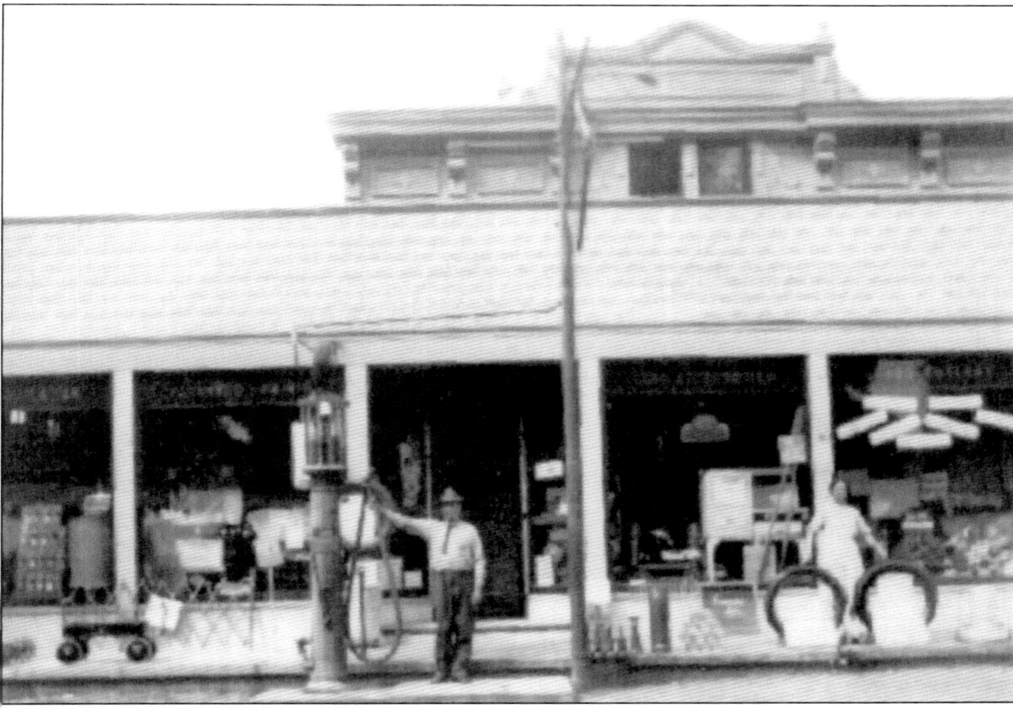

The Lockwood Hardware store opened for business in 1925 at 8251 Colerain Avenue. Here customers could find electrical, plumbing, garden supplies, household wares, roofing materials, paint supplies, hay, straw, flower and vegetable seeds, animal and poultry feeds, guns and ammunition, as well as gasoline and oil products. The store published a monthly magazine to acquaint customers with their service and stocks. In 1930, Fred Lockwood is leaning on the gas pump, and his wife, Emma, is behind the tires. (Courtesy of Janet Lockwood.)

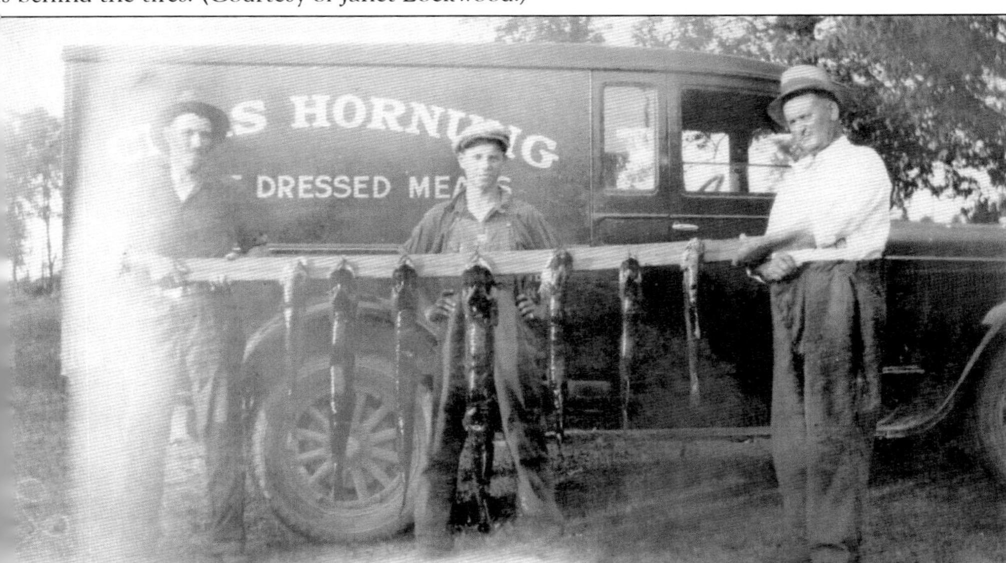

This is a delivery truck for Hornung Meats, but these unidentified gentlemen are more interested showing the northern pike that they caught back in 1930. (Courtesy of Doug Bevis.)

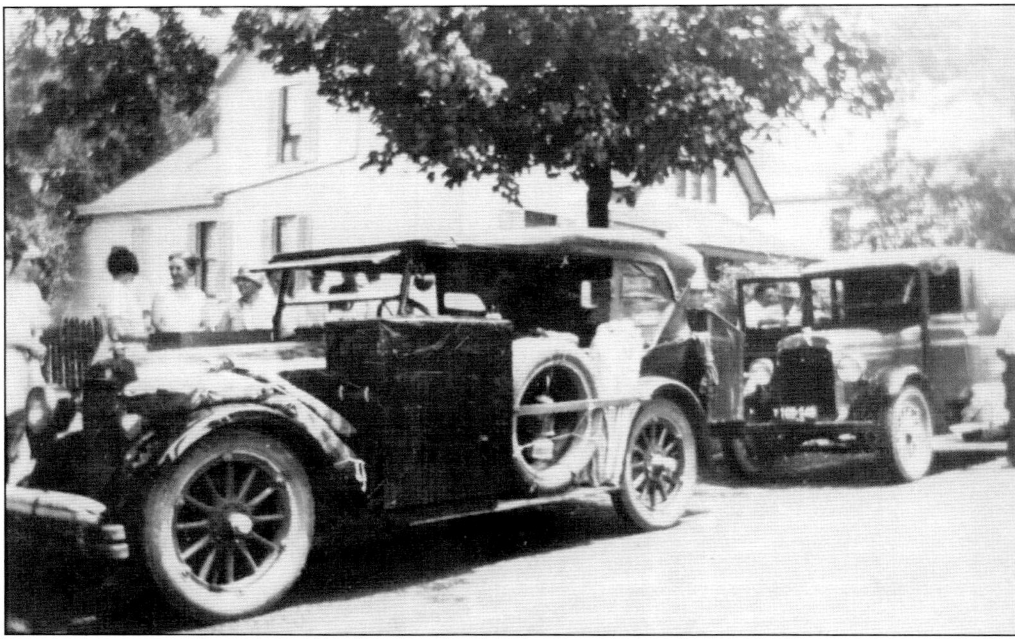

Here are the Bevis and Hornung families from Dunlap preparing for a trip. They are packed and ready. Notice they have utilized just about all the space available to take what they felt they might need. In 1930, there were no trunks on automobiles, so people were very inventive. (Courtesy of Doug Bevis.)

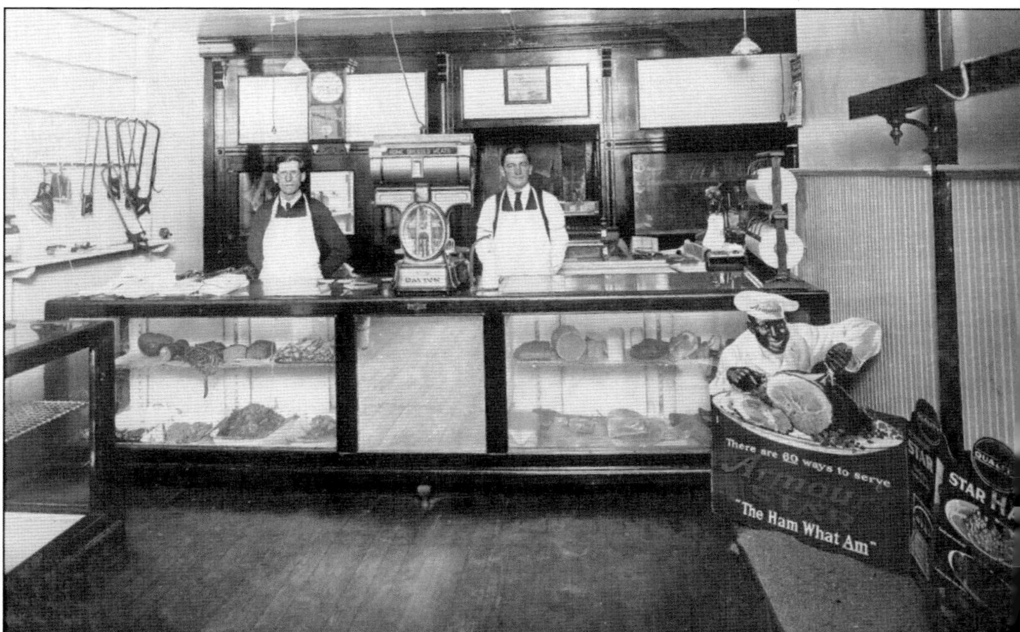

The picture shows the Hornung Meat Market. This business had a store in Dunlap and also i Hamilton. It is believed that this is the Dunlap store. The butchers are very well dressed an ready for customers. (Courtesy of Doug Bevis.)

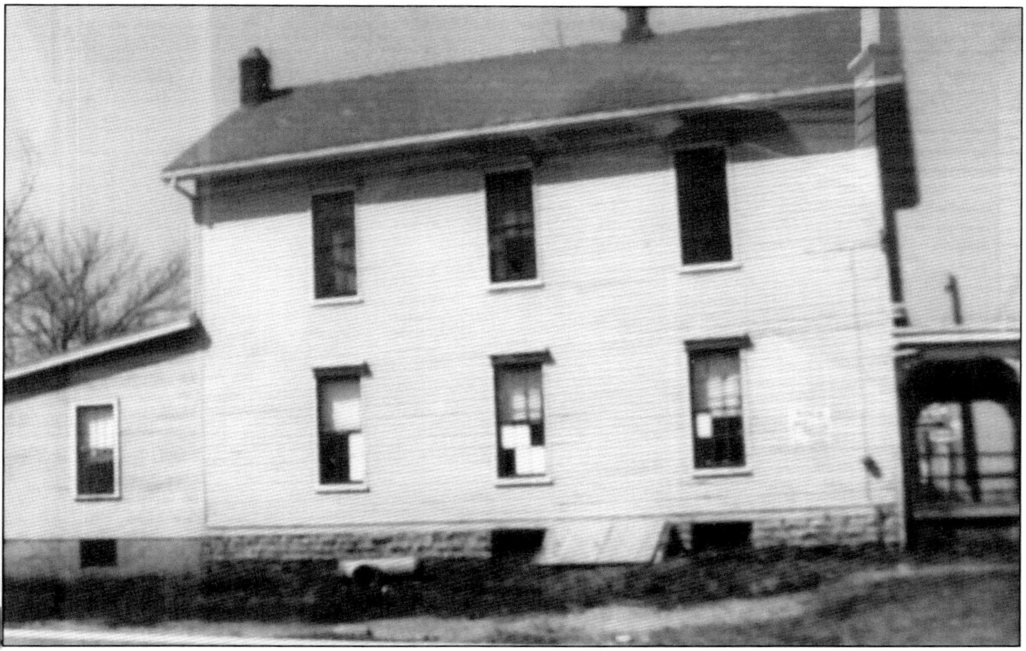

This was the Junior Order Hall, which was built prior to 1900 and razed in 1964. It was occupied by the Odd Fellows until the Colerain Junior Order took over on February 18, 1902. The Groesbeck Improvement Association used the hall prior to 1937. The Groesbeck Volunteer Fireman's carnival was held on the grounds adjacent to the building. Just north of Lockwood Hardware, this site is now occupied by Kentucky Fried Chicken (KFC). (Courtesy of the Coleraine Historical Society.)

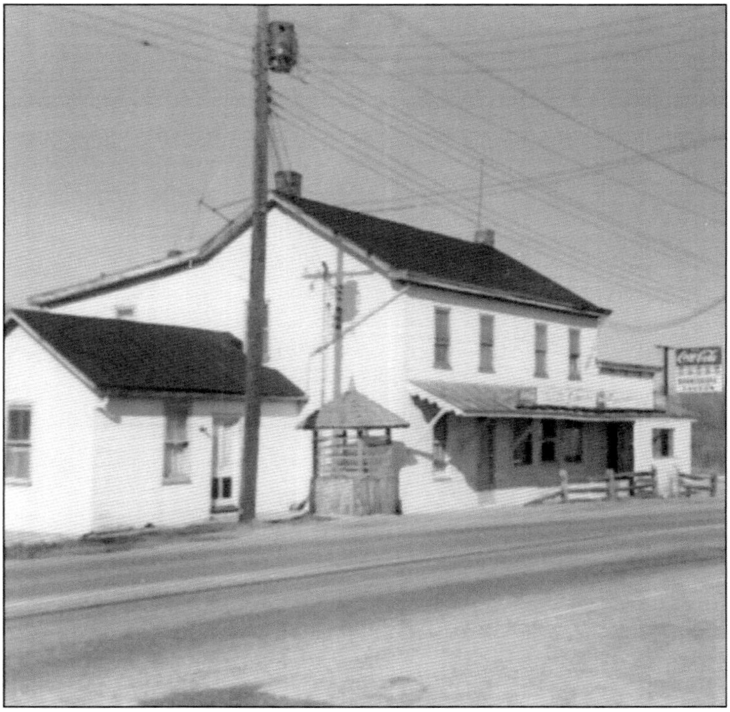

he old Barnesburg Inn pictured here before ie relocation and idening of Blue Rock oad. This building as later demolished. Courtesy of Mel Blust.)

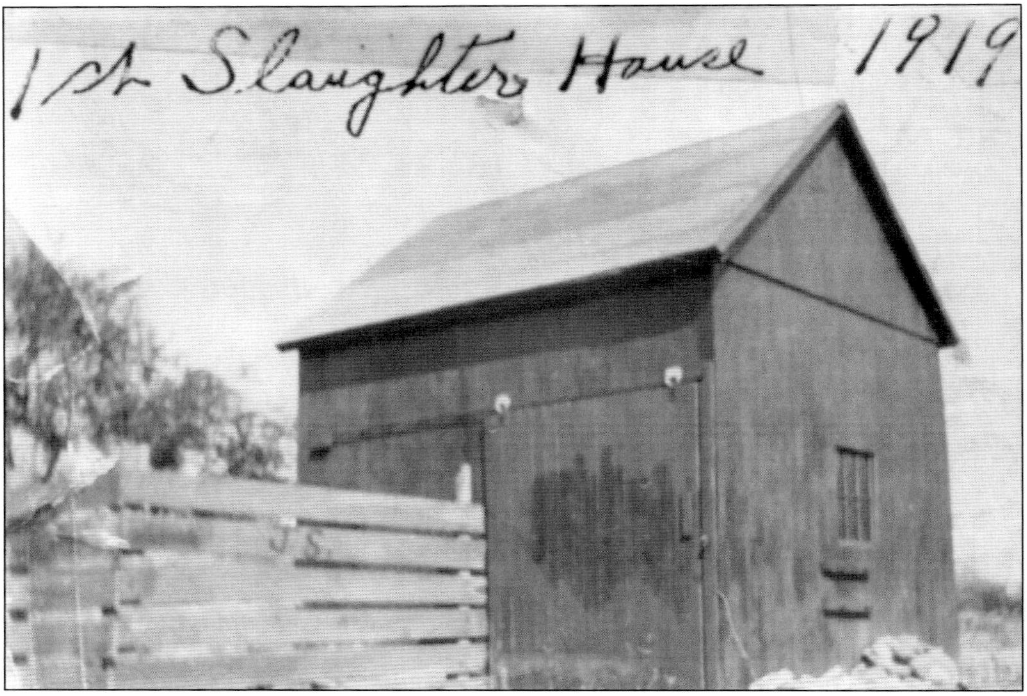

Here is the old barn where Stehlin's Meats began. This was the only meat market and slaughterhouse in Hamilton County outside the city of Cincinnati. (Courtesy of John Stehlin.)

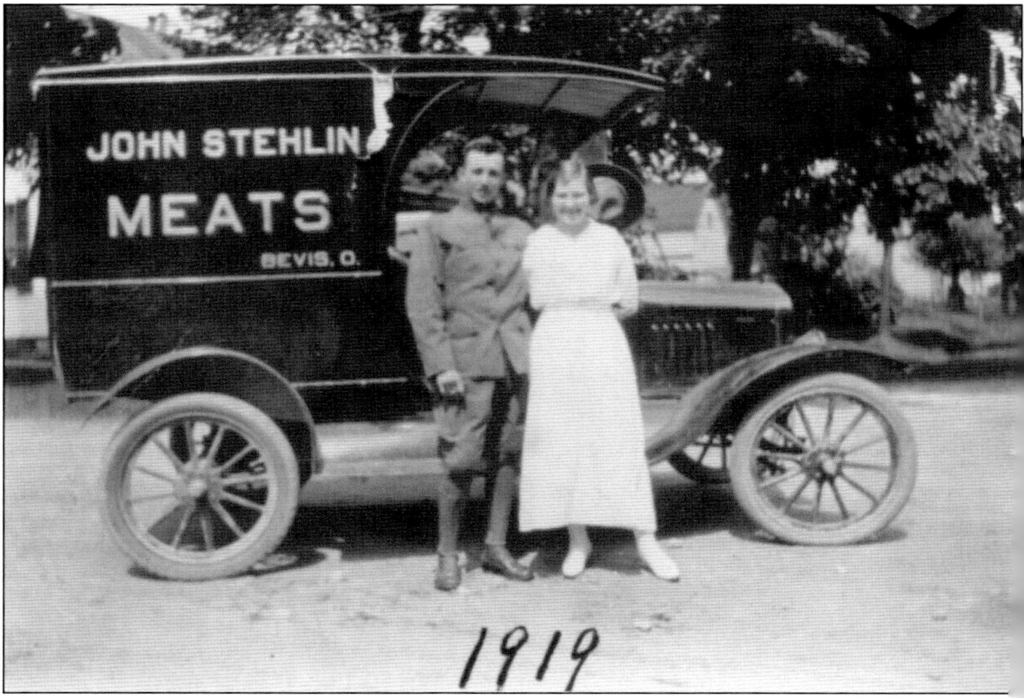

Here is the founder of Stehlin's Meats, John Stehlin, with his wife, Eleonora, after he returne from World War I. (Courtesy of John Stehlin.)

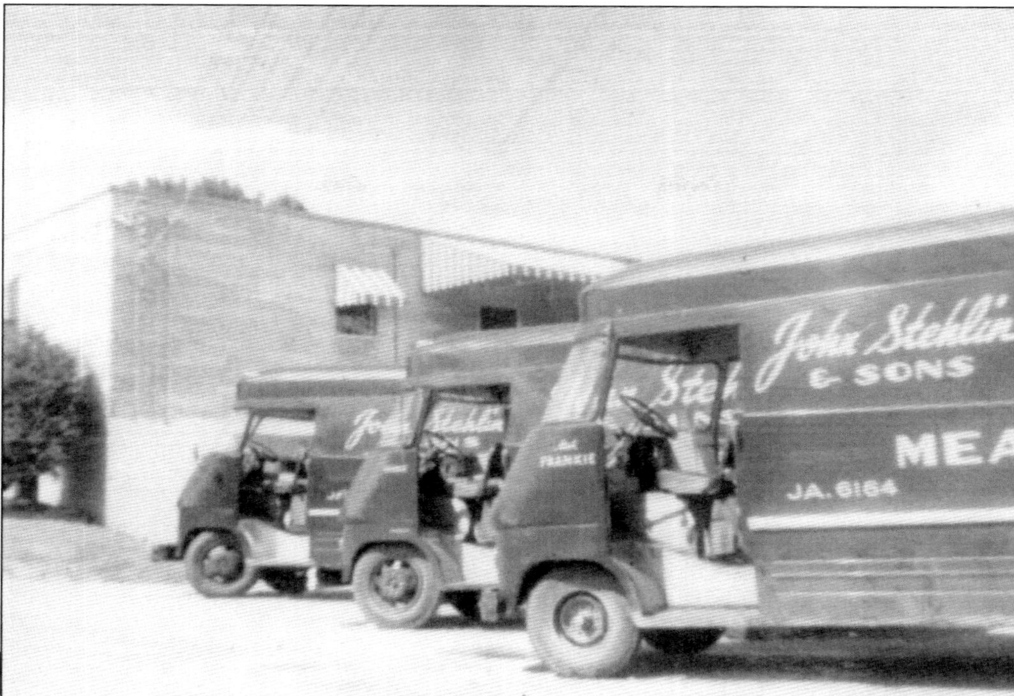

John Stehlin and Sons Company is the official name of Stehlin's Meats. It is tucked away in the northeast corner of Colerain Avenue and I-275. Here are some early Stehlin's meat trucks. (Courtesy of John Stehlin.)

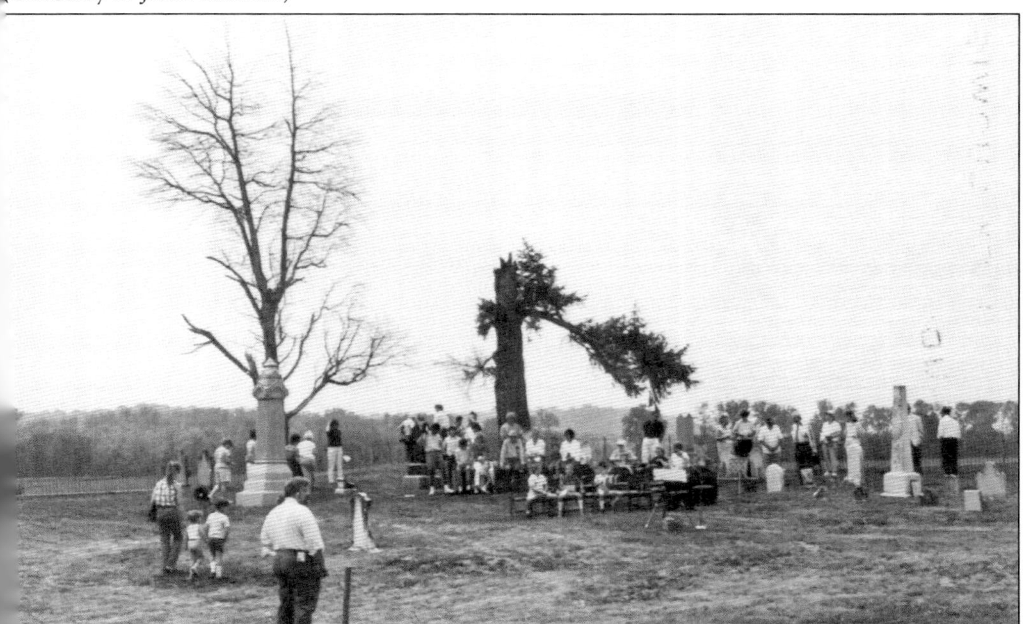

he Coleraine Historical Society members and friends conducted a memorial service at the unlap Station Cemetery in May 1988. (Courtesy of Bob Muehlenhard.)

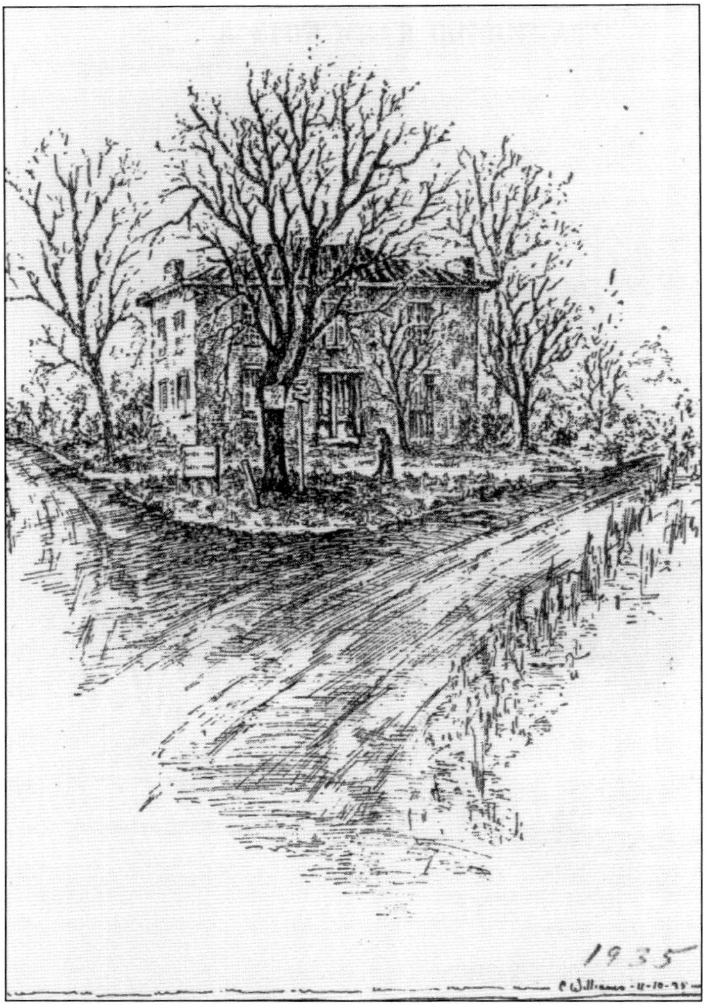

The intersection of Blue Rock and Cheviot Roads was known for many years as Wissel's Corner. This drawing by Caroline Williams appeared in the *Cincinnati Enquirer* on April 10, 1935. The old building, once a tavern, stood for more than 100 years in this triangle. The building was razed in 1938 and replaced by the White Oak Food Market. (Courtesy of the *Cincinnati Enquirer.*)

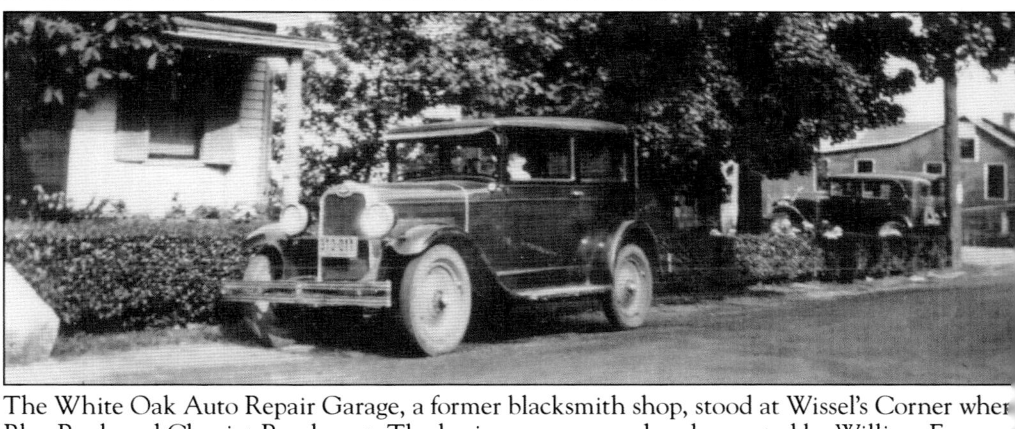

The White Oak Auto Repair Garage, a former blacksmith shop, stood at Wissel's Corner wher Blue Rock and Cheviot Roads met. The business was owned and operated by William Frey, so of Elias Frey. The garage was opened when the automobile began to replace the horse and bugg (Courtesy of the Coleraine Historical Society.)

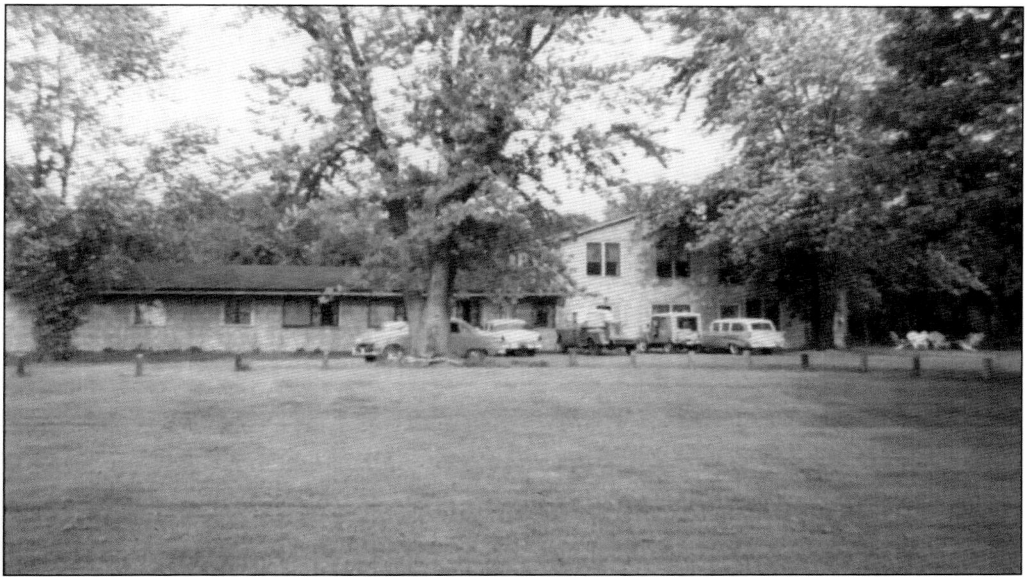

The Bevis Tavern was located at 9890 Colerain Avenue for many, many years. This picture is from the 1960s. The original Bevis Tavern site was on Bevis Lane. That site was abandoned in the mid-1800s. Another tavern was built at Colerain Avenue and Dry Ridge Road. That building was torn down in 1920. The building pictured was built in the mid-1920s and continued to serve the public for many years. (Courtesy of Mel Blust.)

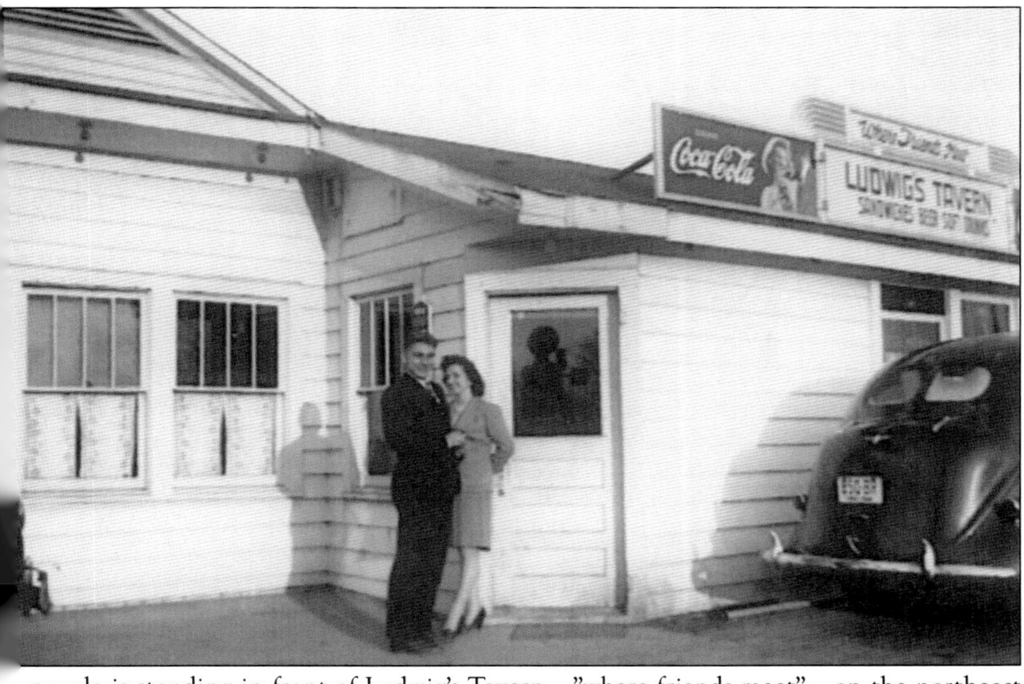

couple is standing in front of Ludwig's Tavern—"where friends meet"—on the northeast orner of Colerain Avenue and Springdale Road. This was also a favorite stop for many of the en associated with the old Mount Healthy airport, which was on the southwest corner of the tersection. (Courtesy of Mel Blust.)

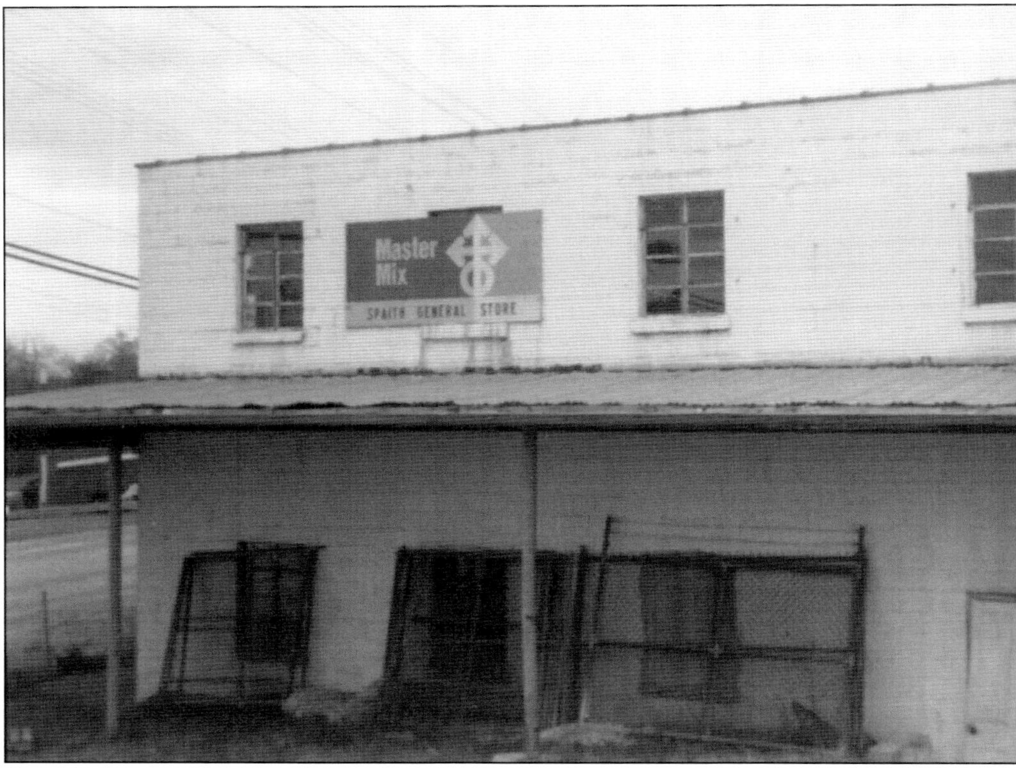

Spaith's General Store, as it was officially known, was a unique operation. The building was constructed in 1947. Spaith's sold feed, grain, hardware, paint, glass, and building materials. Bob Spaith was usually at the register, and his wife, Fran, did all the running for customers' requests. This spot at 6511 Colerain Avenue is now occupied by a Kroger Store. (Courtesy of Greg Snyder.)

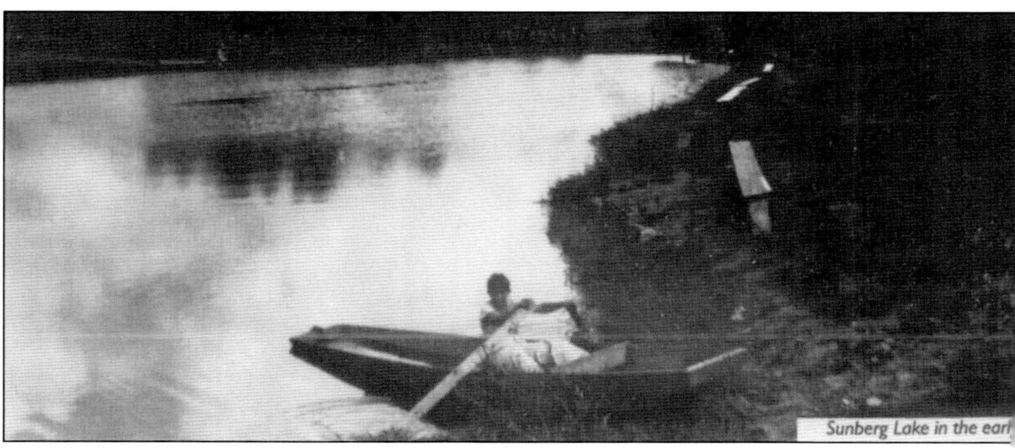

Most area residents are familiar with Lake Nina, but before the name change, the lake was know as Sunberg's Lake. The lake was built in 1938. Originally there were two lakes. One was a car lake, which was later filled in, and the current one, Lake Nina, was always well stocked. Back i those days, people could fish all day for $1. (Courtesy of Sam Sunberg.)

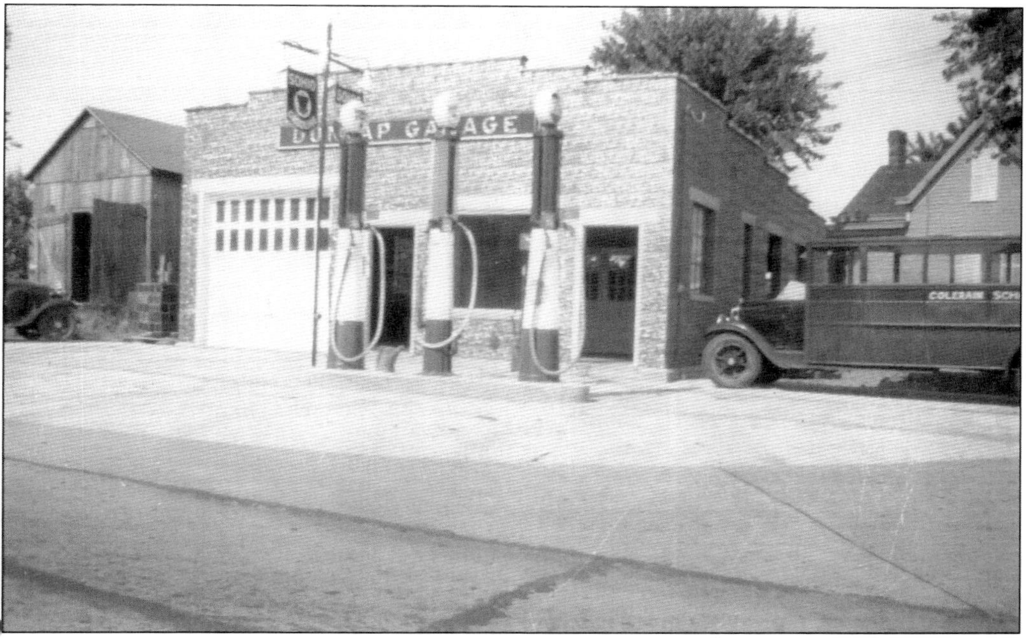

George Matt's Dunlap Garage in the 1930s was on the northeast corner of Colerain Avenue and West Kemper Road. This building later housed the Dunlap Fire Department. Notice the old Colerain school bus to the right. (Courtesy of the Coleraine Historical Society.)

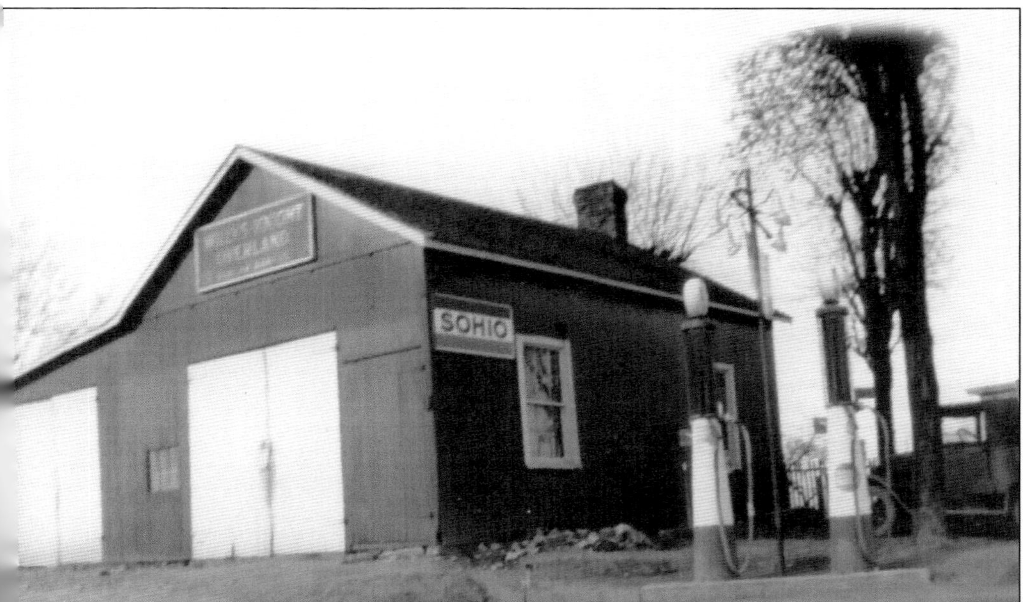

eorge Matt also sold Willys-Knight and Overland automobiles. This building was located on olerain Avenue next to his garage. Notice the old gas pumps where Matt sold Sohio products. Courtesy of the Coleraine Historical Society.)

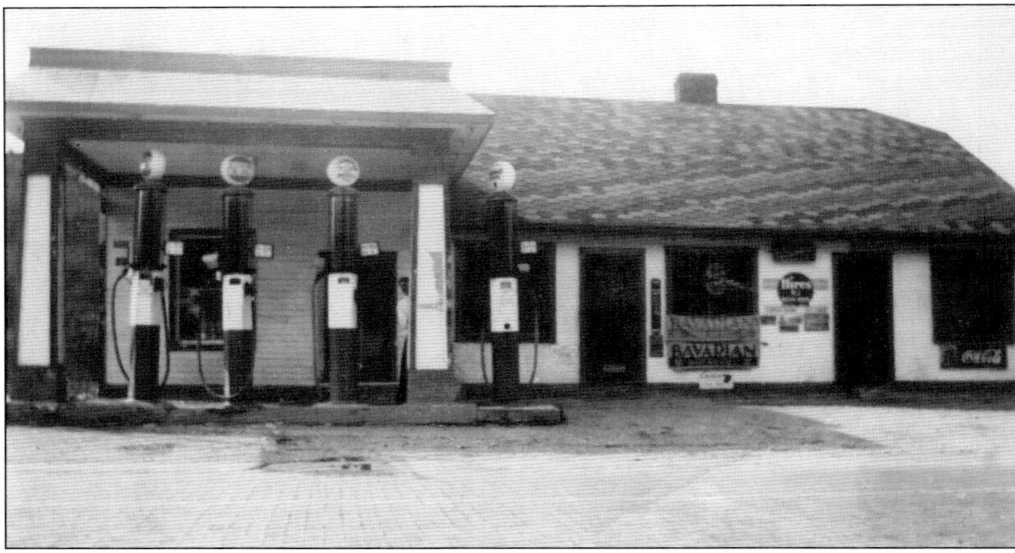

The Flicker Inn gas station is pictured here in 1936. It was located at 7077 Harrison Avenue. The gas station attracted many customers when they needed to "fill 'er up." This was one of the few gas stations in the area. (Courtesy of Marlene Brookbank.)

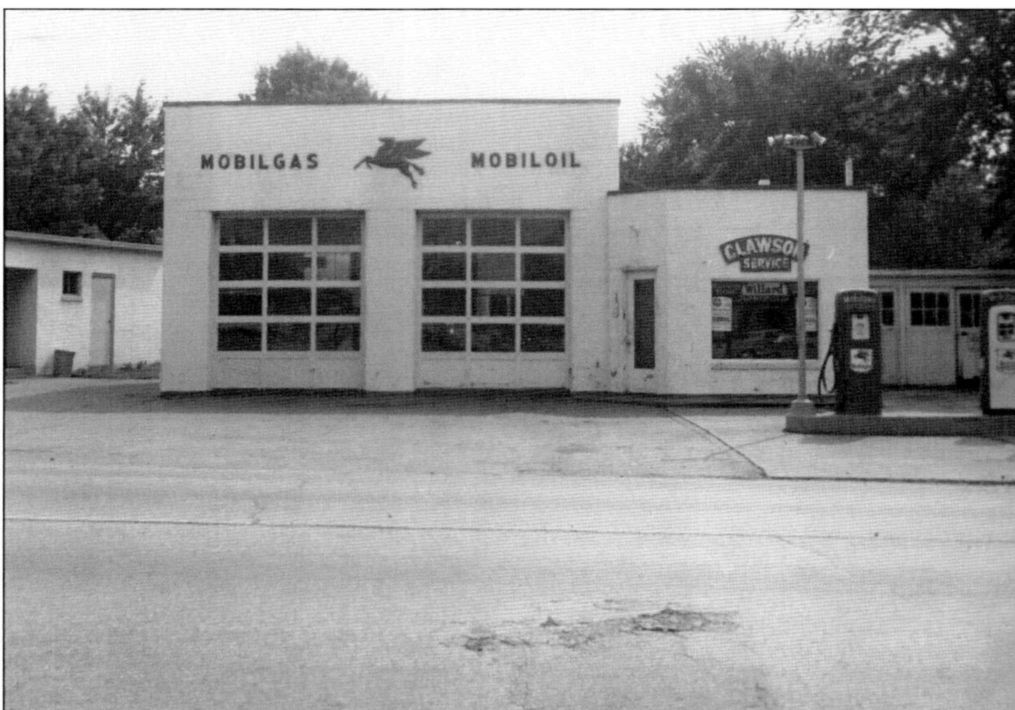

Clawson's gas station was located on the east side of Colerain Avenue just north of Galbraith Road. Armond Clawson was an original member of the Groesbeck Volunteer Fire Department. To the left in the picture is the Groesbeck Improvement Building, home of the Groesbeck Fire Department. (Courtesy of Mel Blust.)

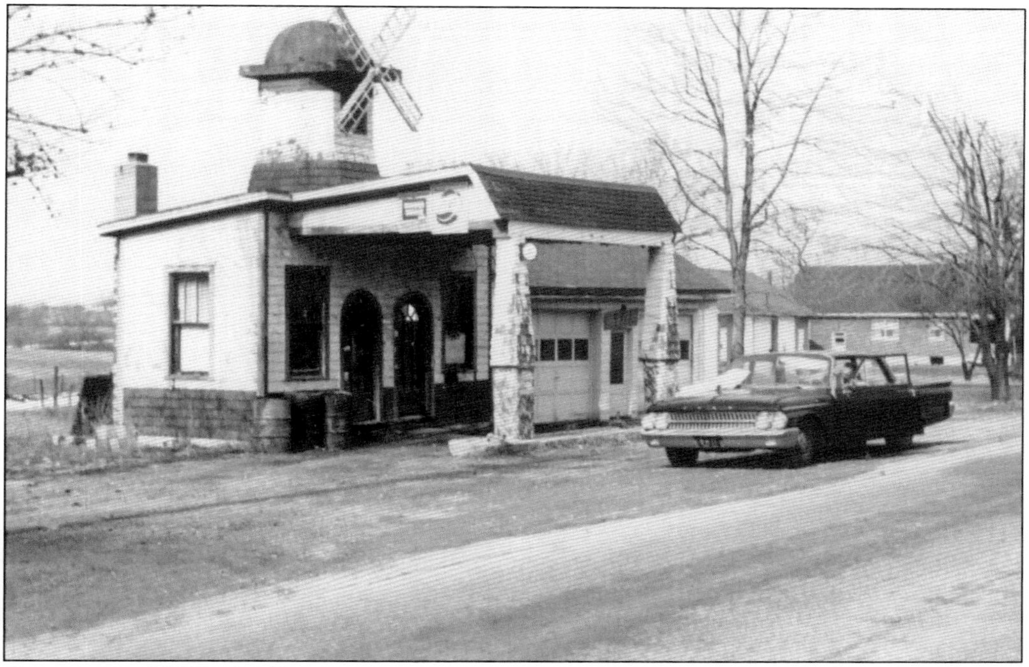

Here is the old Windmill gas station at 9911 Colerain Avenue. It attracted many customers because it was different than most other stations. Many people stopped out of curiosity to see if the windmill actually worked. (Courtesy of Mel Blust.)

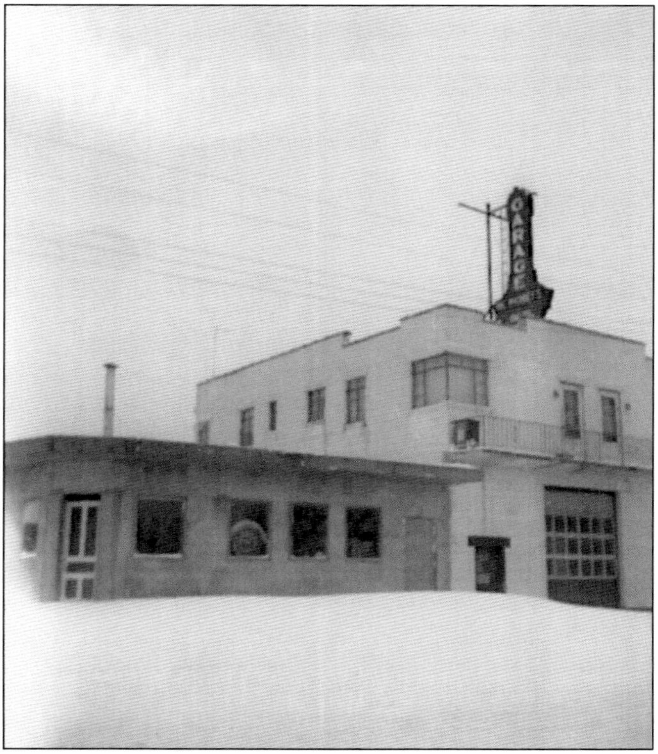

'his garage was home to aner's Auto Garage and later ent Brothers Radiator Shop. here were living quarters ove. It was located at the orthwest corner of Colerain venue and Springdale Road. Courtesy of Mel Blust.)

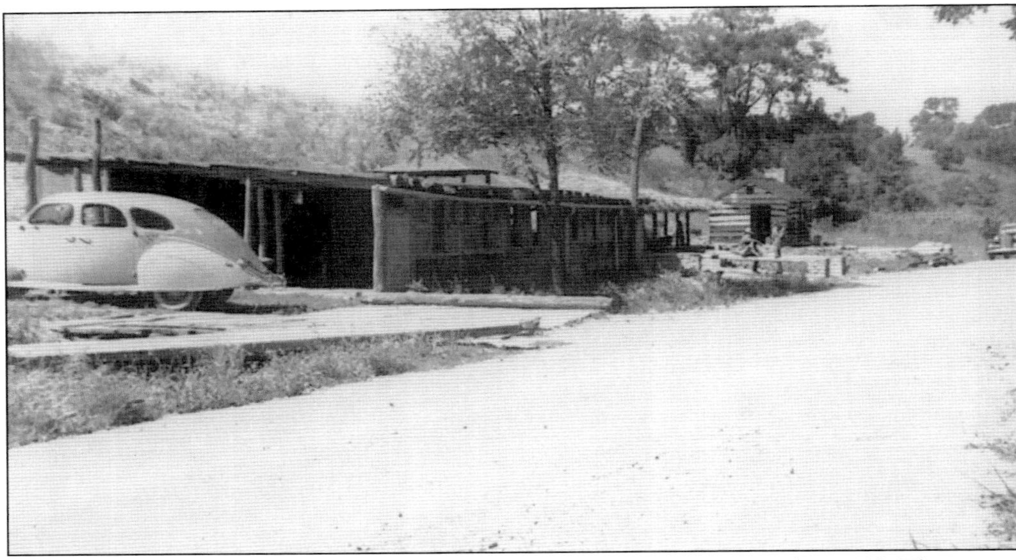

The old Handle Bar Ranch was located at 11317 Hughes Road. It opened in 1937. The owners liked horses, and originally it was a horse farm with 18 horses. But bicycles were a lot cleaner and cheaper, so this prompted the switch from horses to bicycles. The ranch was named after bicycle handlebars. Bicycles could be rented for just 25¢ a half hour. (Courtesy of Anna Ritter.)

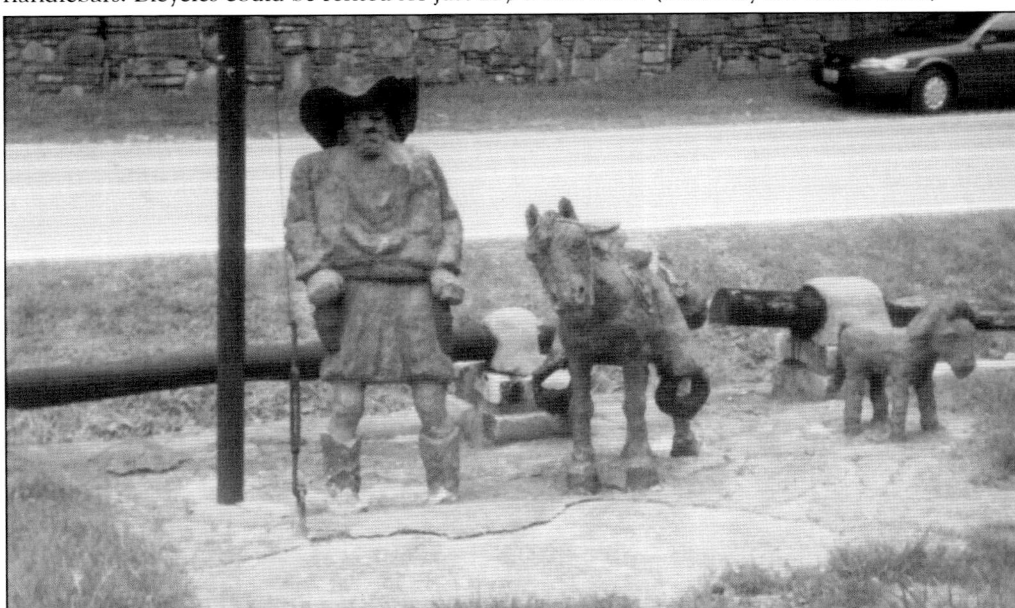

During World War II, the girls left at home would come out to the Handle Bar Ranch, tak hayrides, and have their picture taken on the ugliest concrete cowboy that ever existed. The they would send the pictures to their men in service. Never imitated, never duplicated, it wa quite different—it was the only Handle Bar Ranch. (Courtesy of Anna Ritter.)

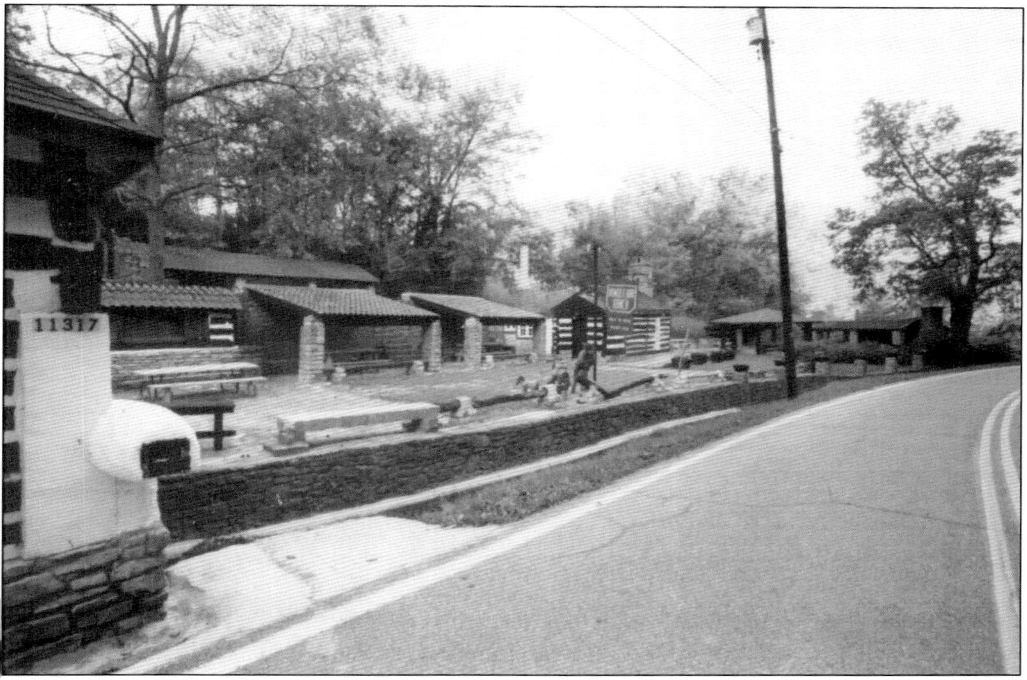

Here is the Handle Bar Ranch in 1998. Many changes have taken place through the years to make it more appealing to younger generations. (Courtesy of Anna Ritter.)

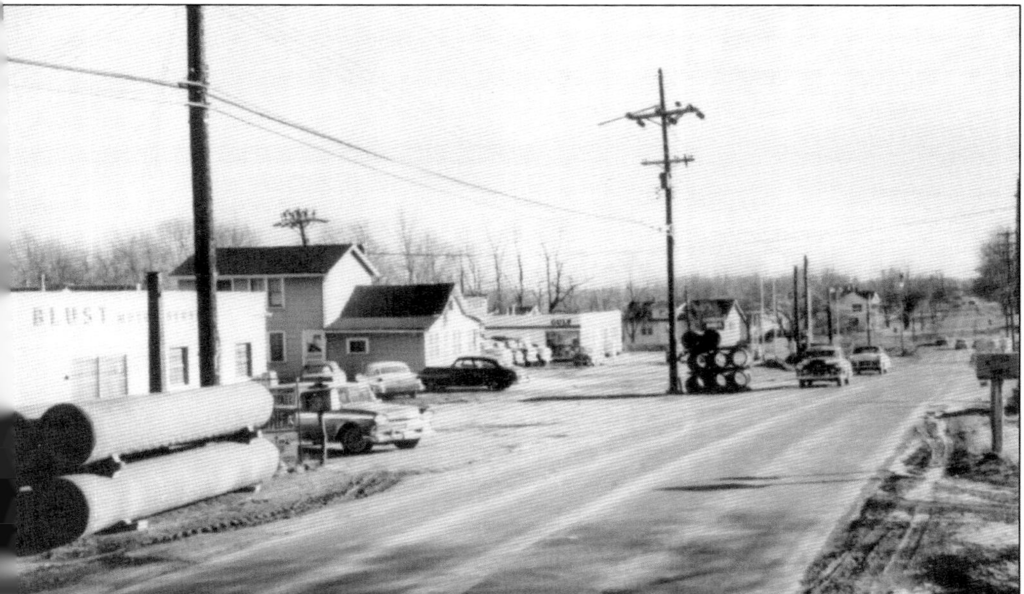

1962, Colerain Avenue underwent a massive widening and renovation. Sewers were being stalled along with curbs and sidewalks, giving the area a new, different look. This is looking uth on Colerain Avenue with Compton Road to the left at the Gulf station. On the left is Blust otor Service, and in the left center is Wagner's Café. (Courtesy of Mel Blust.)

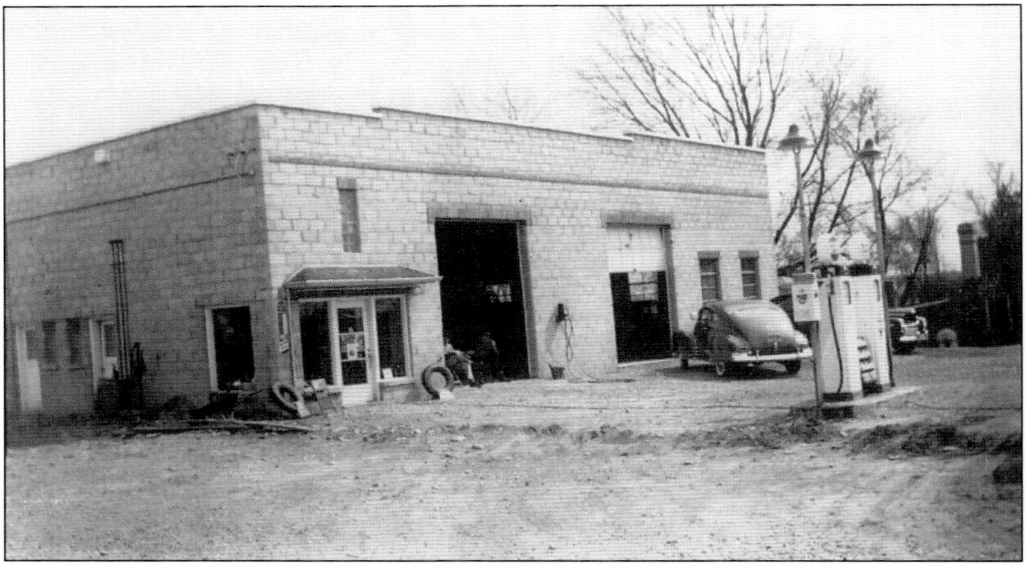

Hardert's Garage was located on the east side of Colerain at 8300 Colerain Avenue. Here is the garage shortly after it opened in 1947. That is Earl Frey's 1947 Chevrolet Fleetline in front and Jack Hardert's Buick to the right. Hardert's remained in business until early 1996. (Courtesy of Earl Frey.)

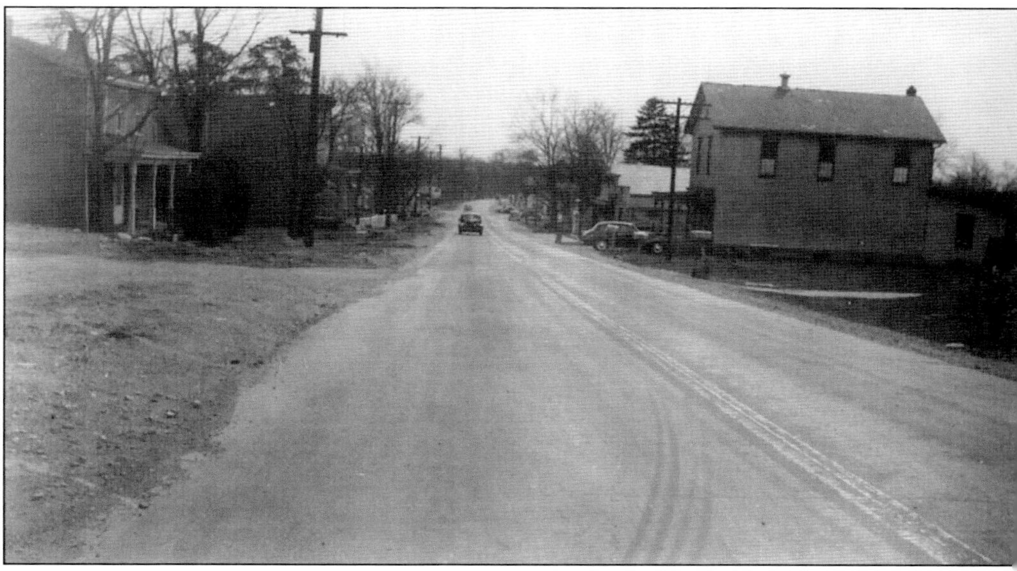

This view looks south on Colerain Avenue toward the intersection of Colerain Avenue an Galbraith Road in 1947. On the left, south of the white fence, is the Groesbeck Improvemen Association building and the Groesbeck Fire Department. Next is Armond Clawson's Mobile ga station. On the northeast corner of the intersection is the Frey building. On the southeast corne was the Galbraith ball field. On the southwest corner was Kurt's Tavern and Fieler's Lounge. Th northwest corner had the Groesbeck Inn and Tavern. (Courtesy of Earl Frey.)

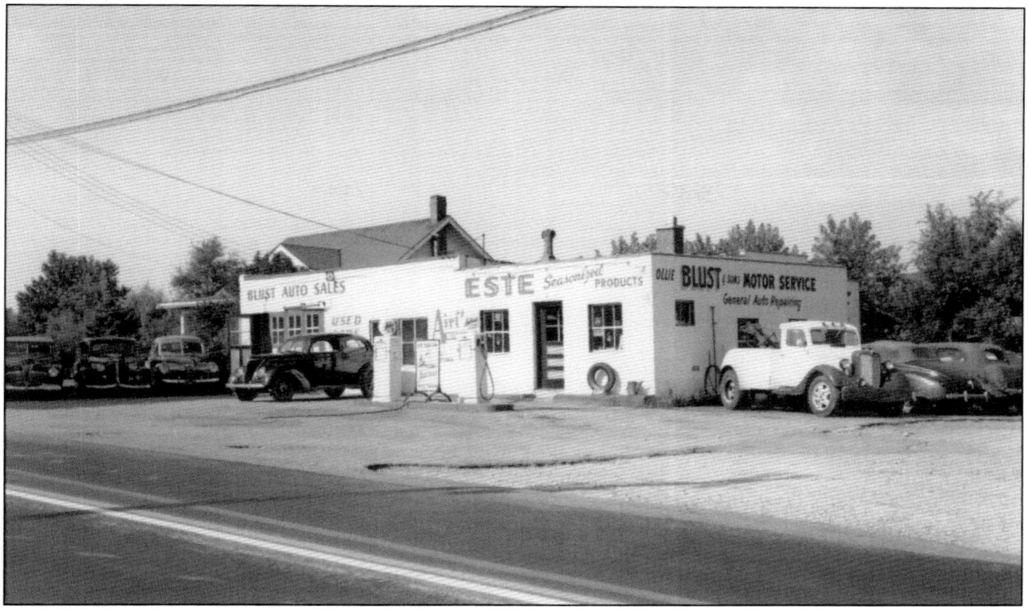

Blust Motor Service has been at 9122 Colerain Avenue in Colerain Township since 1936. The gas station sold Sinclair products and had two gas pumps, but the primary business was repairing automobiles and trucks. Back in 1936, there were only two or three gas stations in the township and no traffic lights. One could drive from Colerain Avenue and Compton Road into the city and not hit a traffic light. (Courtesy of Mel Blust.)

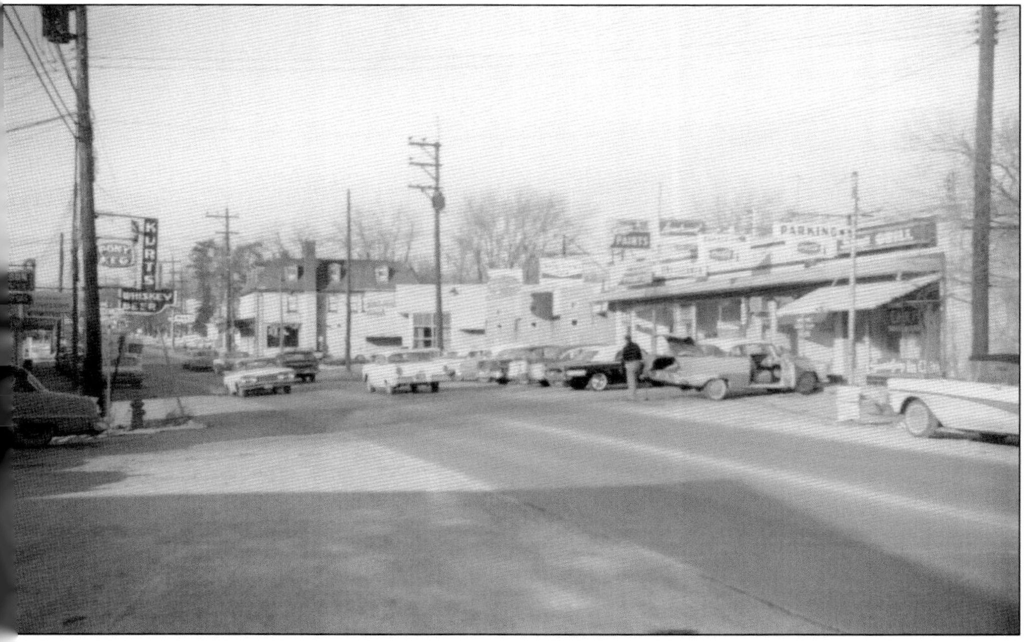

his is Colerain Avenue as it appeared in the 1960s, looking north toward the Galbraith Road tersection. Notice the many buildings that today are just memories. Back in those days, parallel rking was permitted on Colerain Avenue. In the center is the old Provident Bank Building, d further north is the old Frey building. (Courtesy of Mel Blust.)

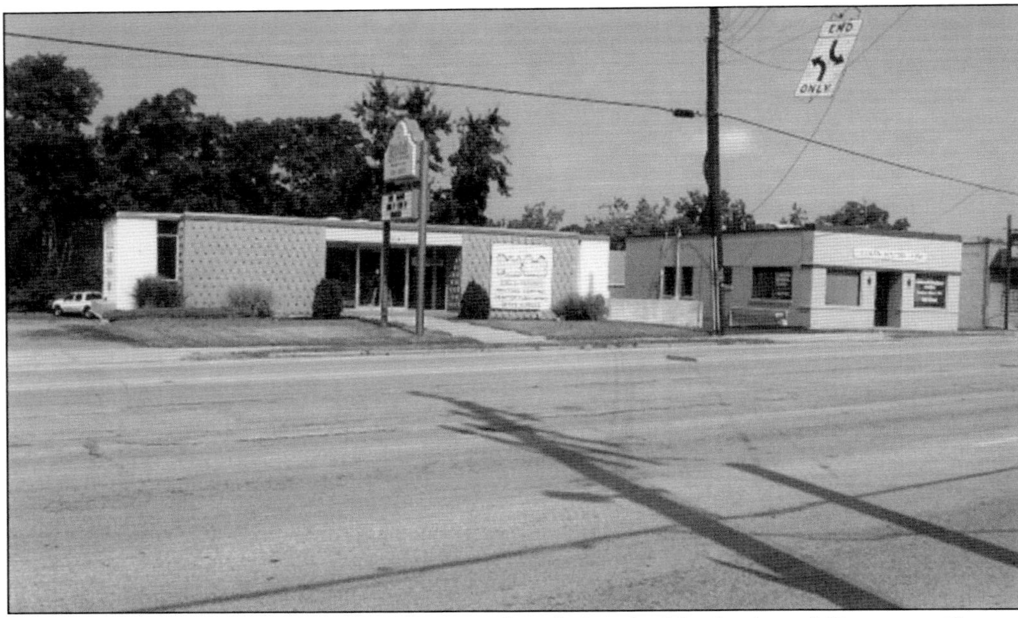

The Elmore Loan and Building Company was founded in the Northside and Cumminsville area in 1907. In 1941, it moved its main office to Groesbeck in Colerain Township. Initially it was housed in the front of a two-family house. In 1941, the building was constructed on the right at 8077 Colerain Avenue. A newer building was constructed as a state-of-the-art bank building (left in the picture at 8045 Colerain Avenue). (Courtesy of Don Linz.)

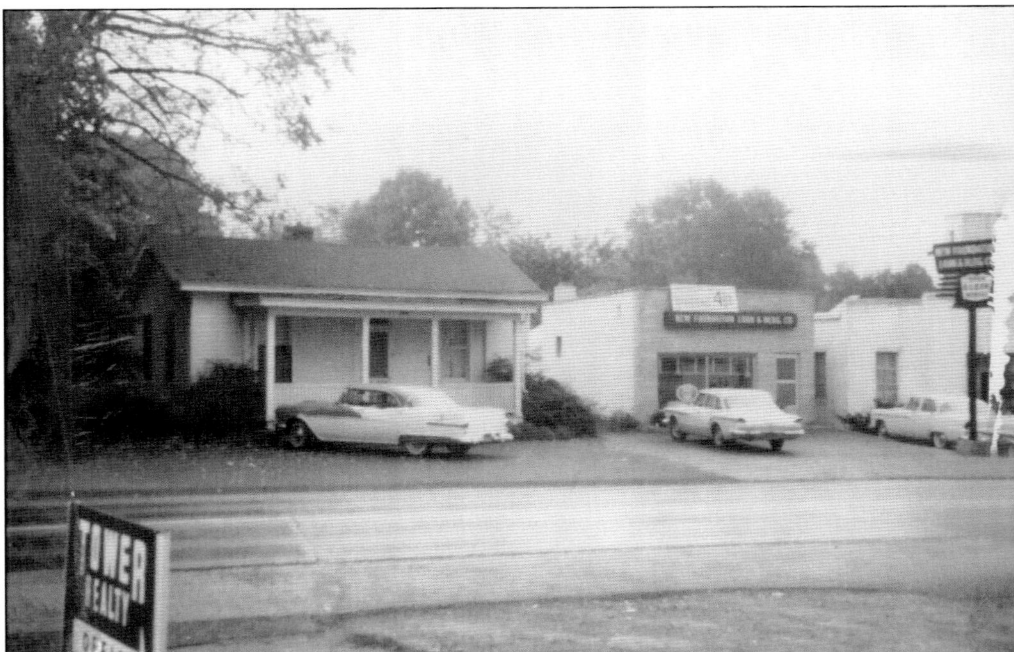

The original New Foundation Loan and Building Company's location was on the east side c Colerain Avenue, north of the Groesbeck Improvement Building. New Foundation later built new building, directly behind the old building on Clara Avenue. (Courtesy of Mel Blust.)

Two

CHURCHES AND SCHOOLS

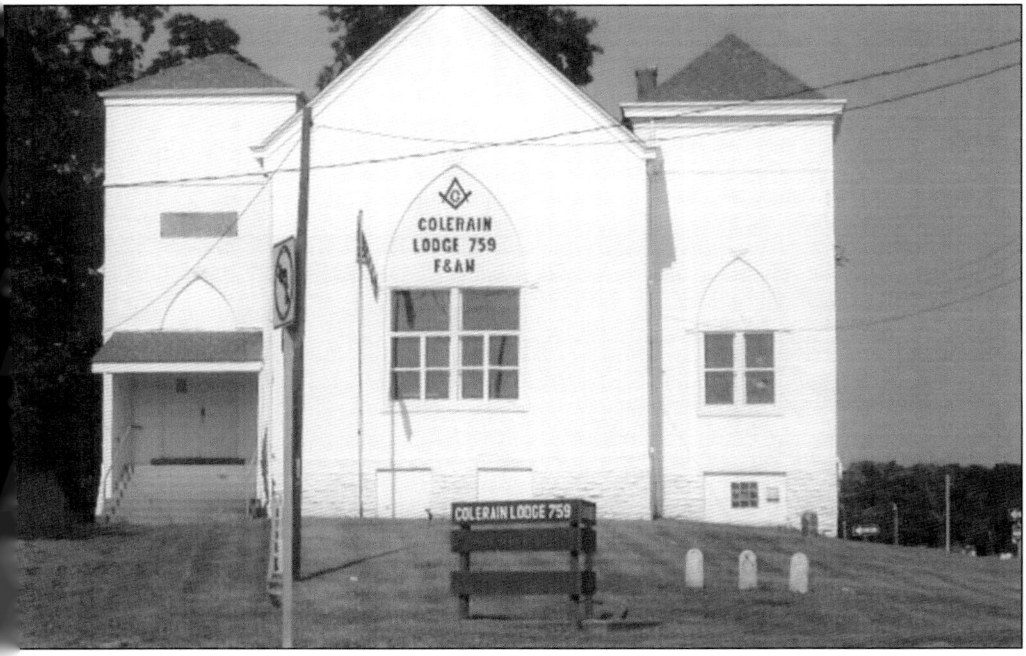

his building, now occupied by the Colerain Lodge No. 759 F. & A.M., is located on the southwest ɔrner of Colerain Avenue and Dry Ridge, on land donated by Jesse and Sarah Bevis. It was the ɔme of what is believed to be the oldest continuous church in the township. Informal meetings ere held as early as 1790. Martin Bevis is said to have been the founder of the church. Back ıen it was called the United Brethren in Christ Church. This building was built in 1893. Today ıis church is known as the Christ Prince of Peace United Methodist Church and is located at)507 Old Colerain Avenue where it moved in 1962. (Courtesy of Don Linz.)

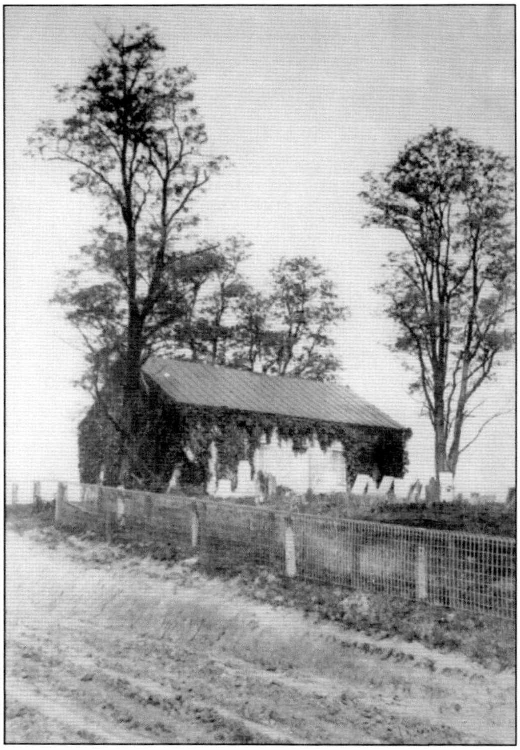

The West Branch Millcreek Church was located at this site on Springdale Road east of Pippin Road in the 1820s. The church has been razed, but the cemetery is still in place. Notice that Springdale Road is unpaved. (Courtesy of the Coleraine Historical Society.)

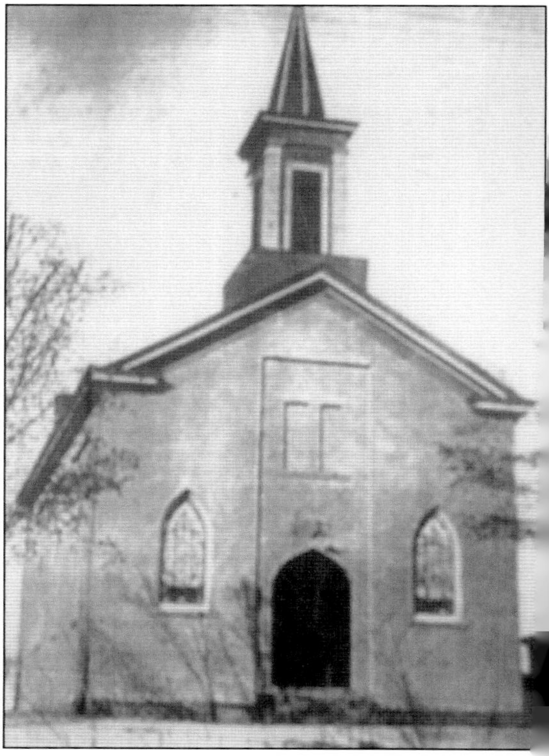

The Old St. Paul Evangelical Church on Blue Rock Road near Springdale Road was established in a small frame building in 1840. A new building was dedicated in 1874. Originally the church had a large German congregation, but times changed and the German services were discontinued in the late 1920s. A complete remodeling and enlargement of the church was completed in 1961. The name was changed to the present St. Paul United Church of Christ. (Courtesy of the Coleraine Historical Society.)

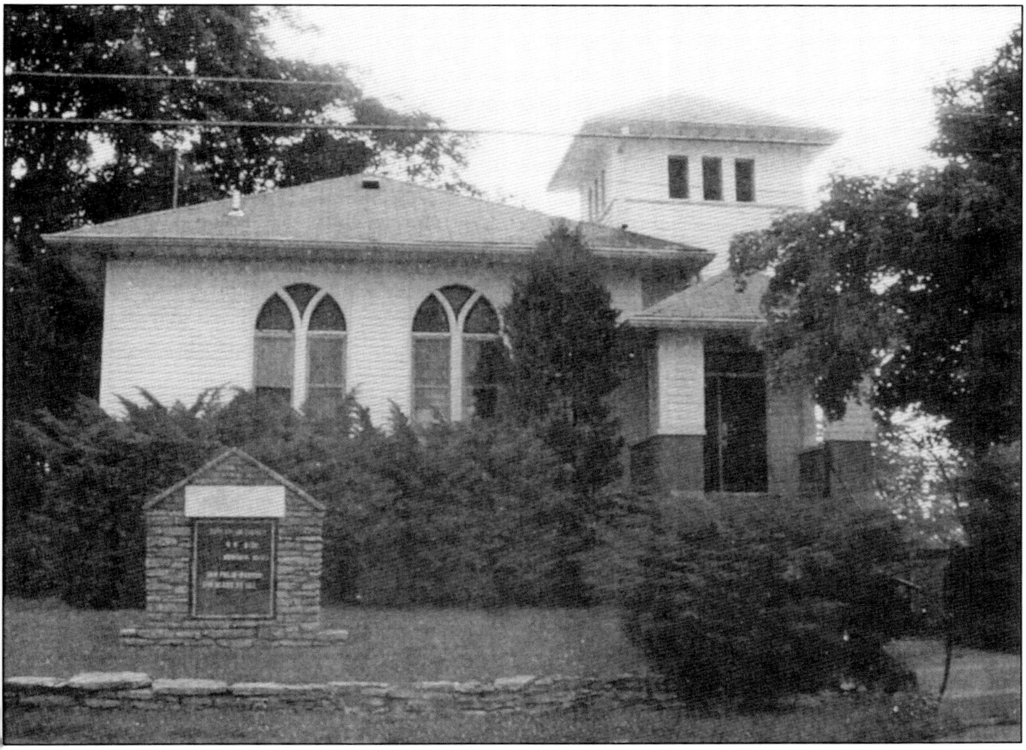

This is the Dunlap United Methodist Church as it appears today. The church has gone through various name changes through the years. The land for the church was donated by Giles Richards in 1860. He also gave 10 acres of woodland so the church would have fuel for future years. In the early years, the horses were tied at a hitching rack in front of the church. When it was cold, the blanketed horses waited until the services were over. (Courtesy of the Dunlap United Methodist Church.)

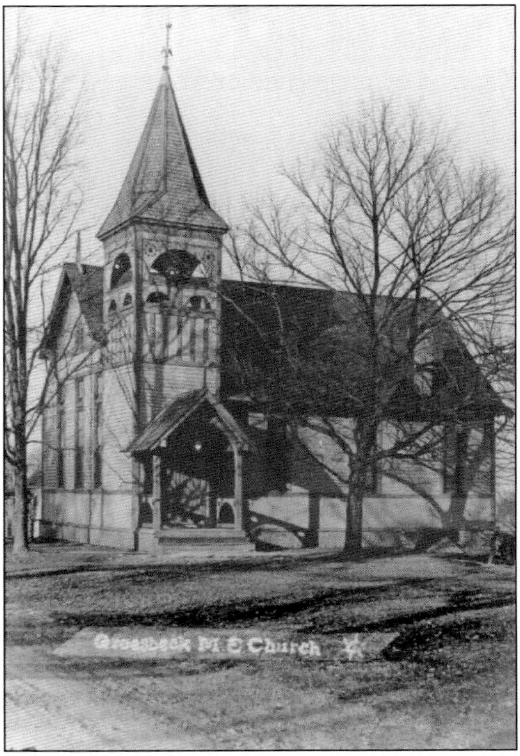

The earliest-recorded Methodist church in Colerain Township is found on Blue Rock Road near Sheits Road. In 1823, Daniel and Rhoda Dean sold a tract of land to the trustees of the Methodist Society. A church on Blue Rock Road near Galbraith Road was a forerunner of the Groesbeck United Methodist Church. This 1910 photograph shows the church built in 1882 on the southeast corner of Colerain Avenue and Compton Road. (Courtesy of Richard Huber.)

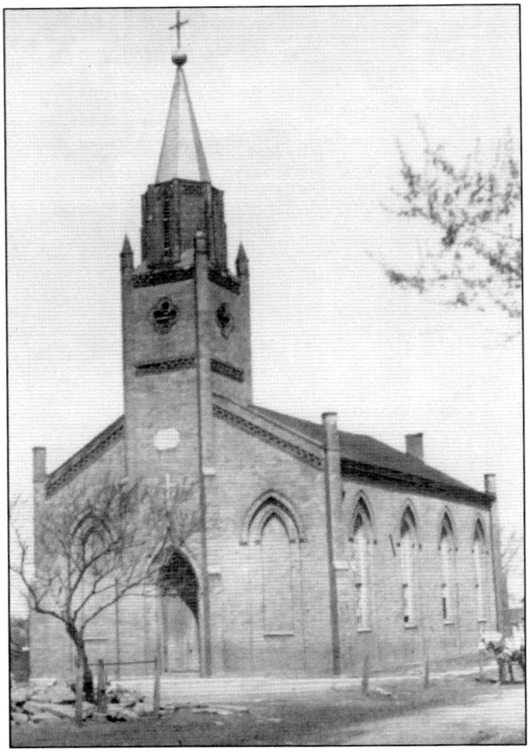

St. John's Catholic Church at 5361 Dry Ridge Road has been home to its congregation since 1846, when a one-room log building was constructed. The cornerstone of the new church (pictured) was blessed on September 2, 1860. St. John's has grown rapidly, and as a result, many changes have occurred. A new and larger church was built in 1997 to accommodate this growing area. (Courtesy of St. John's Catholic Church.)

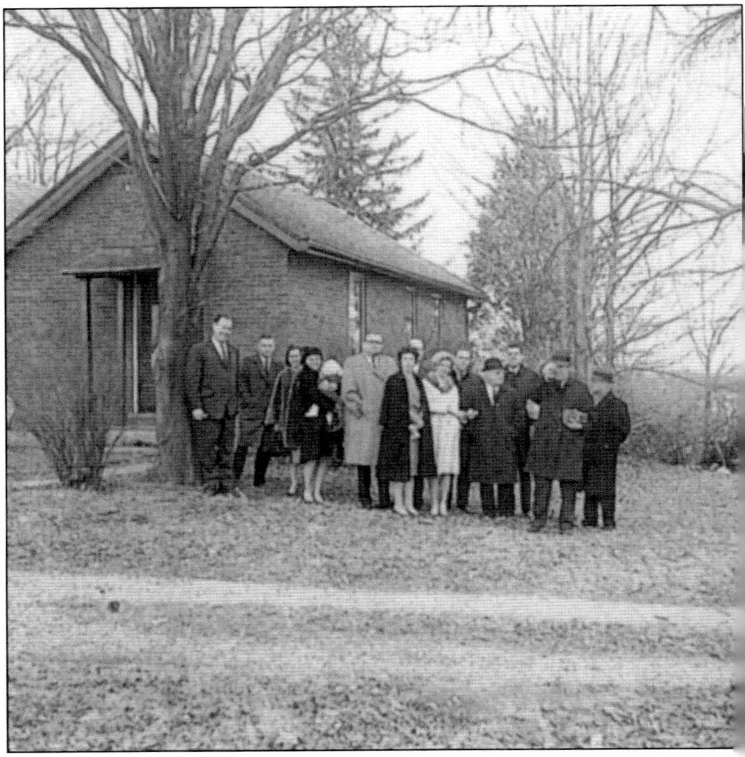

The White Oak Presbyterian Church began its days as a worshipping community in a little house at 3268 Jessup Road in White Oak on February 16, 1964. As the church community grew, they moved to the little theater at Colerain High School. They then broke ground for the new church at 8735 Cheviot Road. The first morning worship was Easter Sunday, March 20, 1970. Today this church is known as the Northwest Community Church. (Courtesy of the White Oak Presbyterian Church.)

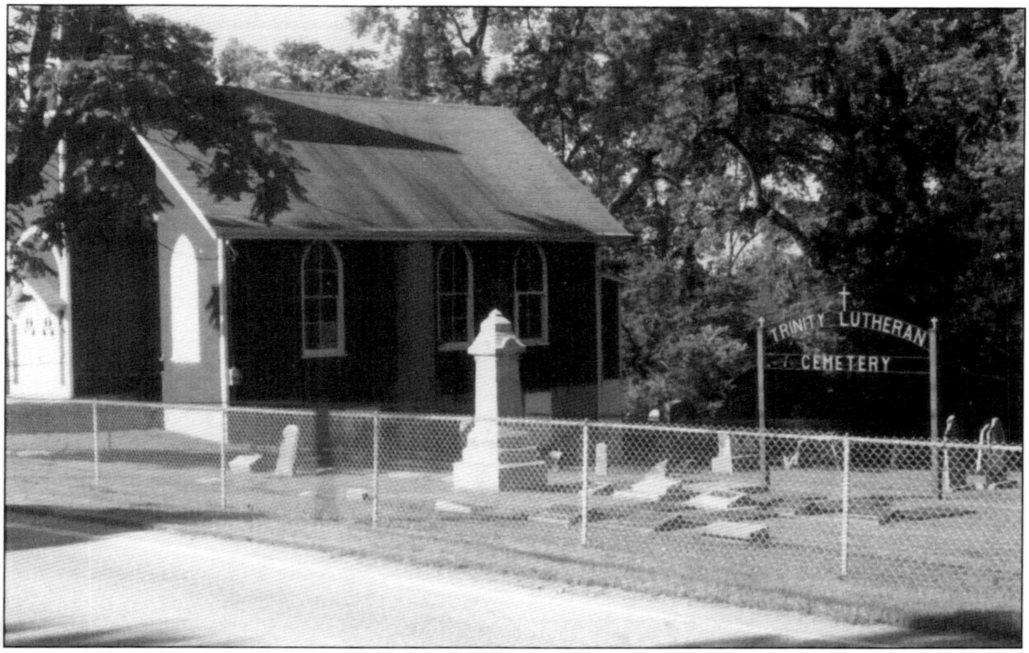

The Trinity Lutheran Church was founded near 7315 Gaines Road in 1851. An old stone church was constructed in the early 1850s. The church was replaced in the early 1920s by the church pictured. Almost all churches in those days had a cemetery nearby. This church was replaced by a beautiful new church in 1958 at 5921 Springdale Road. (Courtesy of Don Linz.)

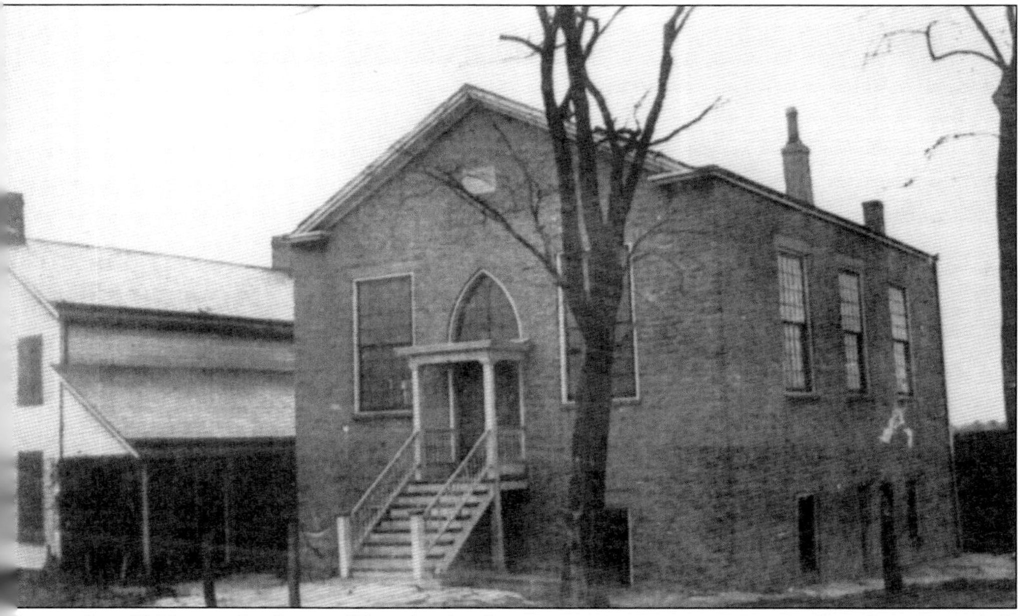

his is the old Trinity Lutheran Church. As the congregation grew, a larger church was needed, ıd that is when they built the new church on Springdale Road. (Courtesy of David Reedy.)

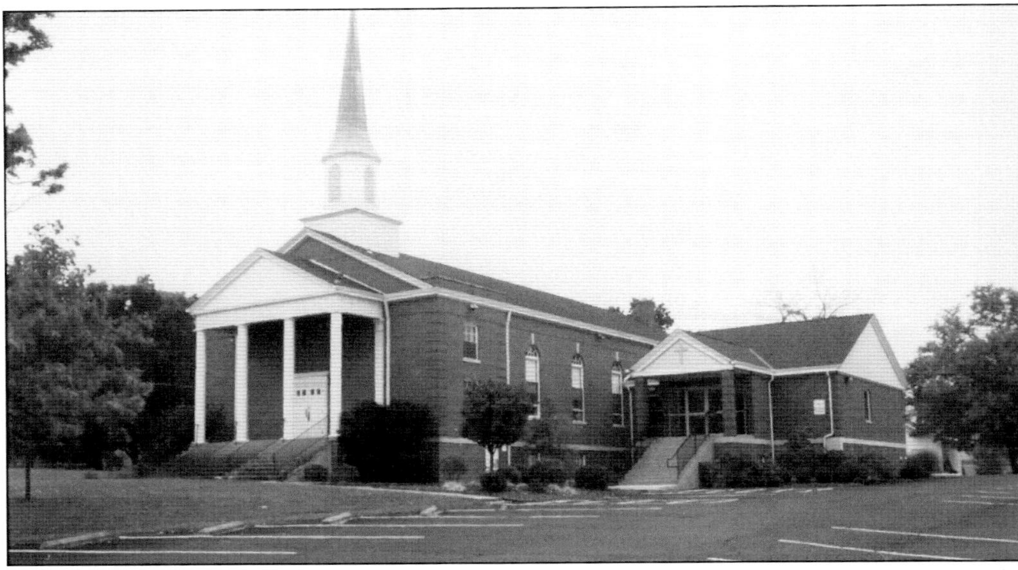

Pleasant Run in Colerain Township is home to the Pleasant Run Presbyterian Church. The church was officially organized on October 16, 1854, with 22 members. The present church was built in 1956 at the corner of Pippin and Crest Roads. The first service in the new building was held on December 15, 1957. One of the proudest moments of the church came with the burning of the mortgage during Christmas 1966. (Courtesy of Don Linz.)

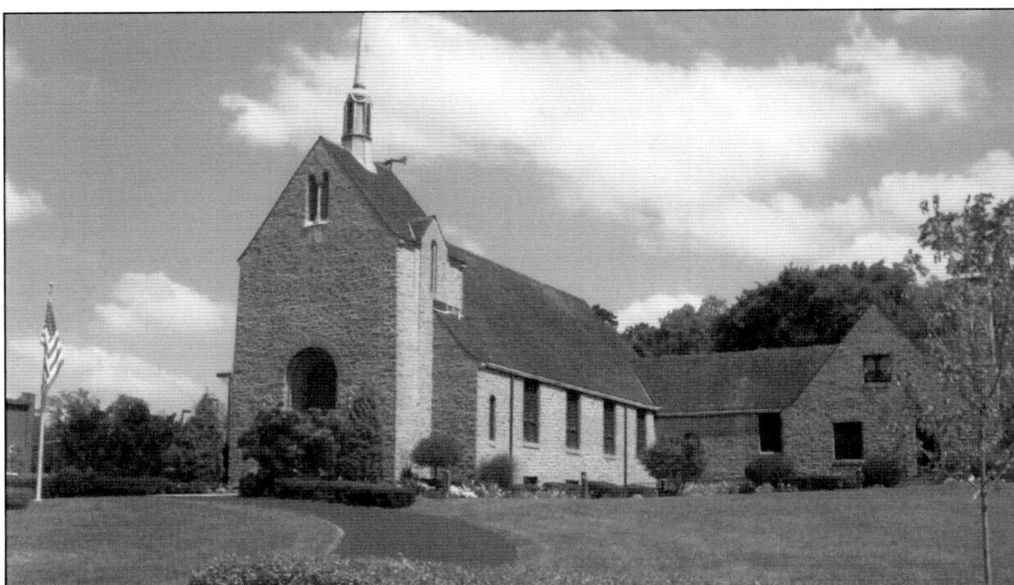

St. Bernard's Catholic Church in Taylor's Creek, at the corner of Harrison Pike and Springdal Road, is a picturesque structure in the English country church style, with interior and exterior wal made from local fieldstone and built in the German Fieldstone style. This parish was establishe in 1867 and has operated a school from the church's beginning. Additions to the school hav occurred as needed. A new rectory and a new parish center building have also been added. Th present church was built in 1935. (Courtesy of Don Linz.)

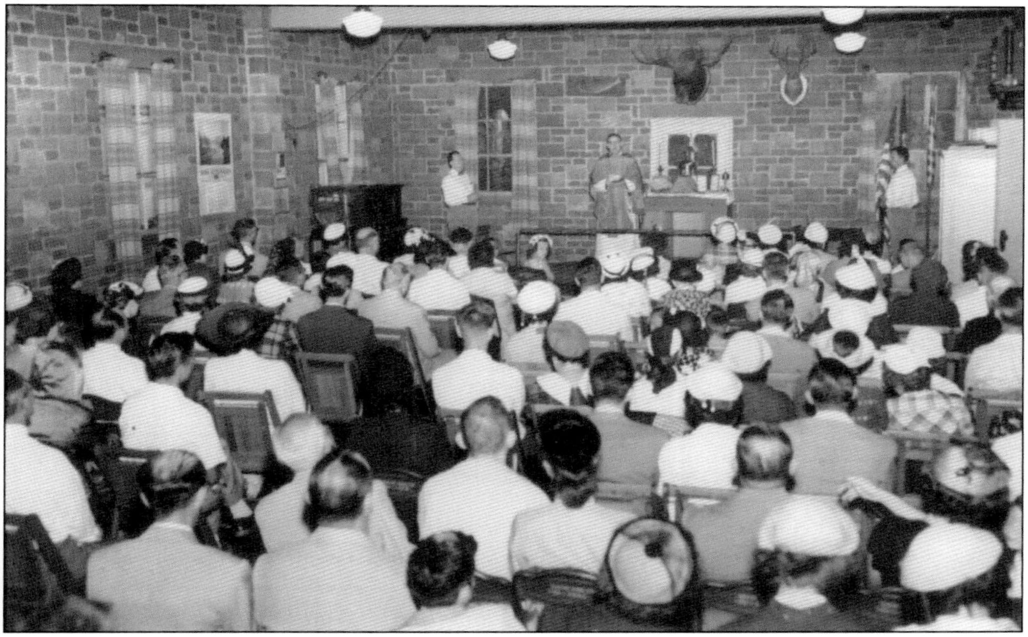

The first masses of the new Catholic parish, St. Ann's of Groesbeck, were held in the Groesbeck Improvement Building on the east side of Colerain Avenue. Fr. James Lunn said mass there from Sunday, June 28, 1953, until November 1, 1953. Notice the moose head above the altar. (Courtesy of St. Ann's Church.)

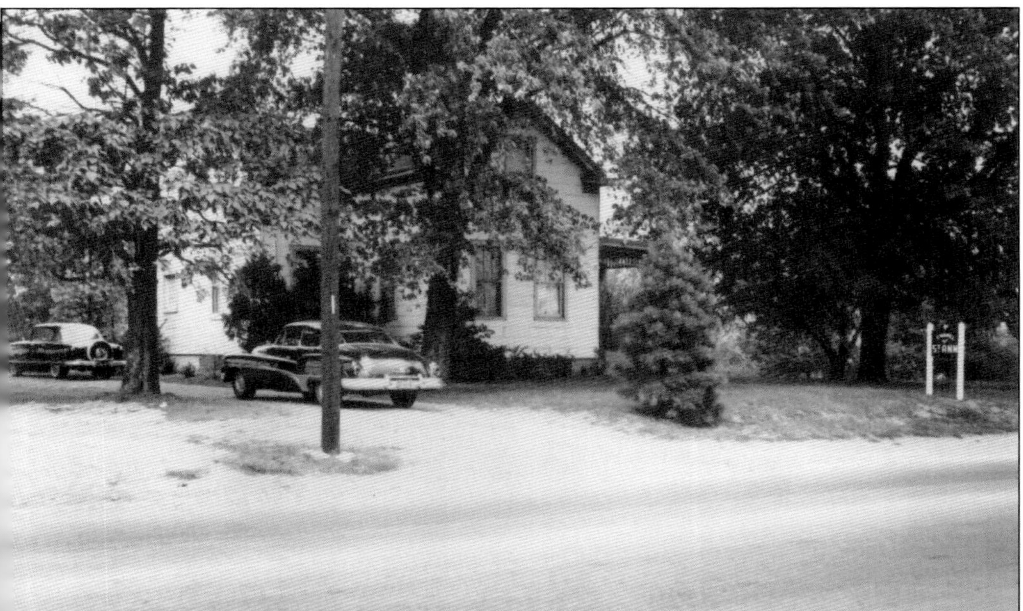

his old farmhouse was located on Galbraith Road on the property St. Ann's bought for e construction of St. Ann's Church and school. After November 1, 1953, daily mass was id here in a devotional chapel. Notice the sign that reads, "Chapel–St. Ann." (Courtesy of t. Ann's Church.)

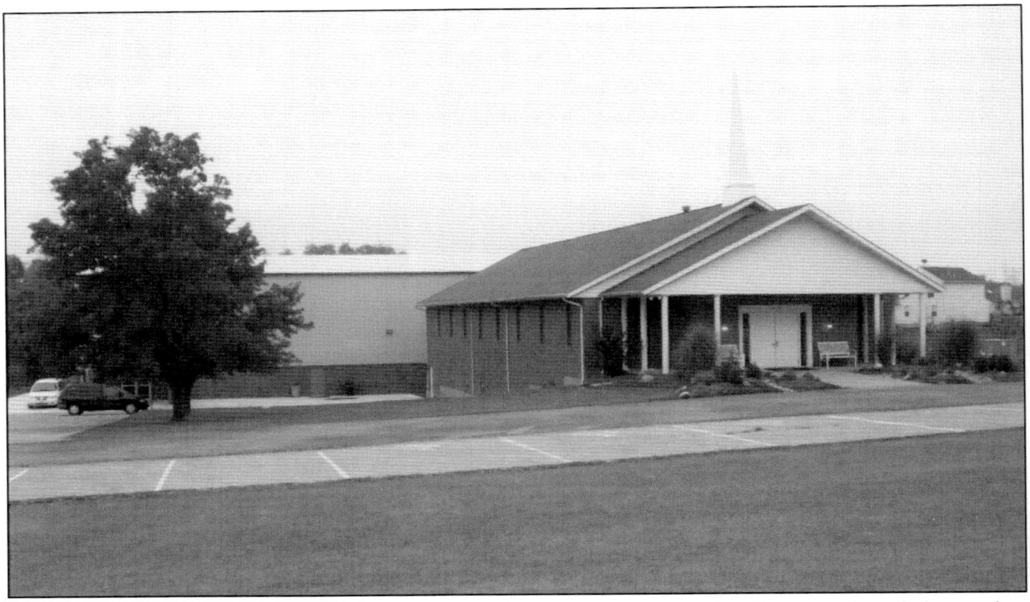

In 1956, the Race Street Mission organized a church called the Bible Baptist Church located at 1822 Race Street. In 1964, the church moved to the suburbs of Fairmount and next, Seven Hills. In the late 1980s, the church bought 10 acres at 2485 Springdale Road, the present site. Now called the Southland Missionary Baptist Church, the church has continued to grow, providing not only religious services but classes for all ages and other services for their congregation. (Courtesy of Don Linz.)

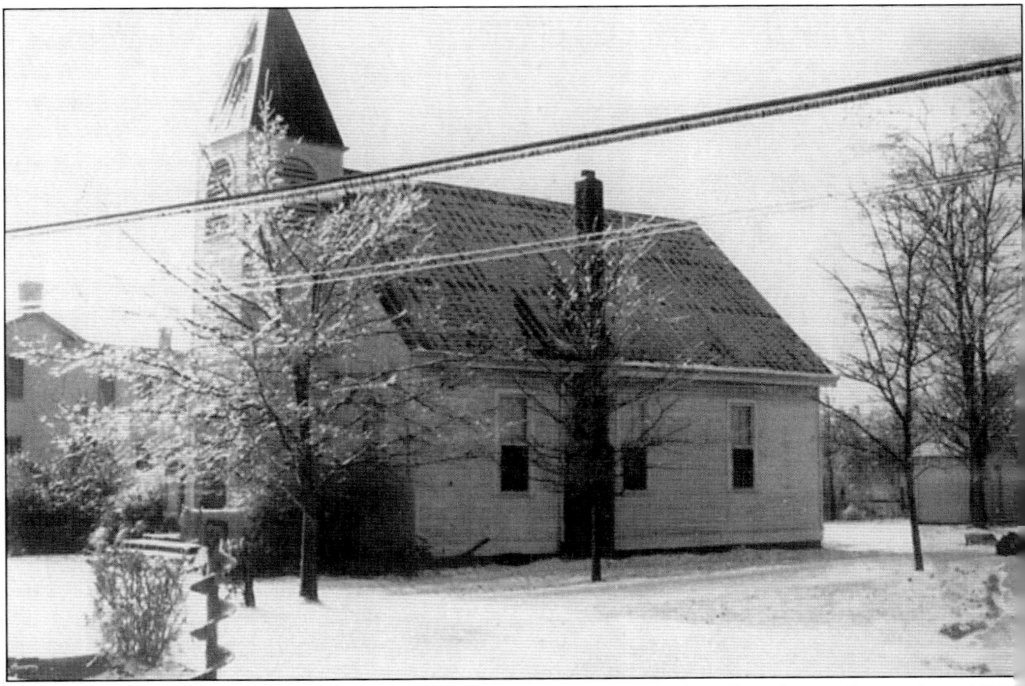

This is the Pilgrim Holiness Church as it appeared in 1961. The church was located at 1027 Colerain Avenue. (Courtesy of Mel Blust.)

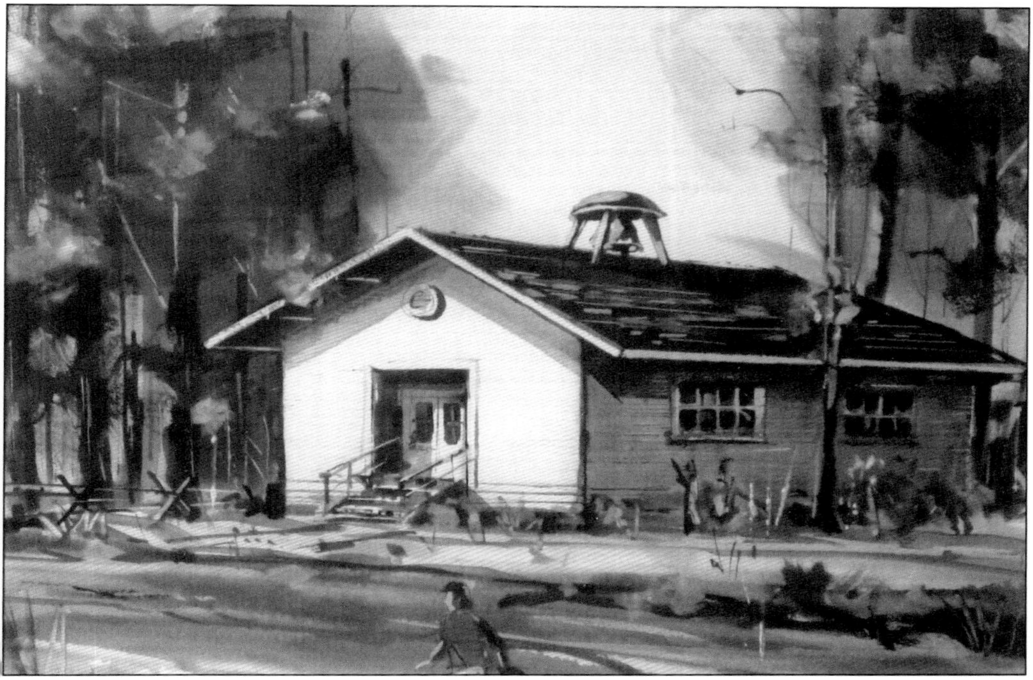

The old Round Top School was so called because the building had a round top tower. It was the first school in the district. This drawing shows a few people playing in the school yard. The building was located on Round Top Road just west of Colerain Avenue. (Courtesy of the Northside Bank.)

The old Colerain High School was built about 1905. The little Round Top School was closed and was used only for trustee meetings. When the new building became overcrowded, the little old school was reopened for a few years. It closed its doors for the last time in 1924 with 7 pupils. (Courtesy of the Coleraine Historical Society.)

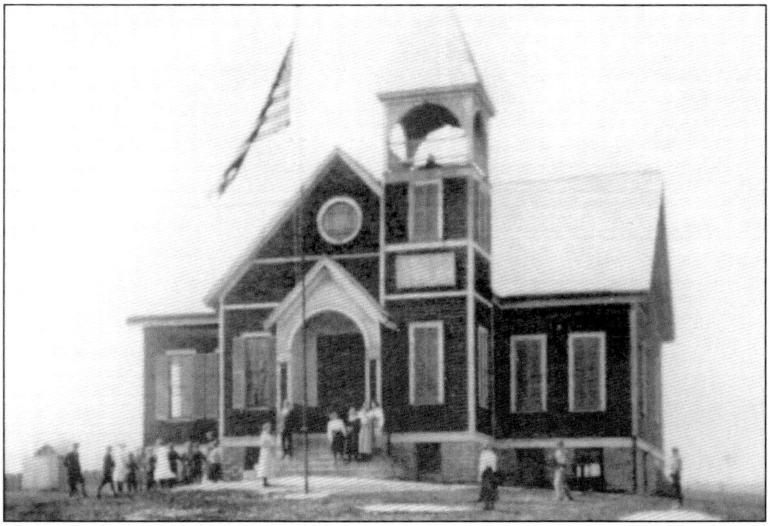

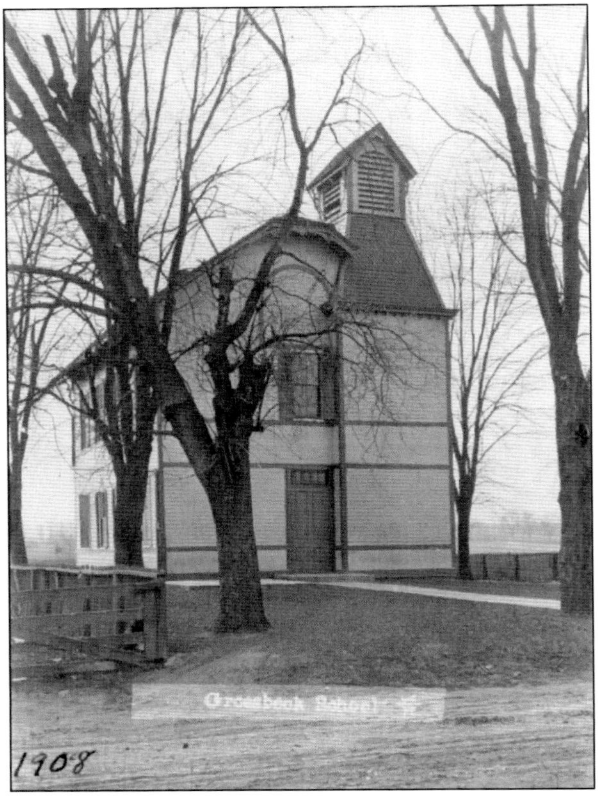

The old Groesbeck school was located on the south side of Galbraith Road, west of Colerain Avenue. This building was erected in 1878. This school closed in the mid-1920s when the one- and two-room schools were centralized. (Courtesy of the Coleraine Historical Society.)

The Blue Rock and Barnesburg schools were both located on Blue Rock Road. The Blue Rock School was located on the north side of Blue Rock Road opposite Flick Road. The school operated from the mid-1800s until it was combined with the Barnesburg school in the 1920s. The building is still standing and is used as a private residence. (Courtesy of the Coleraine Historical Society.)

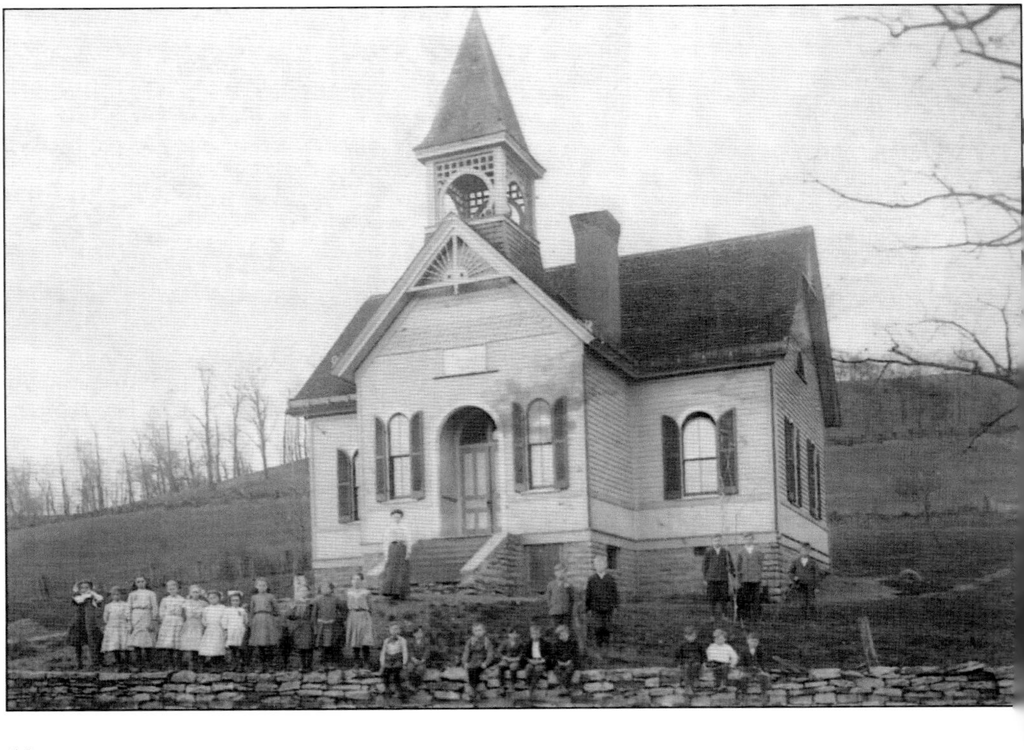

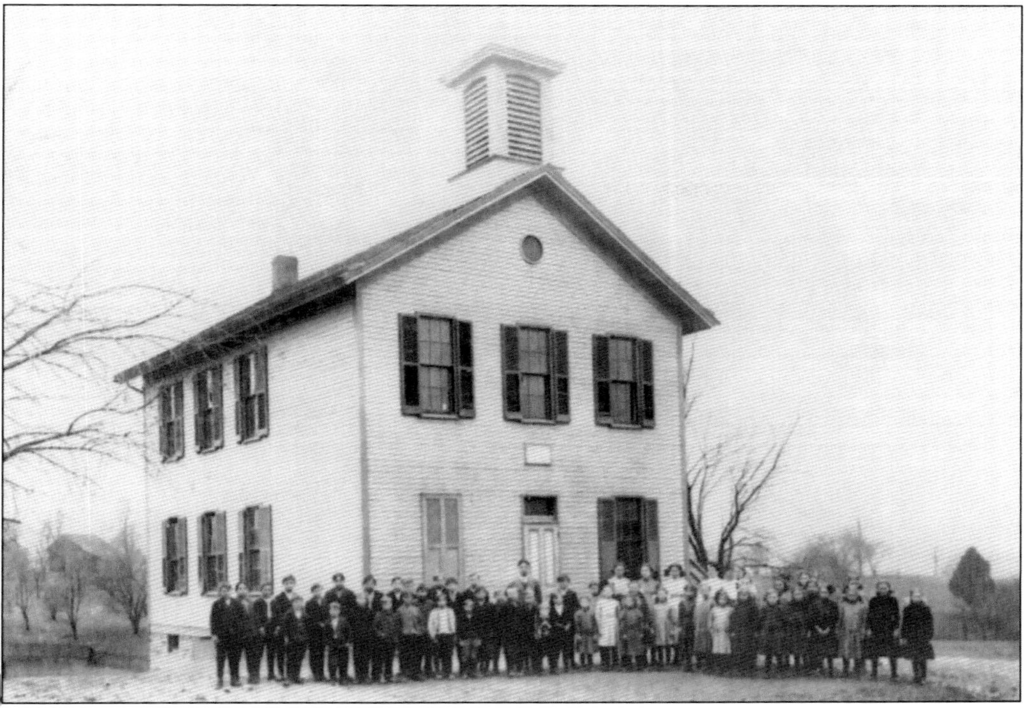

The Barnesburg school was built on land belonging to the Barnes family for whom the village of Barnesburg was named. The two-story building pictured was built in the 1880s. This school was also closed when the schools were voted to centralize to the new school building at Springdale and Poole Roads in 1924. (Courtesy of the Coleraine Historical Society.)

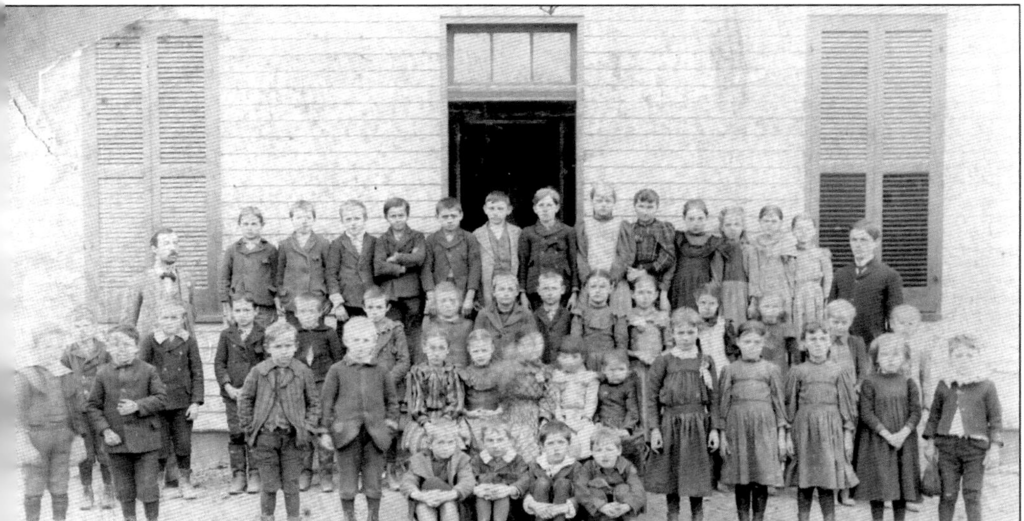

Here are the pupils of the Barnesburg school around 1900. That is John Hammitt on the left and Mr. Cragg on the right. They were teachers at the school at that time. (Courtesy of the Coleraine Historical Society.)

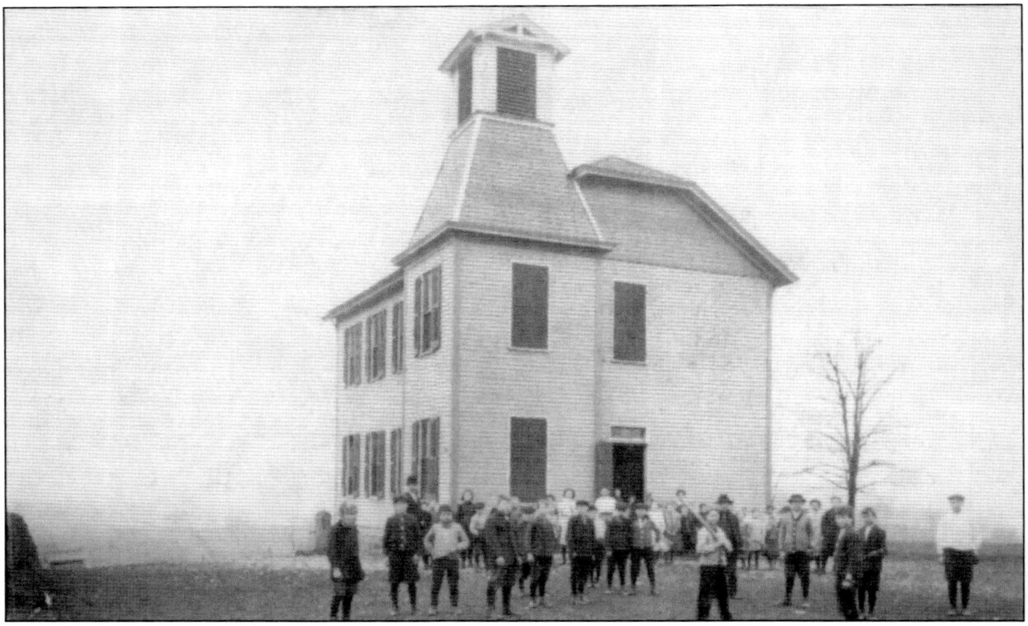

The old Peach Grove school building at the corner of Springdale and Mullen Roads was built in 1880. The school was closed in 1924 when the Colerain schools were centralized. The building later became a private residence and remains so to this day. In the 1950s, there were still two outhouses on the property, one for the boys and one for the girls, as well as a cistern and well to provide water for the students and school. (Courtesy of the Coleraine Historical Society.)

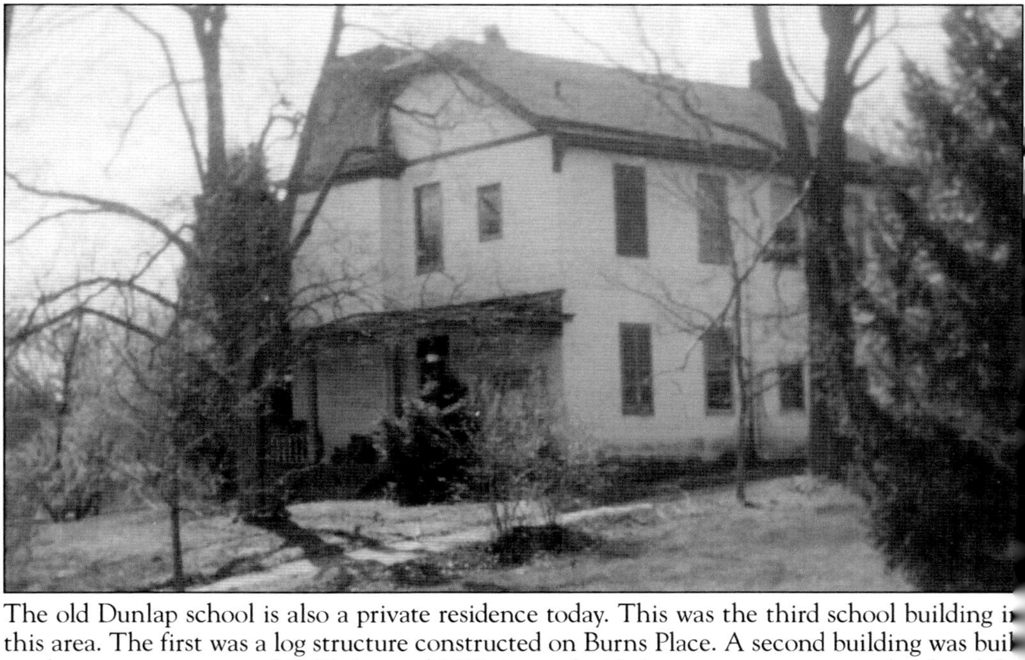

The old Dunlap school is also a private residence today. This was the third school building i this area. The first was a log structure constructed on Burns Place. A second building was buil on the present site around 1865. Around 1885, it was decided to erect a two-room school and th building was sold, moved, and remodeled into a home. This school also closed in 1924. (Courtes of Don Linz.)

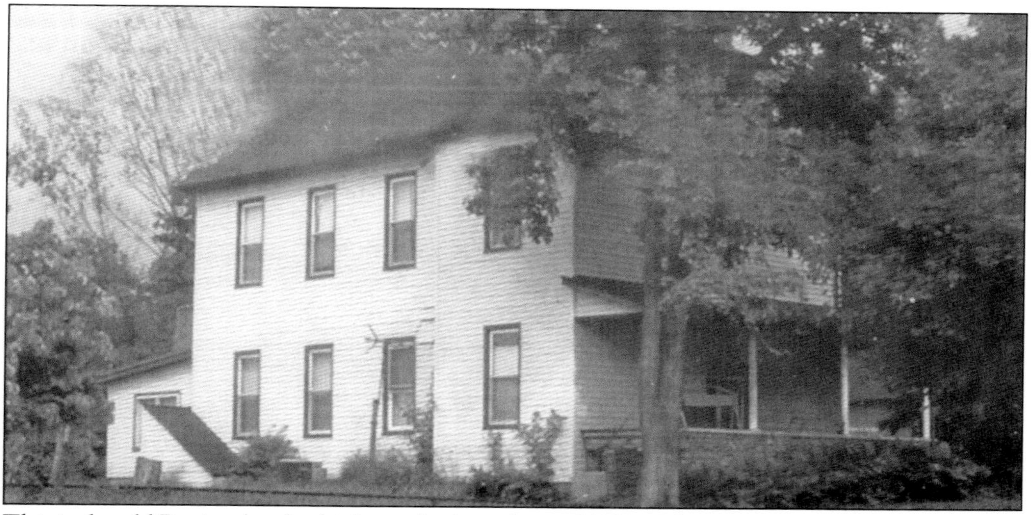

This is the old Bevis school, which was built in the mid-1890s. This was a two-room school. It has been used as a private residence since its closing in 1924. (Courtesy of Don Linz.)

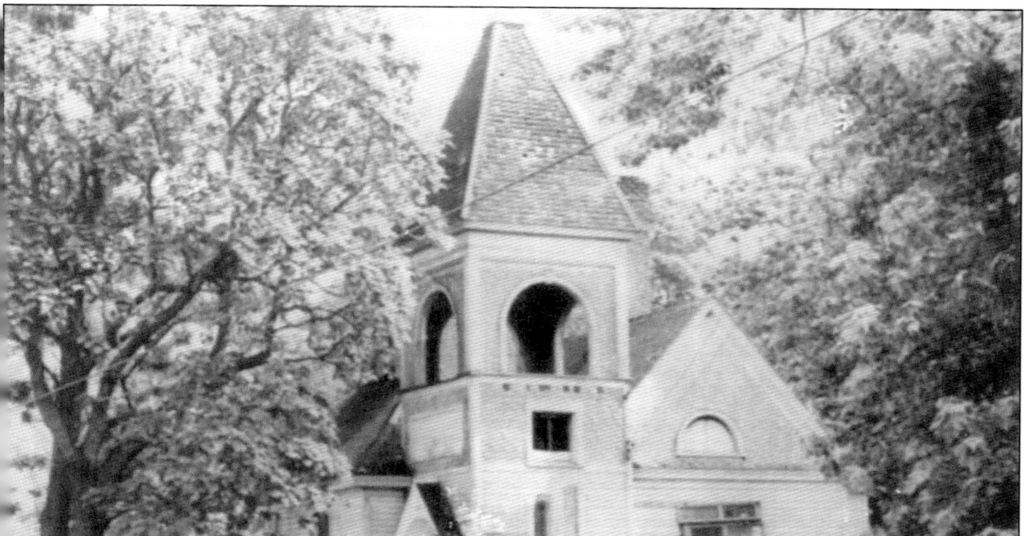

'he Pleasant Run school was built in 1906 on the east side of Pippin Road near Kemper Road. It ›ntinued to operate as a one-room school until it was consolidated into the Northwest School 'istrict in 1950. Early on, the Pleasant Run school sent their high school students to Mt. Healthy efore the consolidation. The Pleasant Run Junior High School stands near this site today. Courtesy of the Coleraine Historical Society.)

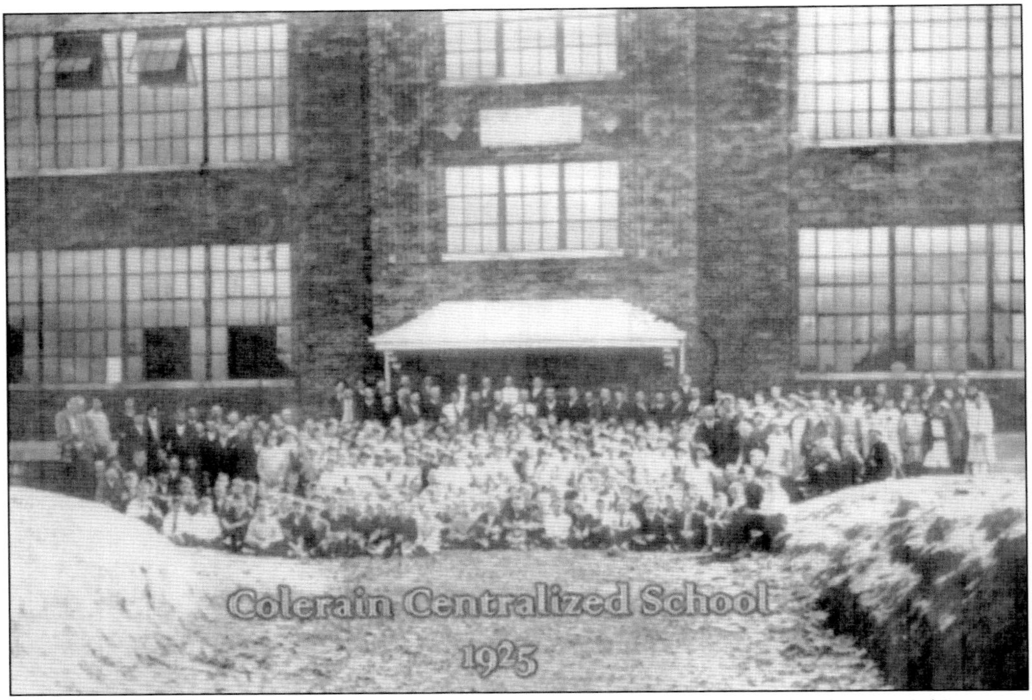

Pictured are teachers and pupils in front of the new Colerain Centralized School in 1925. (Courtesy of the Coleraine Historical Society.)

The first graduating class from the Colerain Centralized School posed for this photograph in 1925. From left to right are Richard Joyce, Lorine Kraus, George Ruoff, Mildred Shaw, Alfred Hutfies, Helen Hoock, Howard Hoock, Helen Craig, and Robert Foster. On the far right is principal Clarence Struble. (Courtesy of the Coleraine Historical Society.)

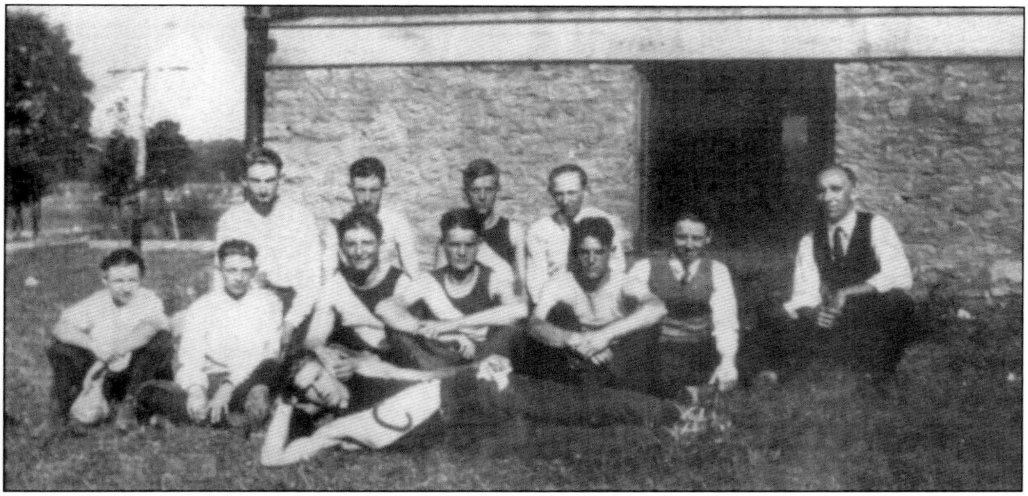

This is the Colerain High School boys soccer team in 1923. (Courtesy of the Colerain High School Alumni Association.)

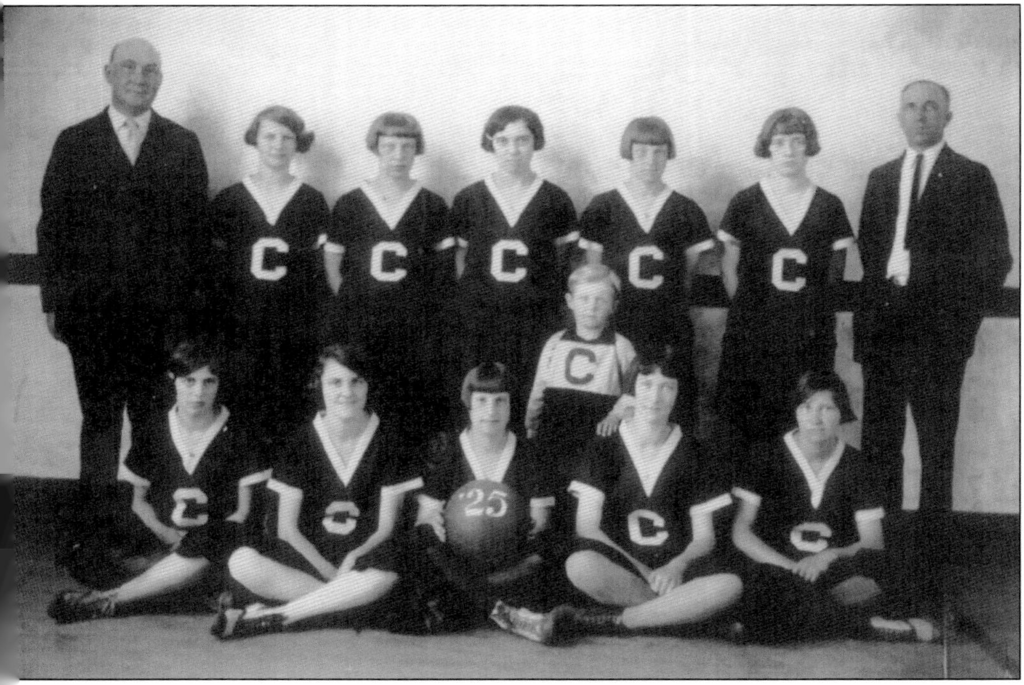

ere is the Colerain High School girls basketball team in 1925. (Courtesy of the Colerain High chool Alumni Association.)

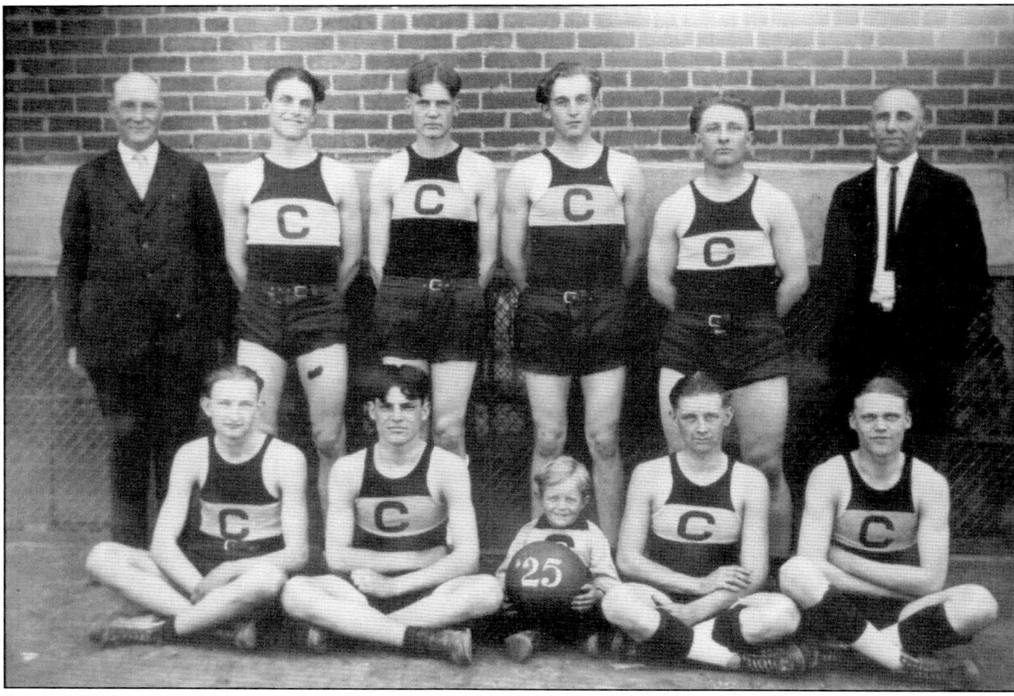

The 1925 Colerain High School boys basketball team poses here for a photograph. (Courtesy of the Colerain High School Alumni Association.)

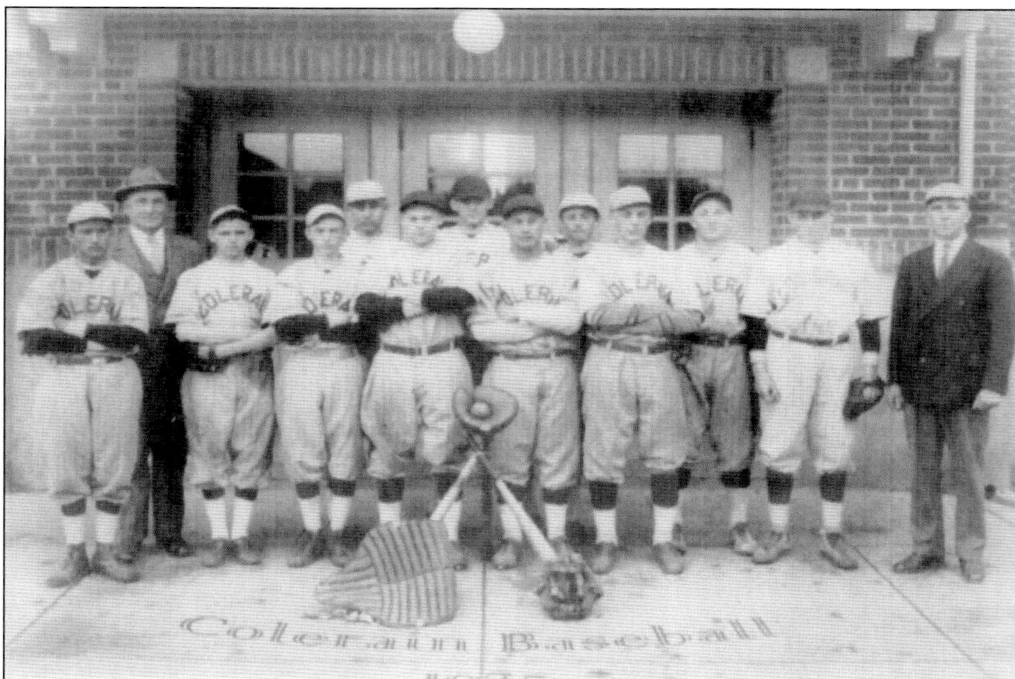

This is the Colerain High School baseball team posing for their team's photograph in 1925
(Courtesy of the Colerain High School Alumni Association.)

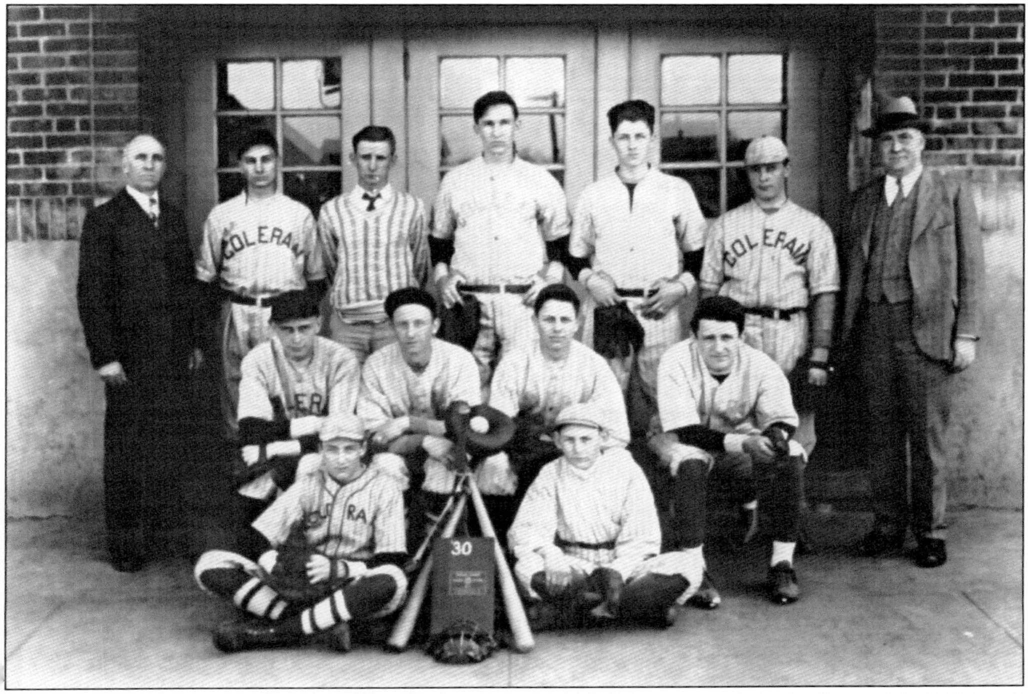

This is the Colerain High School baseball team in 1930. (Courtesy of the Colerain High School Alumni Association.)

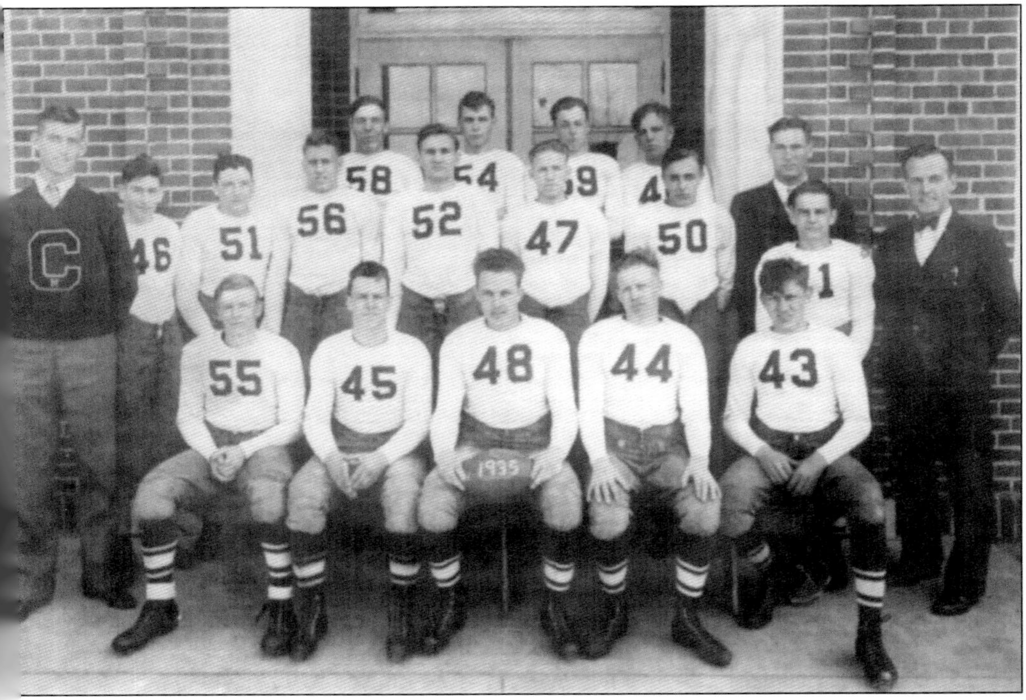

1935, Colerain High School's football team posed for this photograph. (Courtesy of the Colerain igh School Alumni Association.)

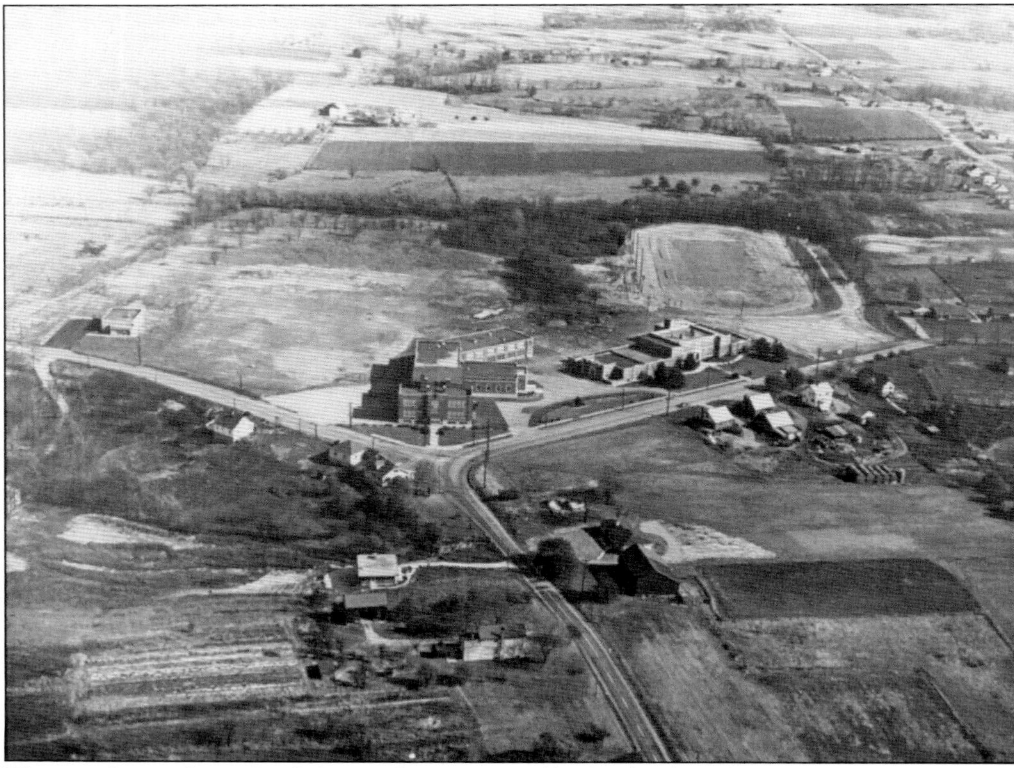

This aerial view shows the Colerain elementary and high schools as they appeared in the 1950s at the intersection of Springdale and Poole Roads. (Courtesy of the Northwest School District.)

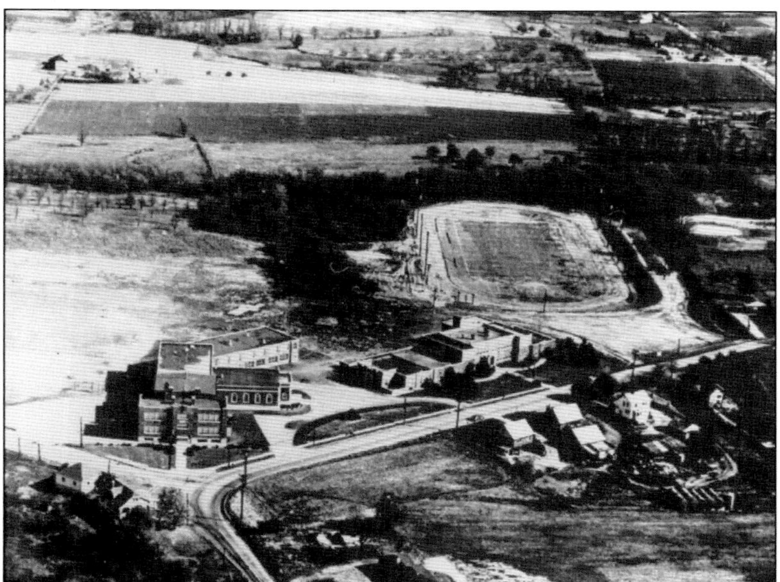

Here is another view of the elementary and high school at Springdale and Poole Roads. (Courtesy of the Northwest School District.)

Three

To Protect and Serve

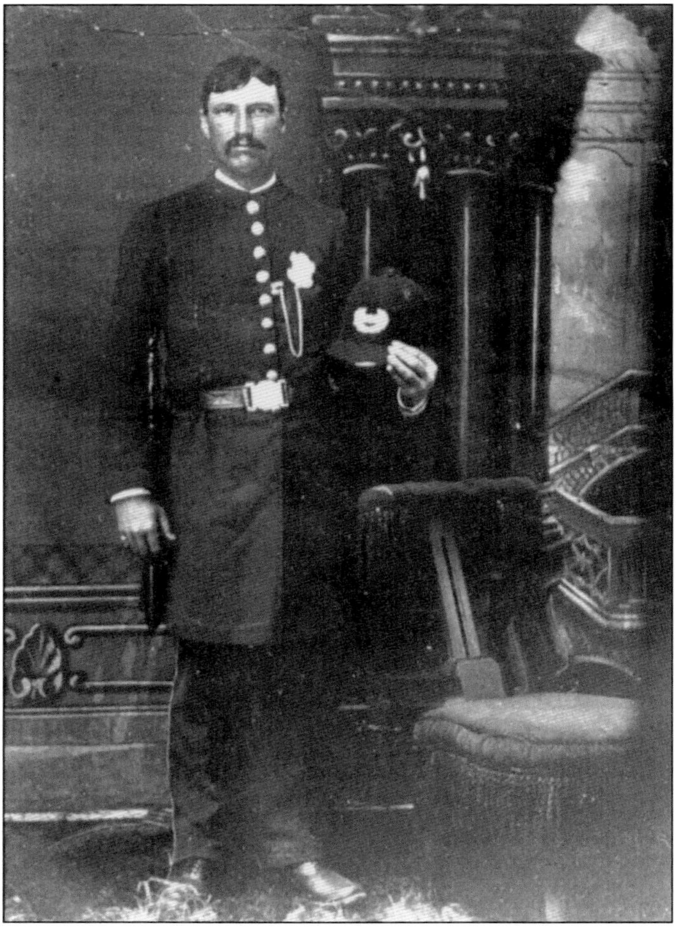

Colerain constable John W. Wilsey was shot and killed in an ambush inside his home on August 15, 1918. Wilsey had returned from the market with a lot of money and was apparently killed for the cash. His assailant was later identified as Orville Ogg. Ogg was arrested and found guilty of second-degree murder. Ogg threatened the Willsey family and everyone else at his trial. He escaped from prison in 1944 and was never found. The Willsey family lived in fear for many years because of Ogg's threats. (Courtesy of the Colerain Township Police Department.)

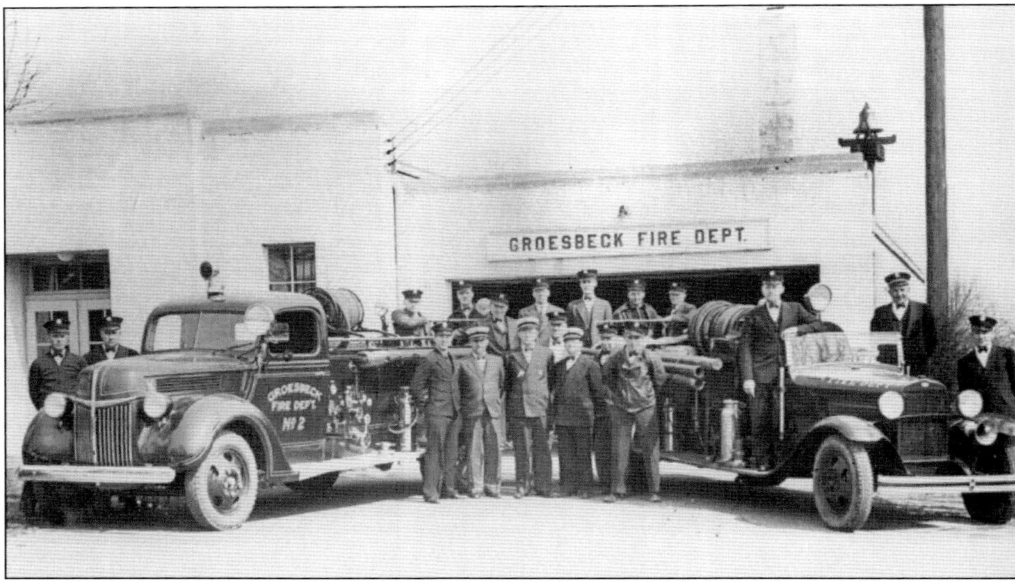

The Groesbeck Volunteer Fire Department poses here in the 1930s. From left to right are (first row) Joe Kramer, Bud Harris, Ed Hirsch, assistant chief John Frey, marshall Ivan Johnson, Henry Fieler, chief Fred Finke, Chris Ruehl, Armond Clawson, Capt. Herman Tieman, John Hermann, and Bill Lengerich; (second row) Ralph Lockwood, Herb Heithacker, Martin Frey, Bud Aston, Carl Thole, Art Bailey, and Carl Huber. (Courtesy of the Coleraine Historical Society.)

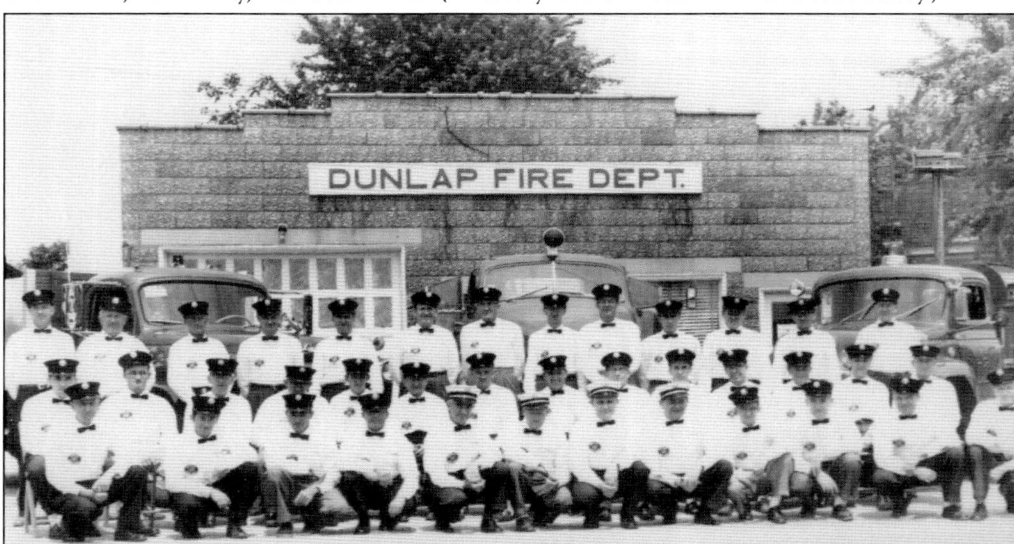

The Dunlap Volunteer Fire Department was, from left to right, (first row) R. Weber, C. Sunderhaus G. Brown, N. Crawford, G. Matt, R. Walters, G. Taylor, H. Hornung, H. Stehlin, E. Williams A. Dorrman, and R. Bowman; (second row) G. Botts, W. Stepaniak, G. McNeil, W. Thompson F. Harris, S. Diefenbacher, G. Schiering, J. Fieter, T. Underwood, Ni. Crawford, W. Hite, D Diefenbacher, L. Shad, and S. Schiering; (third row) Wm. Solneker, S. Knabe, G. Pottenger, R Westrich, R. Ryan, E. Sortman, O. Steiner, E. Moeller, C. Yerkes, A. Kreuzmann, R. Richards, F. Hil and R. Distler. The Groesbeck and Dunlap Fire Departments merged in January 1975 to form th Colerain Township Fire Department. (Courtesy of the Colerain Township Fire Department.)

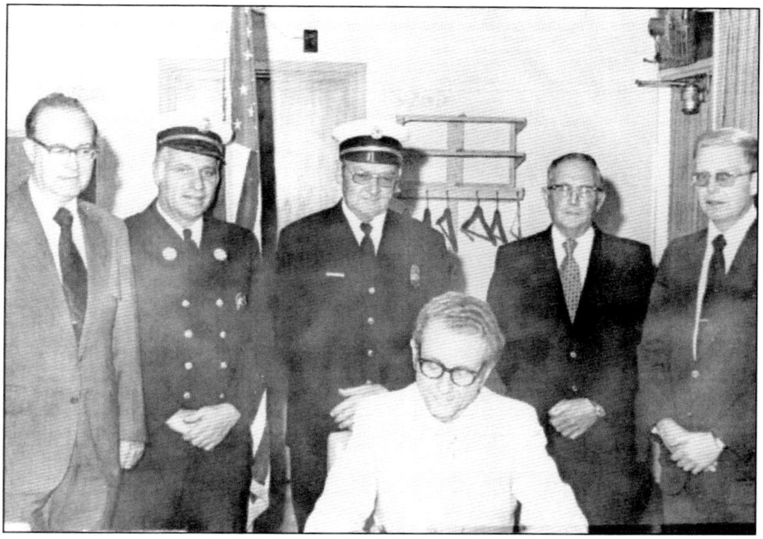

This is the signing of the merger of the Groesbeck and Dunlap Fire Departments in January 1975. From left to right are township clerk Gil Maringer, Groesbeck fire chief Cloyce "Corky" Snyder, Dunlap fire chief Bud Williams, trustee Dale Diefenbacher, and trustee John Schwerling. Seated is trustee Norm Muehlenhard. (Courtesy of the Colerain Township Fire Department.)

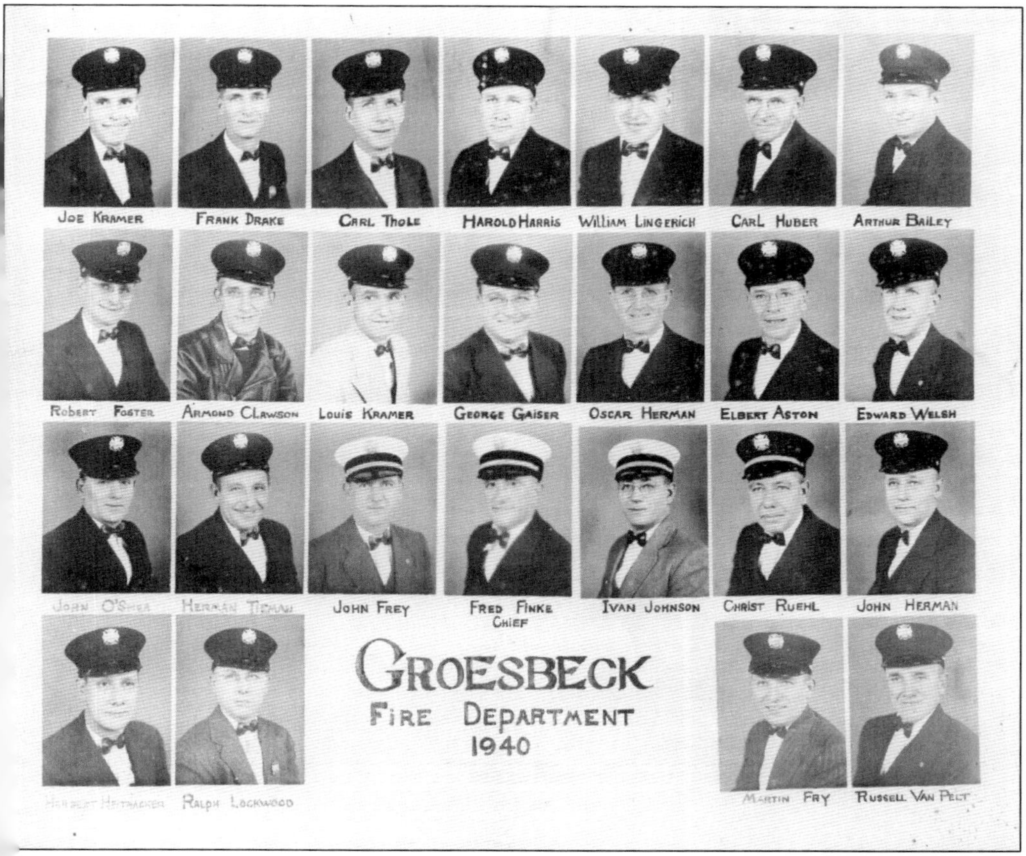

he Groesbeck Fire Department is pictured here in 1940. Many of these volunteer firemen were embers for many years afterwards. (Courtesy of the Colerain Township Fire Department.)

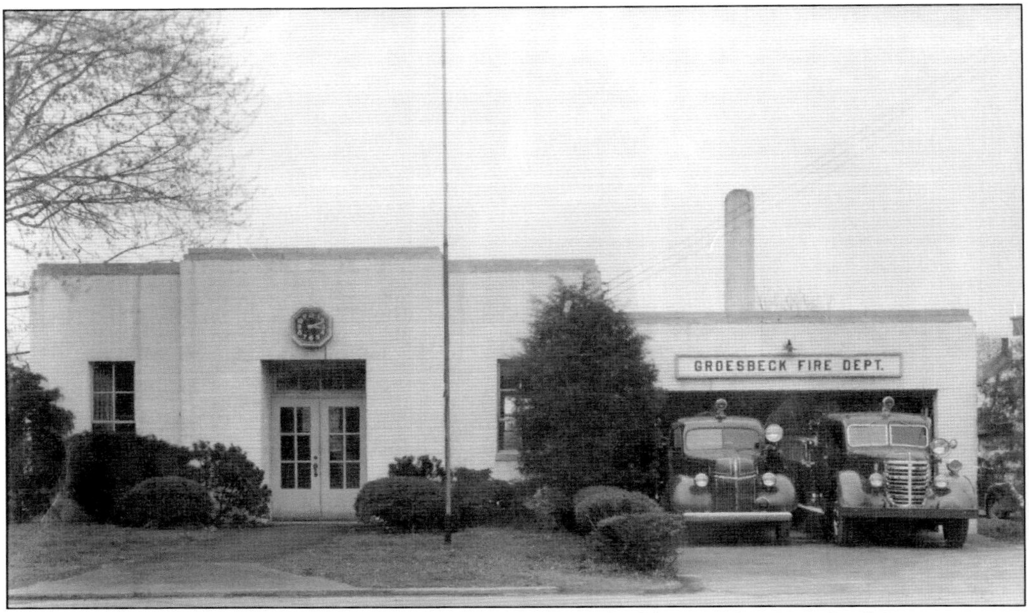

The Groesbeck Fire Department was housed in the same building as the Groesbeck Improvement Association on the east side of Colerain Avenue just north of Galbraith Road. (Courtesy of the Colerain Township Fire Department.)

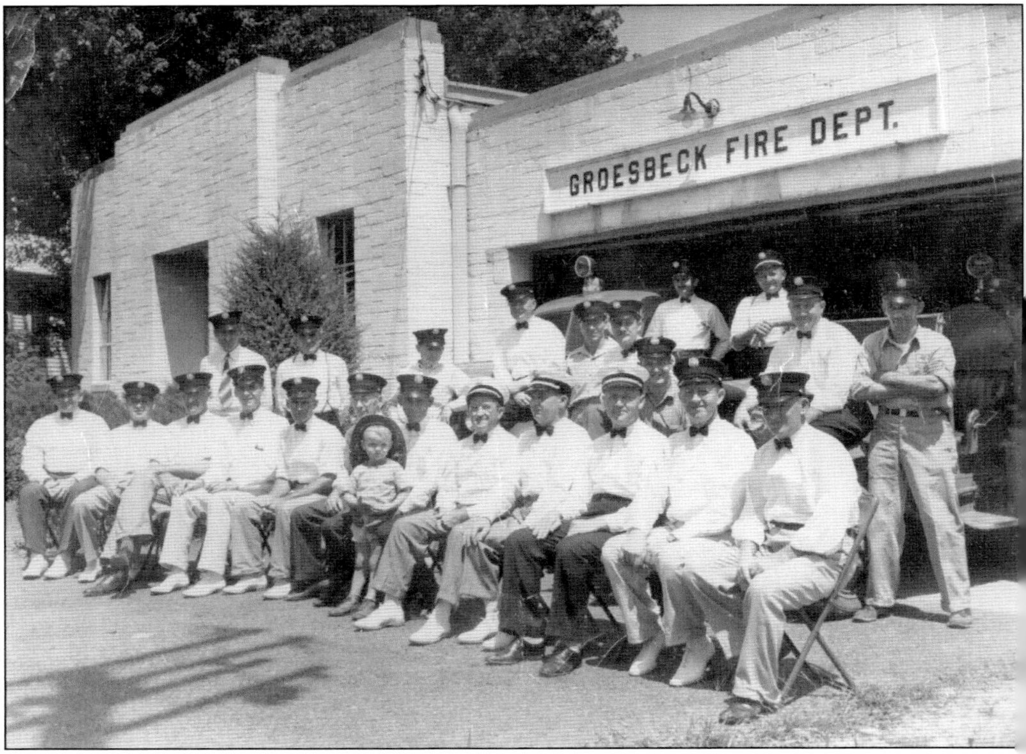

This undated picture shows the members of the Groesbeck Fire Department. (Courtesy of the Colerain Township Fire Department.)

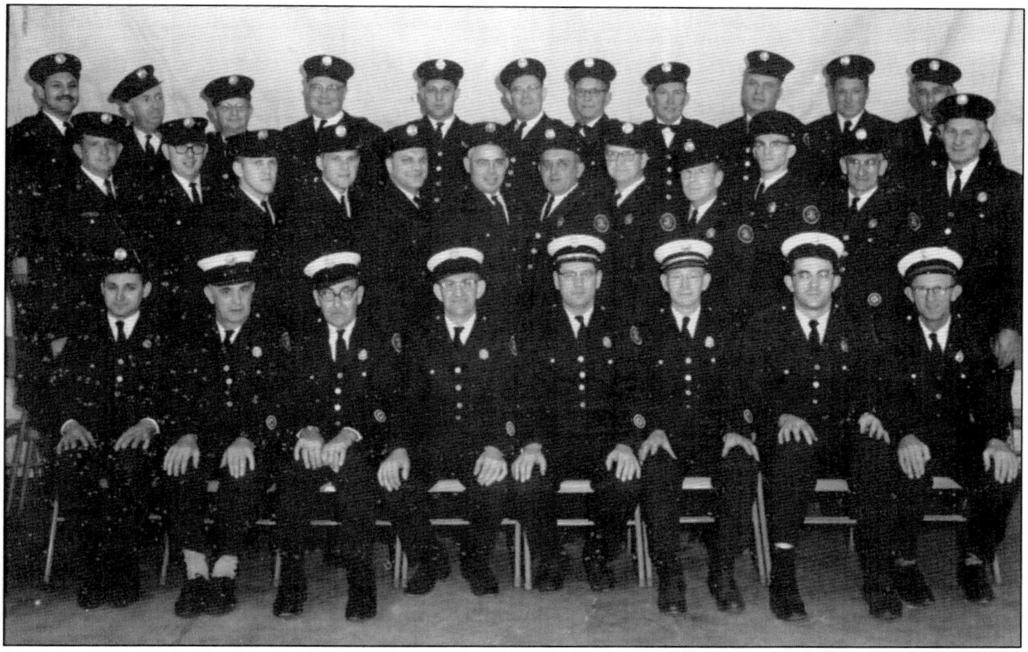

The Groesbeck Fire Department on March 5, 1964, was, from left to right, (first row) Bob Loichinger, Life Squad 1st lieutenant Wes Jones, marshall A. Zoellner, captain Lee Hammitt, chief Leroy Johnson, assistant chief Ivan Johnson, squad captain Armond Clawson Jr., and Life Squad 2nd lieutenant Ed Rapking; (second row) Bruce Price, Jack Hafer, Lyle Ranson, Norm Parker, Ray Ressa, Stan Kramer, Ed Hansert, Vince Walter, Bruce Haskins, clerk Don Kline, Al Wolk, and Joe Linnemann; (third row) Martin Sherwood, Art Hase, Rob Foster, George Gaiser, Art Addcock, Ed Hirsh, treasurer Joe Kramer, Carl Lierer, Cloyse "Corky" Snyder, Rick Gaiser, and Armond Clawson Sr. Lee Hammitt and Bruce Price both died in the line of duty on October 19, 1964, in a major fire at Western Cabinet on Colerain Avenue. Lt. Charlie Palm died in a house fire on November 29, 1977. Lt. Robin Broxterman and firefighter Brian Schira died fighting a house fire on April 4, 2008. (Courtesy of the Colerain Township Fire Department.)

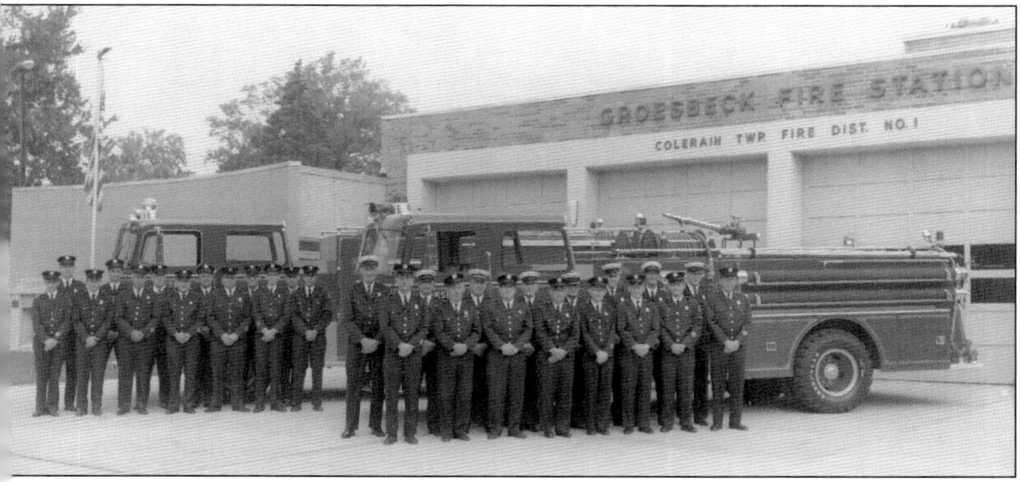

'hese are fire trucks used by the Groesbeck Fire Department to protect the community. (Courtesy f the Colerain Township Fire Department.)

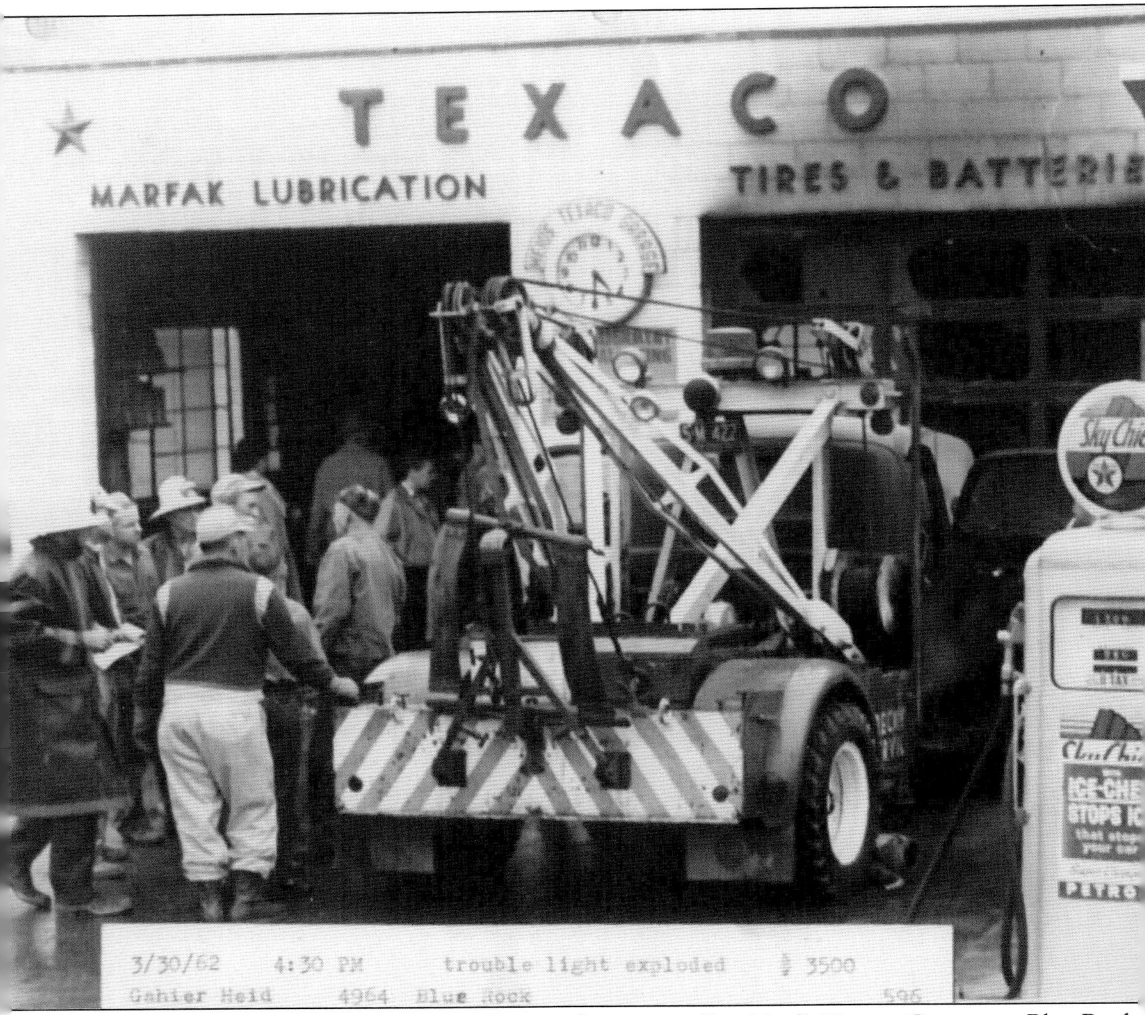

The Groesbeck Fire Department is responding to a call at Heid's Texaco Garage on Blue Rock Road in 1962. (Courtesy of the Colerain Township Fire Department.)

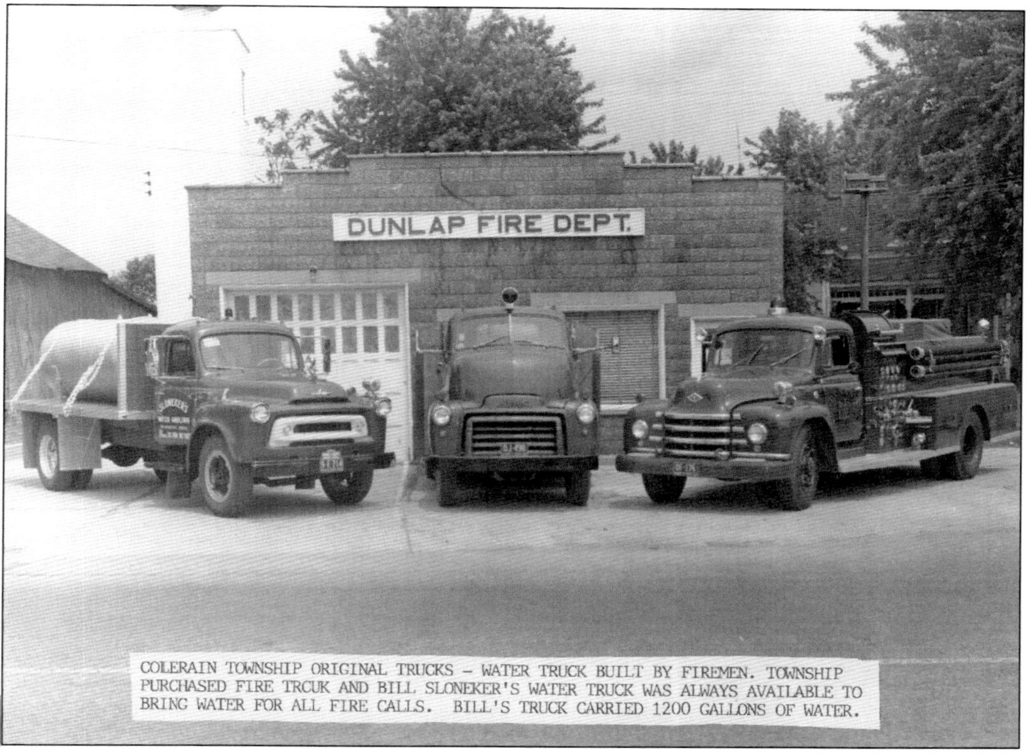

These are Dunlap's original fire trucks. The truck on the left was owned by Bill Sloneker and carried 1,200 gallons of water. When he was not fighting fires, Bill hauled water for the township residents. The truck in the center was a water truck built by the firemen. At that time, Dunlap had no waterlines or fire hydrants. The firemen had to bring water to fight any fires. The truck on the right was the only real piece of firefighting equipment. (Courtesy of Larry Shad.)

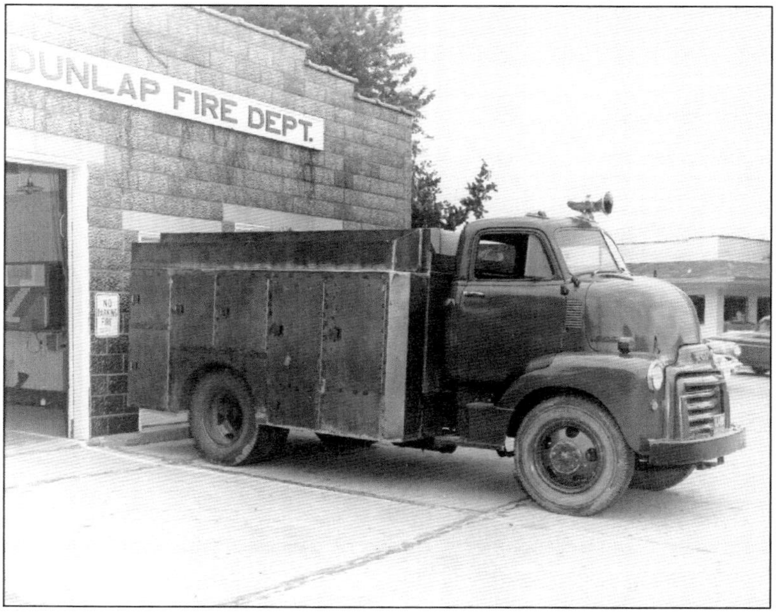

Pictured is the water truck built by the Dunlap firemen. The Dunlap Fire Department was housed in George Matt's old garage. Matt's old sign was repainted to read "Dunlap Fire Dept." (Courtesy of Larry Shad.)

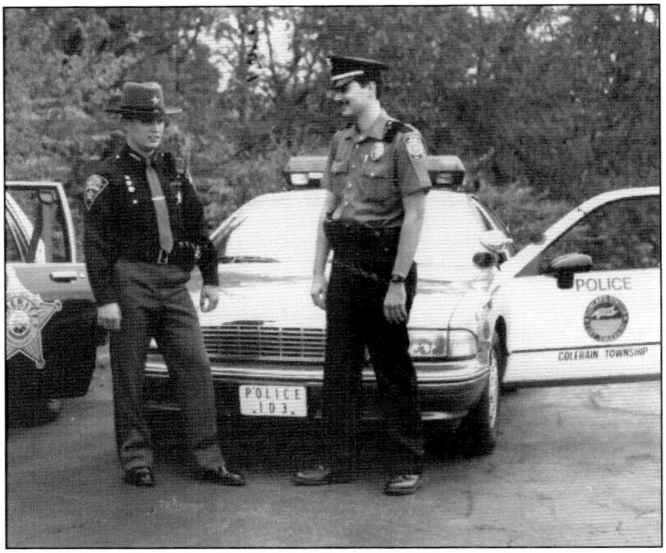

In the 1950s, the constabulary handled law enforcement. Charlie Losacker is thought to have been a part-time marshal or constable in 1951. Bill Terrell, Charlie's son-in-law, joined him in 1957. When a major problem arose or the constables were off duty, police from neighboring jurisdictions and the sheriff's office helped. Hamilton County deputy Vince Clark (left) is discussing safety with Colerain Township officer Denny Deaton in 1991. (Courtesy of the Colerain Township Police Department.)

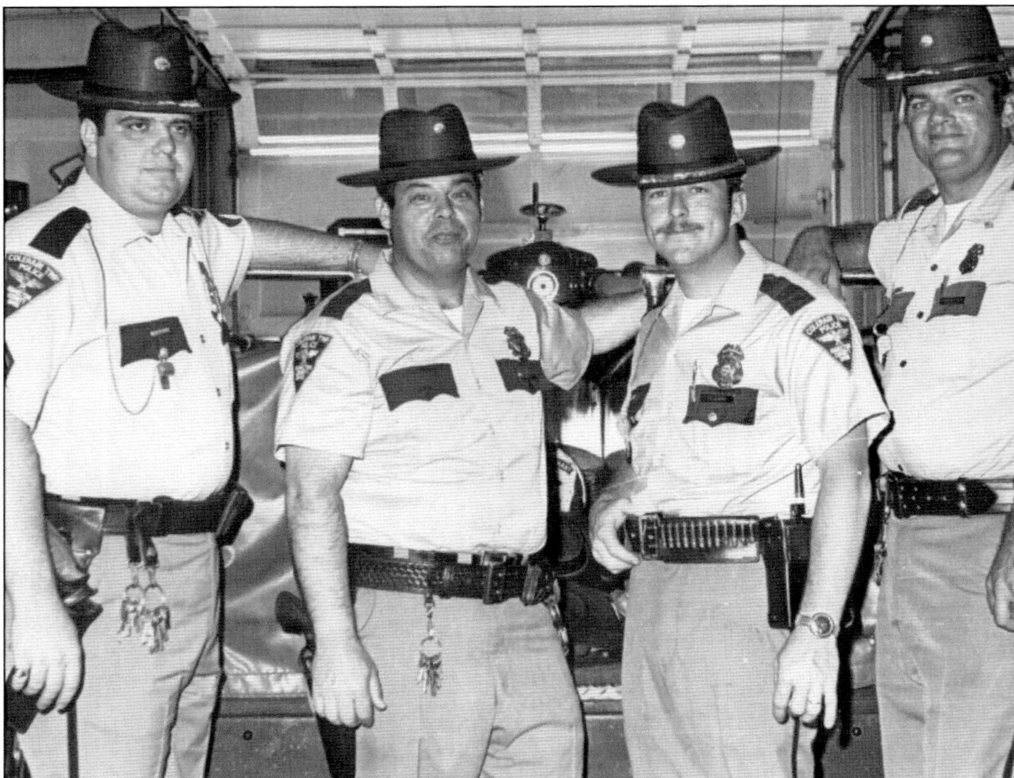

One of the major problems was that the jurisdiction of constables was limited. They could not writ tickets on state highways, such as Colerain Avenue, only on county roads. They were permitted t write tickets for DUIs and vehicular homicides. Four officers from the Colerain Township Polic Department in the 1970s are, from left to right, Edward "Butch" Frey, Sam Russo, Jim Ruhl, an Tom McDowell. (Courtesy of the Colerain Township Police Department.)

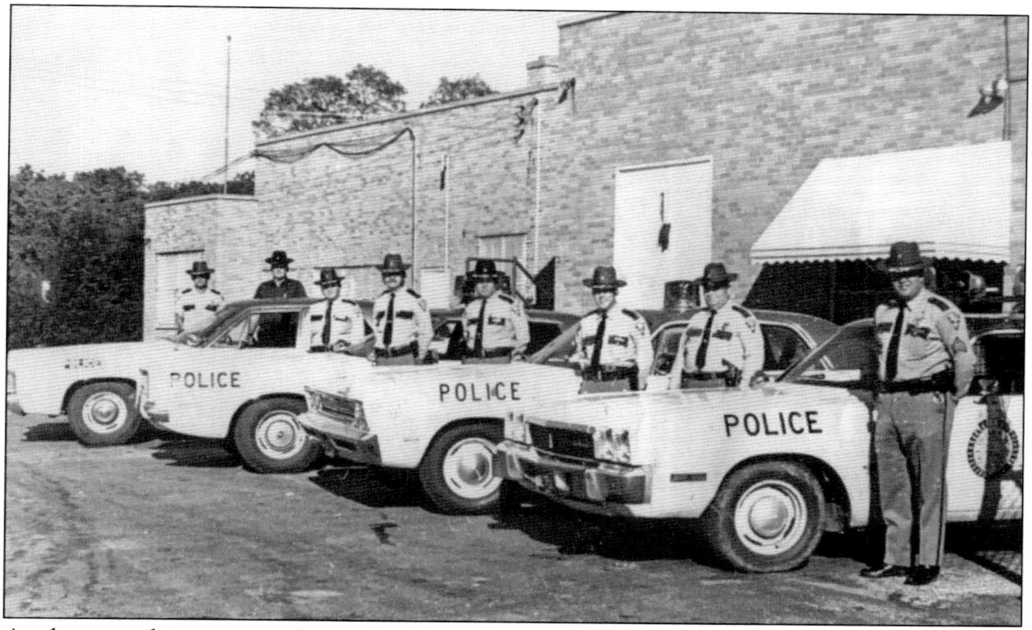

As the township grew to almost 51,000 residents, the need for a definite jurisdiction became more apparent. Township trustees granted jurisdiction in 1977. The police department consisted of eight full-time and seven part-time officers. Here are chief Bill Terrell and seven officers with their patrol cars in the 1970s. From left to right are Sgt. Edward "Butch" Frey, chief Bill Terrell, Jim Ruhl, Dan Totten, unidentified, Wayne Fricke, unidentified, and Marvin Adams. (Courtesy of the Colerain Township Police Department.)

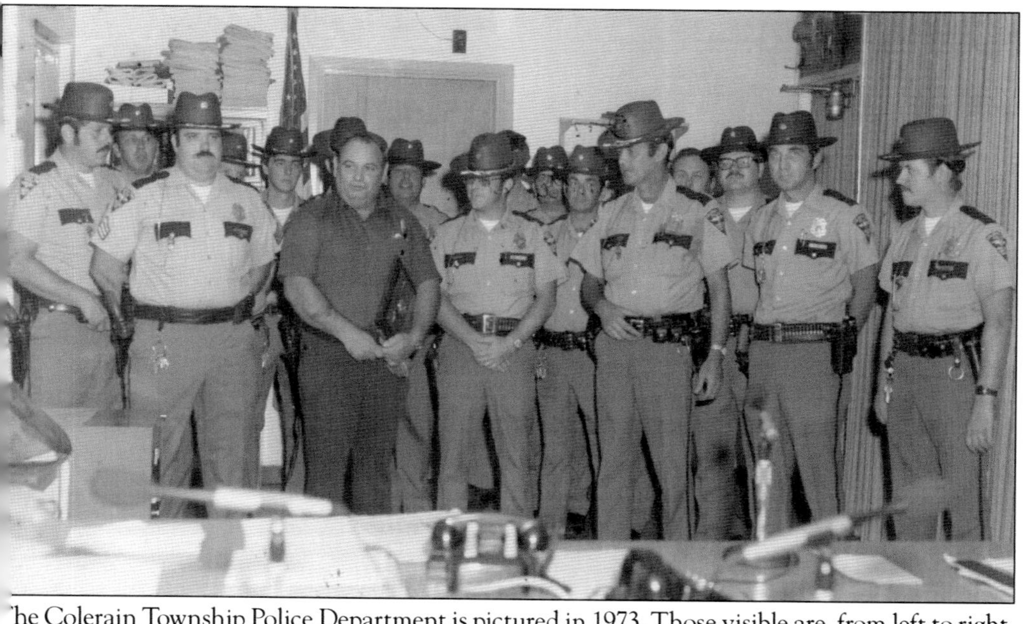

'he Colerain Township Police Department is pictured in 1973. Those visible are, from left to right, .ndy Demeropolis Sr., Dan Totten, Edward "Butch" Frey, Wayne Fricke, Jim Martin, Bill Terrell, am Russo, Jim Ruehl, Ray Roginski, Rhon Hadsell, Marvin Adams, Jim Siefert, Gary Hummeldorf, en Baker, and Rick Niehaus. (Courtesy of the Colerain Township Police Department.)

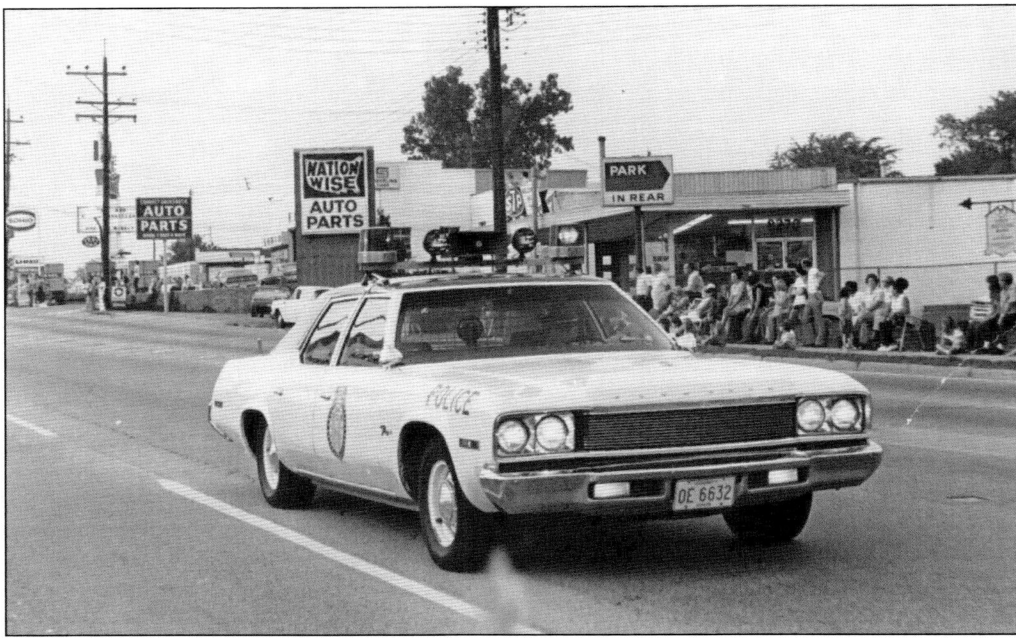

This 1974 Plymouth patrol car, driven by officer Jim Ruhl, is taking part in a township parade traveling south on Colerain Avenue toward the Galbraith Road intersection. (Courtesy of the Colerain Township Police Department.)

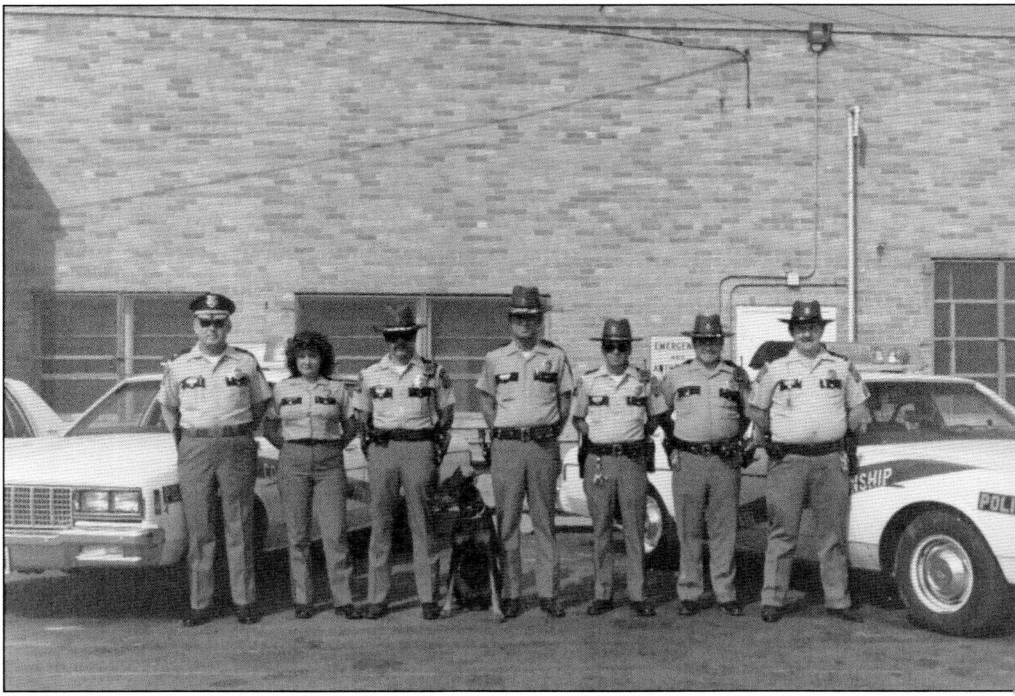

From left to right, chief Roger Johannes and officers Dolores Capadagli, Bob Judy, Lord (the dog), Ken Baker, Rohn Hadsell, Terry Zinser, and Jim Siefert are at police headquarters in Dunlap in the early 1980s. (Courtesy of the Colerain Township Police Department.)

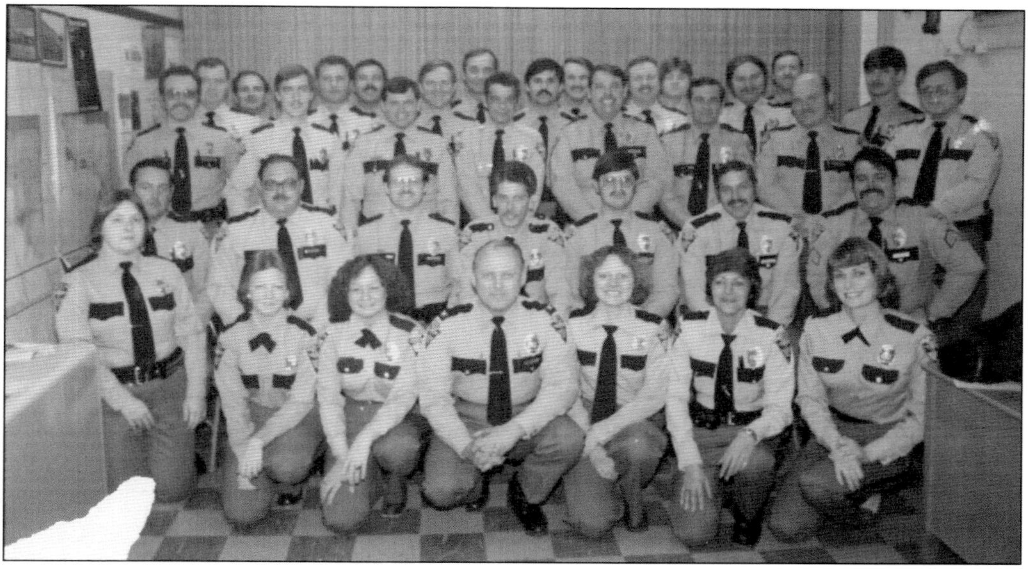

The Colerain Township Police Department in 1983 was, from left to right, (first row) Donna Hauserman (Stegeman), Jenny Busam (Poole), Delores Bierman (Capadagli), chief Roger Johannes, Pam Schedel, Mary Powers, and Donna Meyer; (second row) Marvin Adams, Roger Olsen, Gary Hummeldorf, unidentified, Andy Demeropolis Jr., Andy Demeropolis Sr., and Edward "Butch" Frey; (third row) Bob Judy, Jim Martin, Terry Zinser, Fred Montgomery, Sam Russo, Rhon Hadsell, Wayne Fricke, and Ken Klayer; (fourth row) Warren Tudor, Ray Roginski, unidentified, Dick Dwyer, Bob Walker, Ken Baker, Fank Kandil, Charlie Mayes, Jim Seifert, Jay Schnitt, Bob Cummins, Rick Niehaus, and Dave Kelley. (Courtesy of the Colerain Township Police Department.)

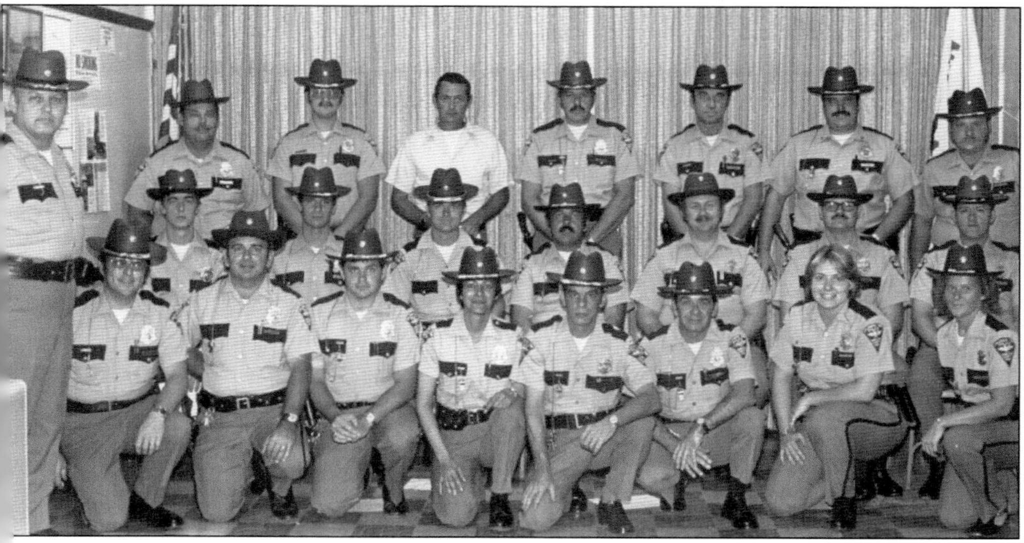

'he Colerain Police Department in the 1980s was, from left to right, chief Roger Johannes (standing) nd (first row) officers Jim Ruhl, Ray Rofinski, Terry Zinser, Mary Power, Fred Montgomery, hon Hadsell, Donna Troscher, and Connie Tiemeyer; (second row) Jim Martin, David Kelly, ob Walker, Richard Dwyer, Jim Seifert, Gary Hummeldorf, and Rick Niehaus; (third row) Sam usso, Andy Demeropolis Jr., Marvin Adams, Andy Demeropolis Sr., Ken Baker, Edward "Butch" rey, and Wayne Fricke. (Courtesy of the Colerain Township Police Department.)

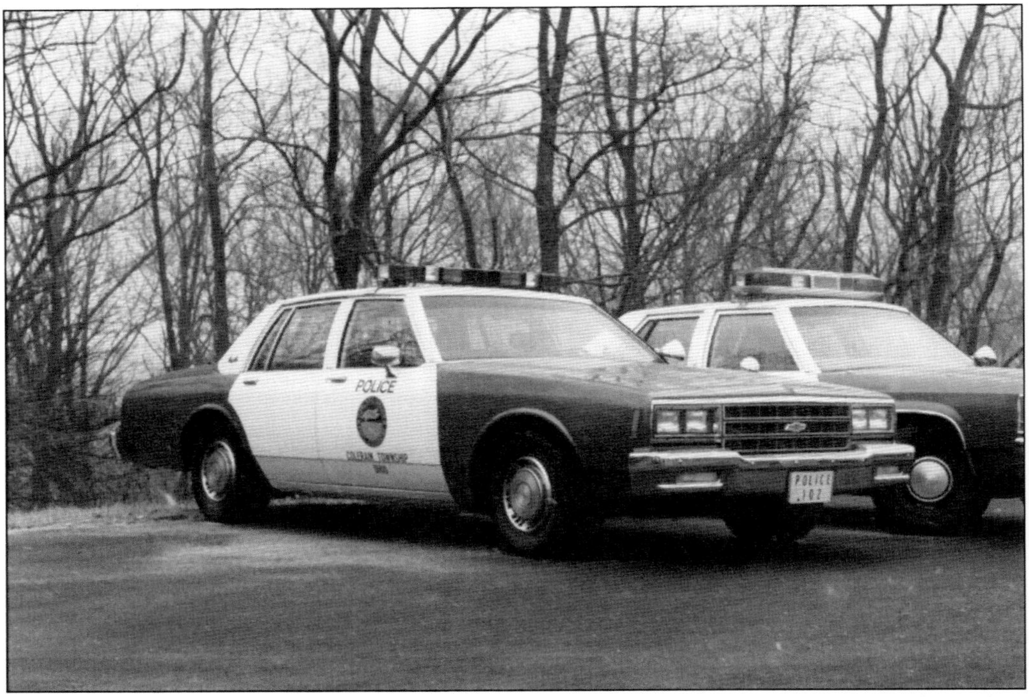

This 1987 Chevrolet Colerain Township patrol car is ready to respond to calls from people needing a police officer's help. (Courtesy of the Colerain Township Police Department.)

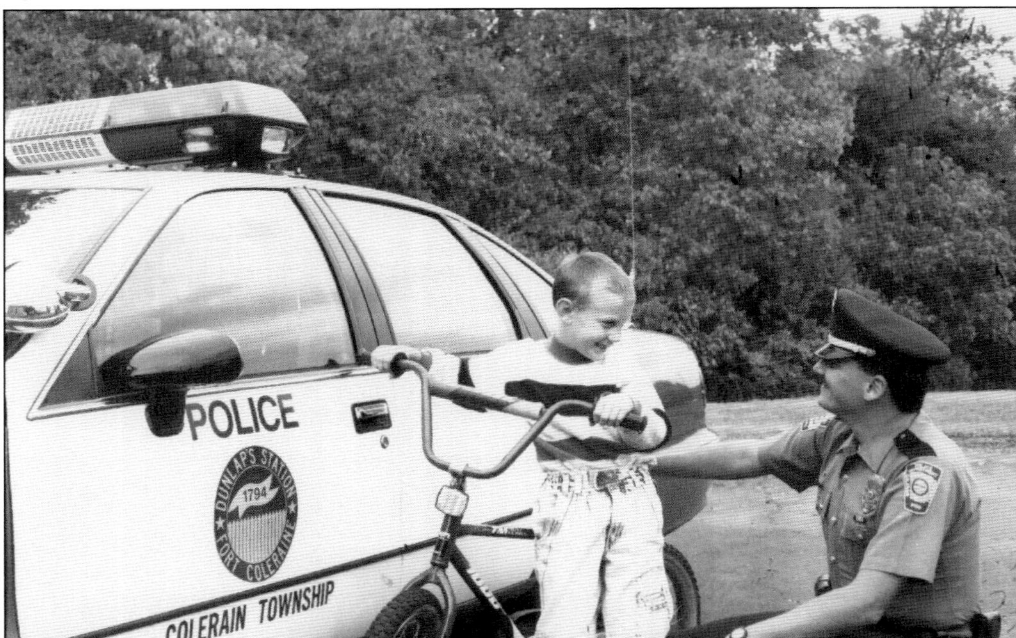

Colerain Township police officer Mark Meyer speaks with Cody Human in 1991, possibly abou bicycle safety. (Courtesy of the Colerain Township Police Department.)

Four

Home Sweet Homes

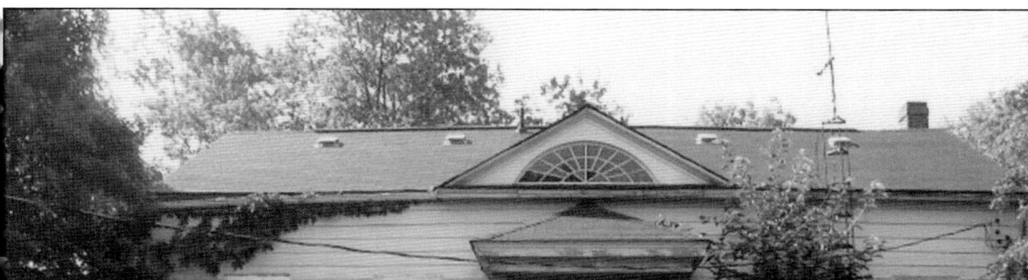

'his is Elland, the home of Giles Richards, one of the early settlers of Colerain Township. The ome is named in honor of Richard's wife, Eleanor, and his daughter, Elizabeth. The home stands ke a sentinel on the crest of one of the highest hills in the area, overlooking the Great Miami iver. (Courtesy of Don Linz.)

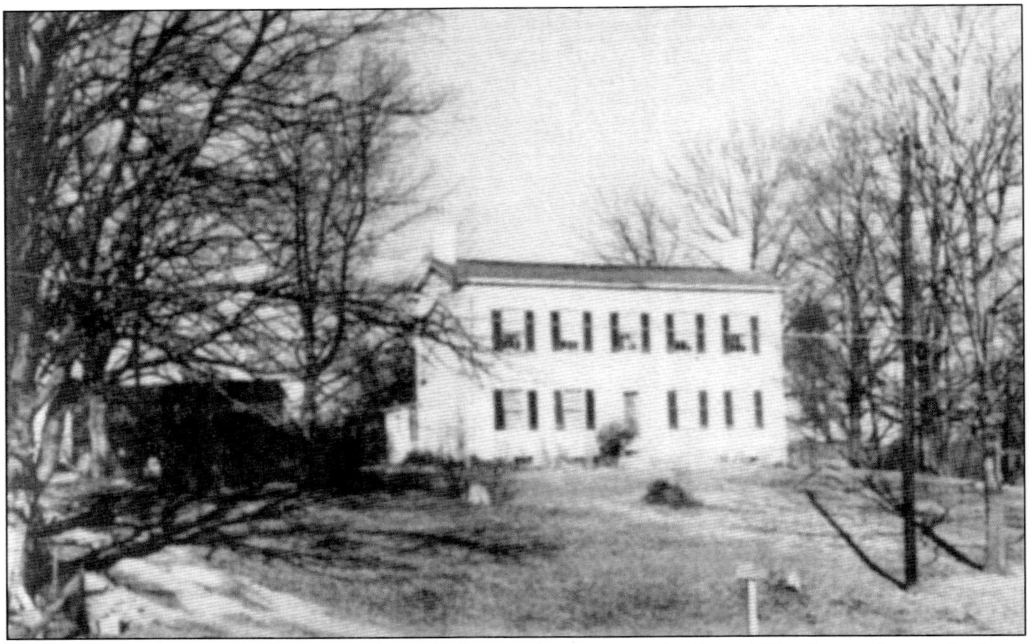

The old West home on the west side of Colerain Avenue was built in 1824. It was located where Walmart is today. Charles West was a Methodist lay preacher who donated land on the east side of Colerain, opposite his home, for the new Methodist church. (Courtesy of the Coleraine Historical Society.)

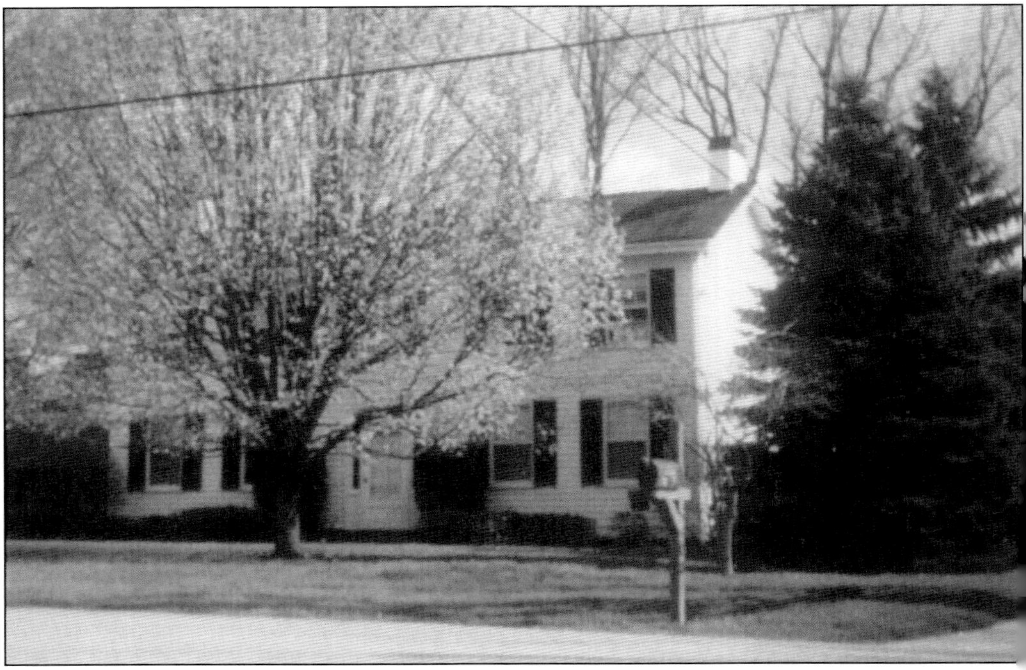

This beautiful two-story home at 4428 Blue Rock Road is said to be the oldest home still standing in Colerain Township. The home was built in 1831 and has been renovated extensively through the years. (Courtesy of Tom Walters.)

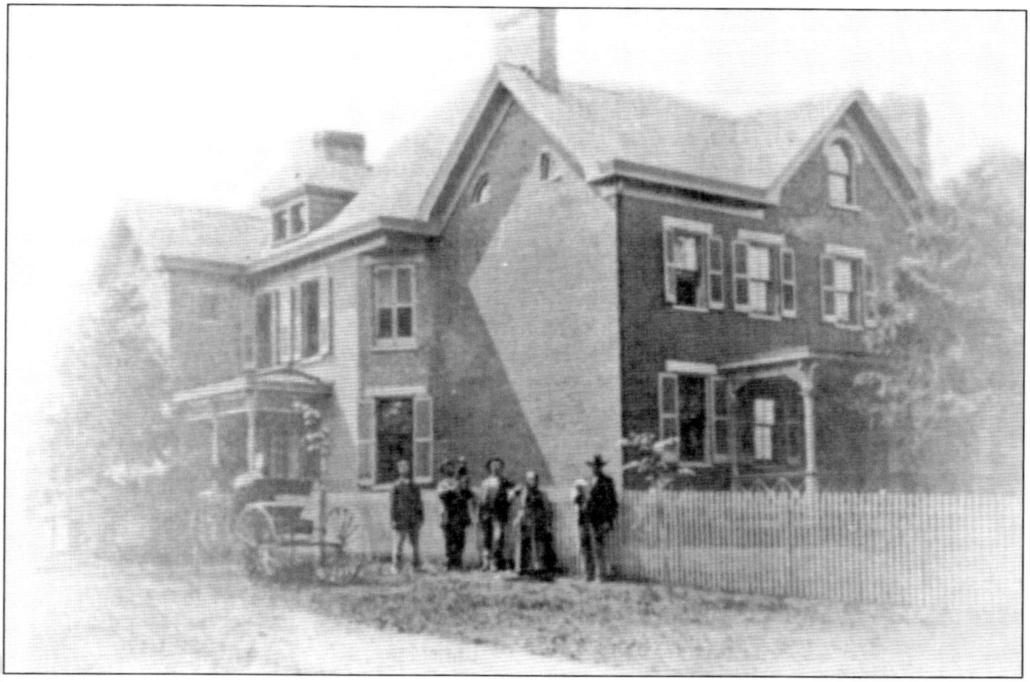

This was the home of Jim and Andy Huston. It is believed to have been built around 1835. For many years, it was home to one of the earliest pioneer families in the area. The home was demolished in the Pleasant Run area to build a subdivision. It was located on the west side of Pippin Road north of Crest Road. (Courtesy of the Coleraine Historical Society.)

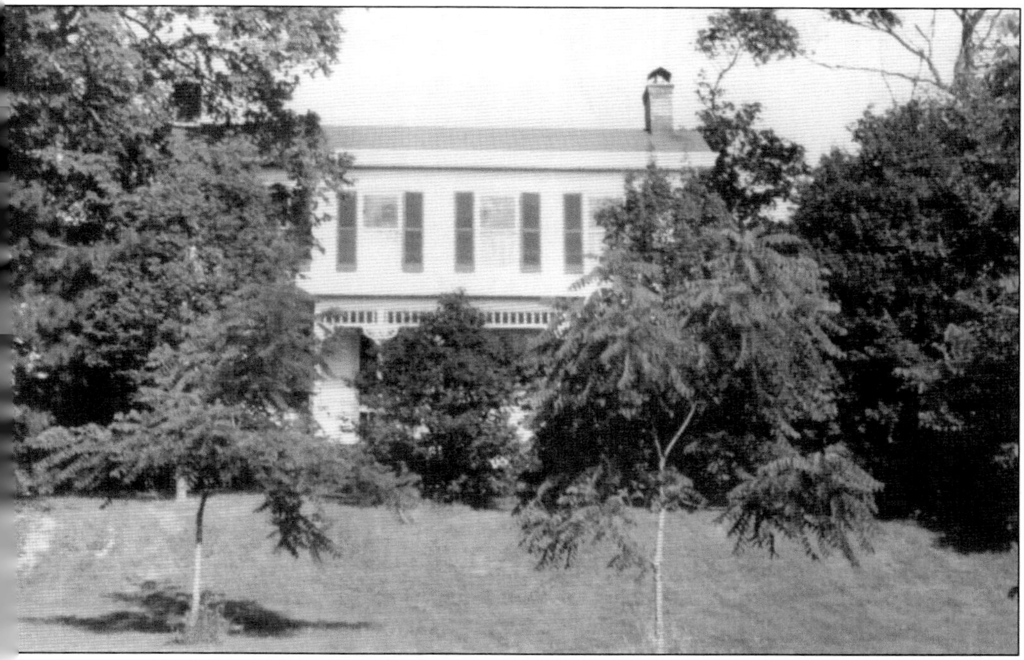

his home at 11499 Pippin Road was built in 1835 and is still used as a private residence. (Courtesy Don Linz.)

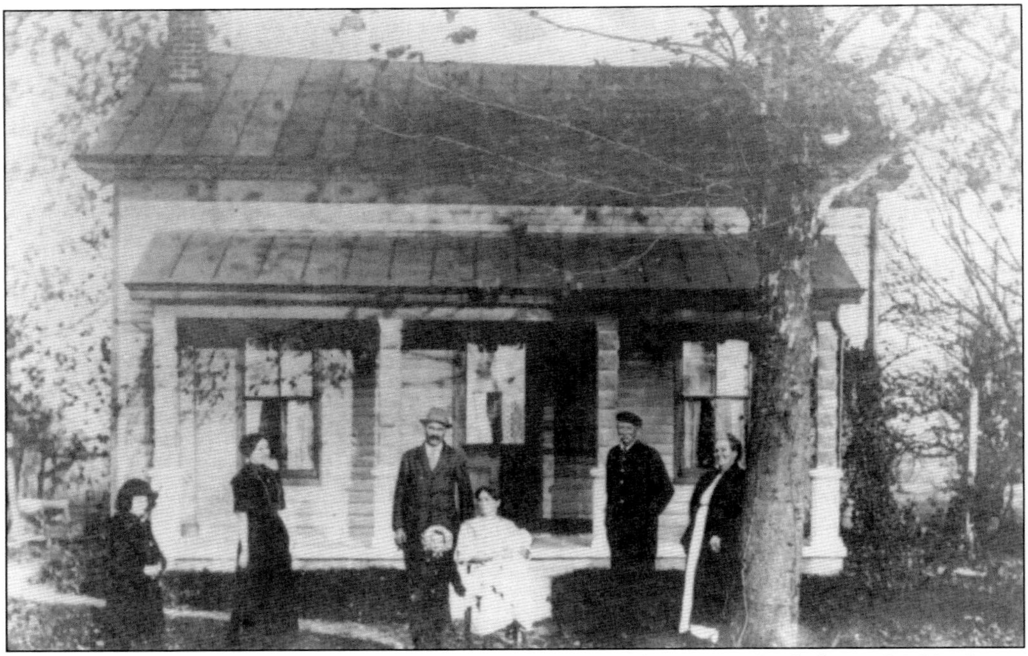

The Aston Family (pictured here) are, from left to right, Helen Aston Backelman, Mable Aston Tumey, Archie Aston, Mary Evan (in front), Lillian Aston, Thomas Owen Aston, and Lottie (Underwood) Aston. The family lived on the east side of Colerain Avenue in Groesbeck. (Courtesy of the Coleraine Historical Society.)

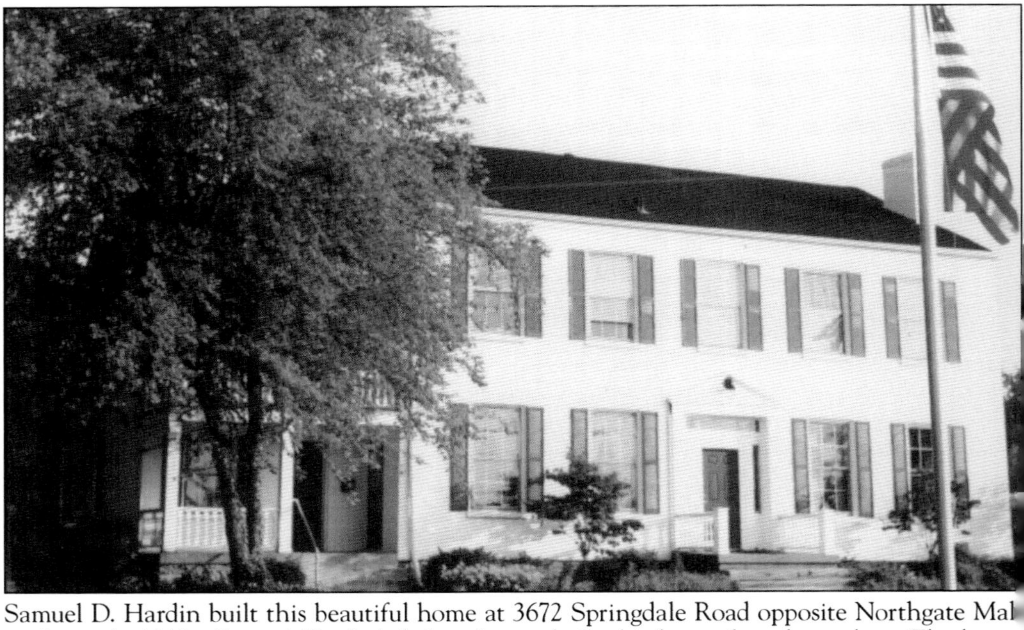

Samuel D. Hardin built this beautiful home at 3672 Springdale Road opposite Northgate Mal in the early 1840s. Samuel Hardin's father, James, built this home from hewn logs. The hous was used to hold the presidential election of Thomas Jefferson. Since so few settlers lived in th township at that time, a constable was sent to bring them in to vote in order to ensure it was legal election. (Courtesy of Don Linz.)

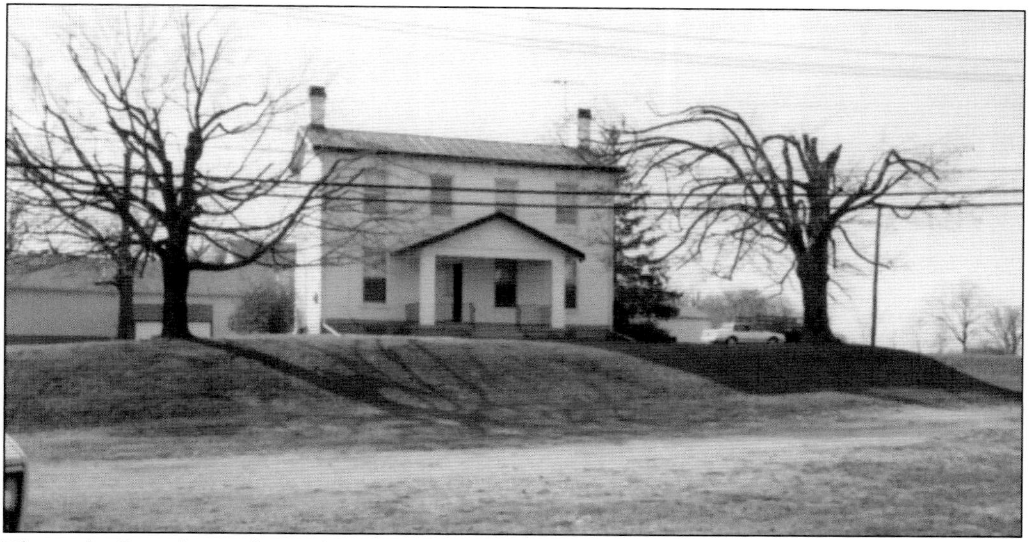

This is the Bevis house, located on the southwest corner of Colerain Avenue at 10345 Colerain and old Colerain Avenues. This home, built in 1845, was the home of David Bevis, believed to be the son of Martin Bevis. At one time, it was home to Dr. Howard Bevis, who in 1933 became an associate justice on the Ohio Supreme Court for an unexpired term. He was also the seventh president of Ohio State University. Appointed in 1940, he served for 16 years. (Courtesy of Dennis Klei.)

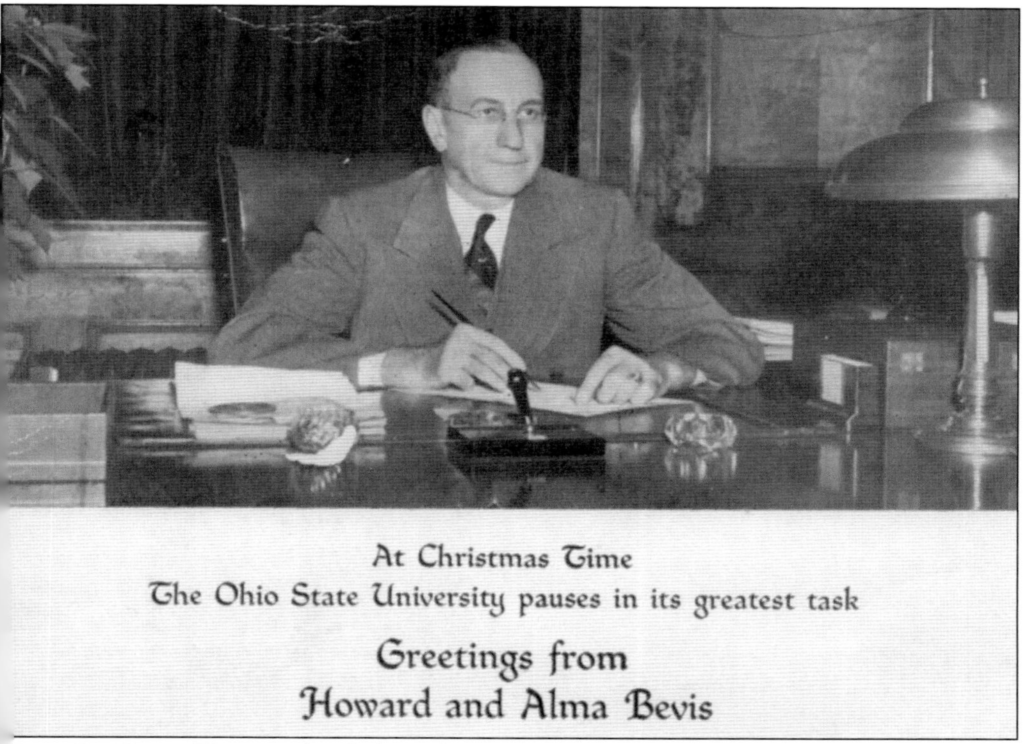

his is Dr. Howard Bevis at this desk at Ohio State University during Christmas time. (Courtesy f Doug Bevis.)

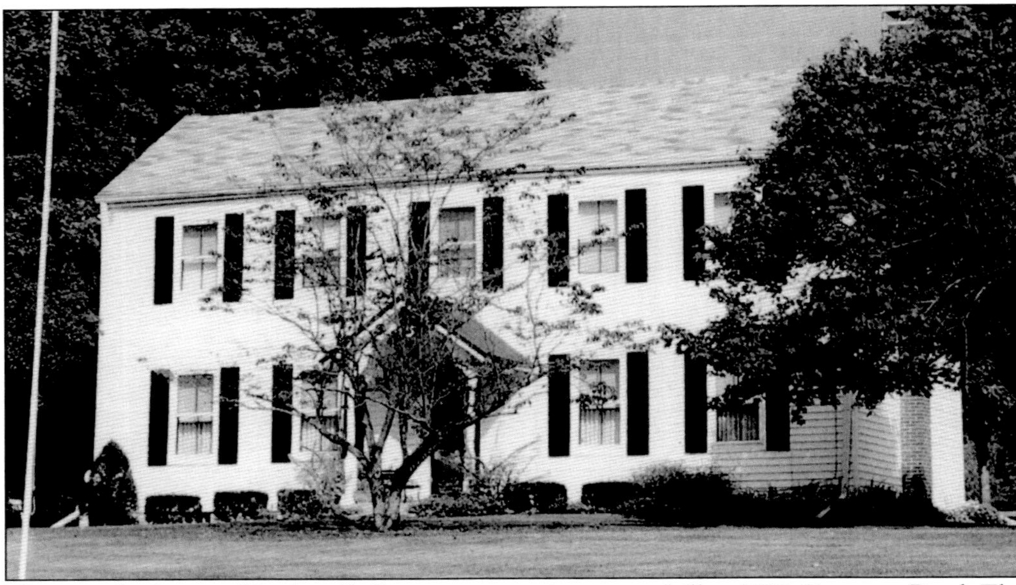

This was the home of Reuben S. Compton on a picturesque hill at 2620 Compton Road. The Compton family was very involved in the community and helped with the organization of the Mount Healthy Christian Church in 1848. Reuben Compton was the church clerk. The Compton home was demolished to make room for a subdivision. (Courtesy of Don Linz.)

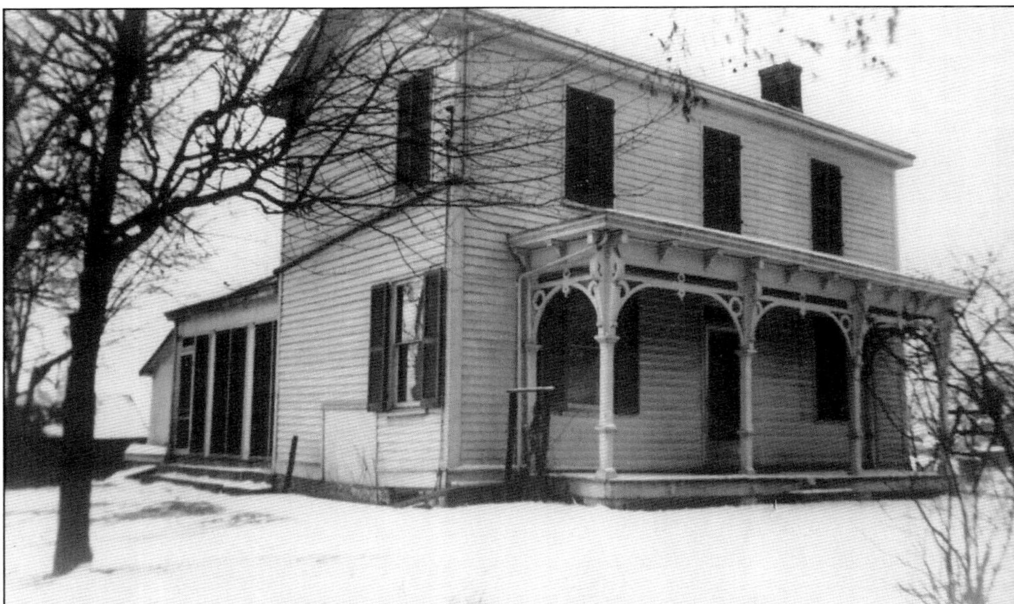

The Blair-Klein house, built in 1850, stood at the corner of Blue Rock and Hanley Roads unti it was razed in 2009. The house sat on high ground at the top of the watershed, and the well or the property was quite deep. One had to go down 18 feet to reach the water, which was about 1 feet deep. The family used to keep milk cold by lowering filled milk cans down into the well. O the well side, the water flows to the Great Miami River an on the other side of Blue Rock Road the water flows to the Ohio River. (Courtesy of Dr. William Klein.)

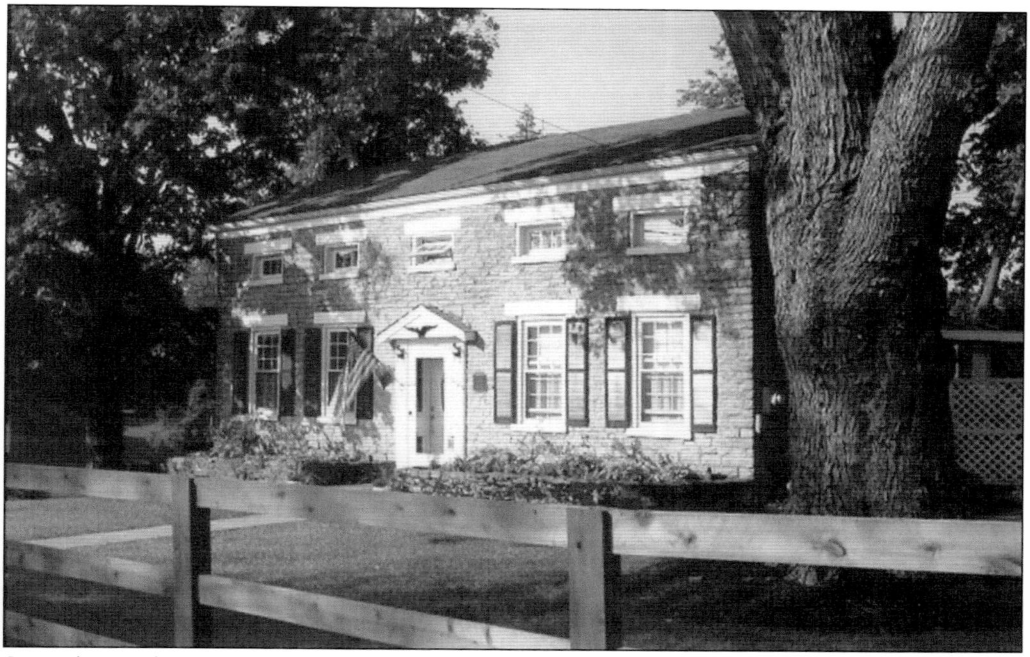

Several stone homes were built along Thompson Road by German immigrants, many of whom settled in Colerain Township. This home is at 6143 Thompson Road and is an example of their work. (Courtesy of Don Linz.)

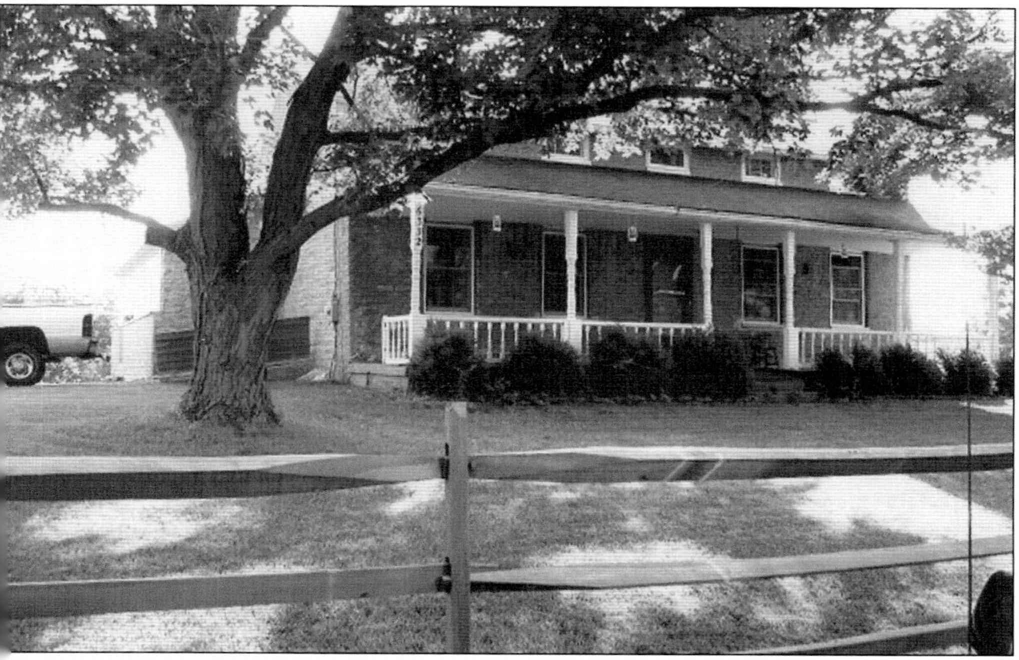

his home is located at 6332 Thompson Road. The homes were built with stones gathered from earby streams and fields in the 1800s. (Courtesy of Don Linz.)

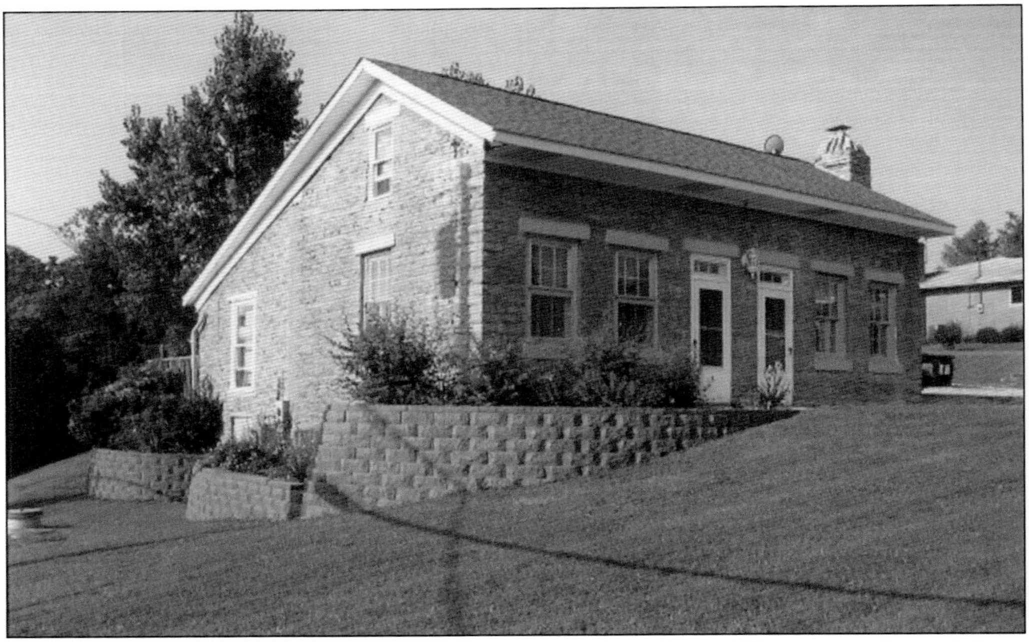

The stone homes are still standing and are in very good condition. They are used as well-kept, private residences. This home is at 6607 Thompson Road. (Courtesy of Don Linz.)

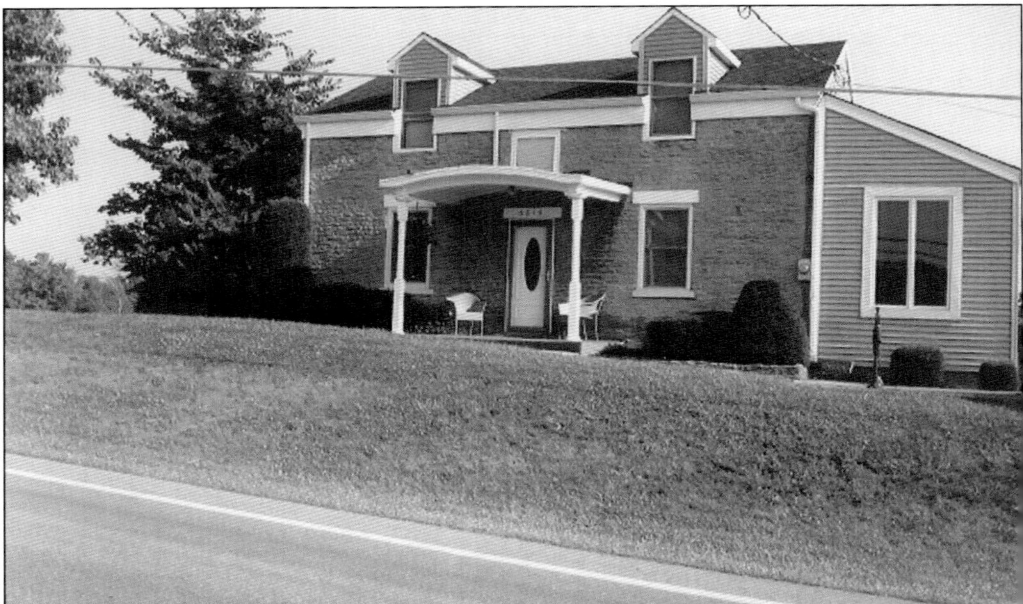

This stone home, similar to some of the others, has had additions built onto it. It is easy to se that the beauty of the home is still maintained. This home is found at 6614 Thompson Road (Courtesy of Don Linz.)

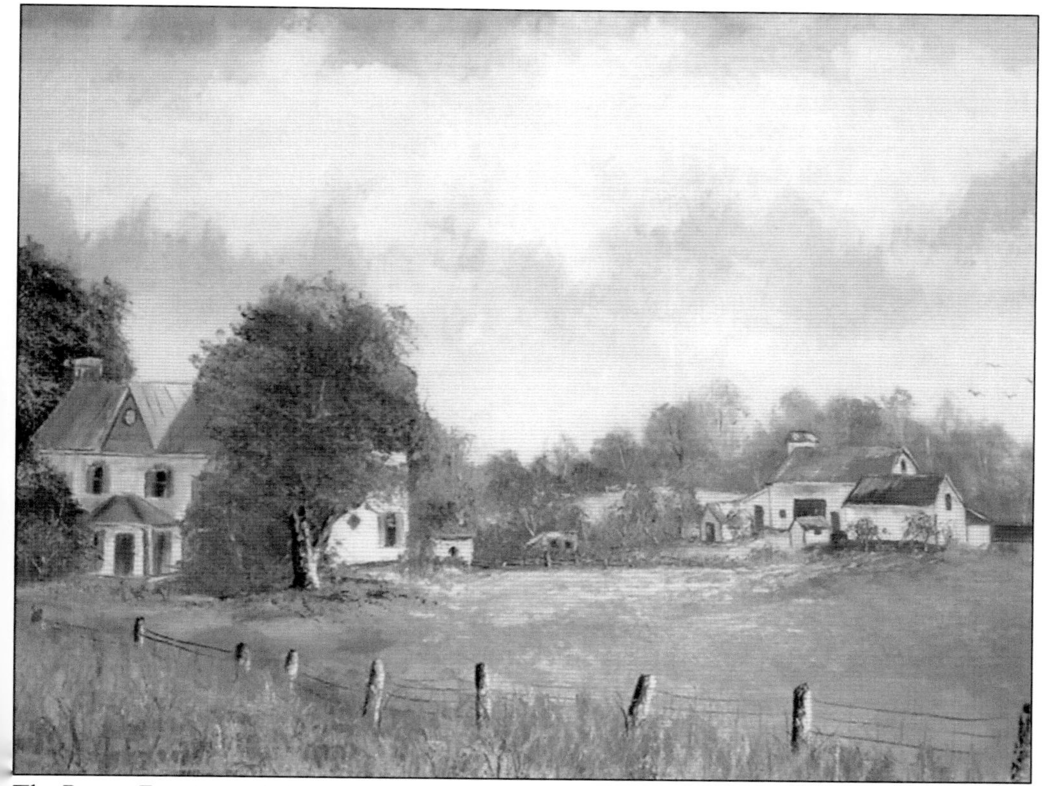

The Burger Farm's stately home at 2385 Springdale Road was built in three stages. The front part with extremely thick walls was built in 1858 with bricks that were made on-site. The back part was added in 1902, and a new porch and bathroom were added in 1944. This was primarily a working dairy farm. The farm had 83 acres and five outbuildings. (Courtesy of the Burger Family.)

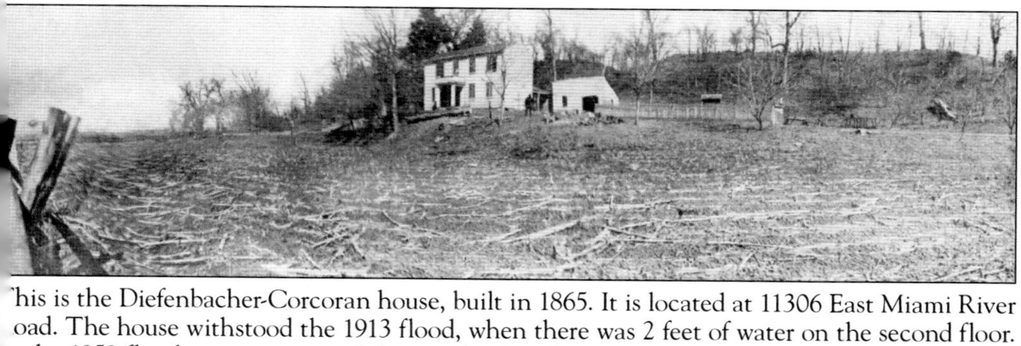

'his is the Diefenbacher-Corcoran house, built in 1865. It is located at 11306 East Miami River oad. The house withstood the 1913 flood, when there was 2 feet of water on the second floor. ı the 1959 flood, water came up 2 feet on the first floor. When it floods in the spring, the river ın cover the highway and the front yard. This was a working farm for many years. (Courtesy f Hazel Brown.)

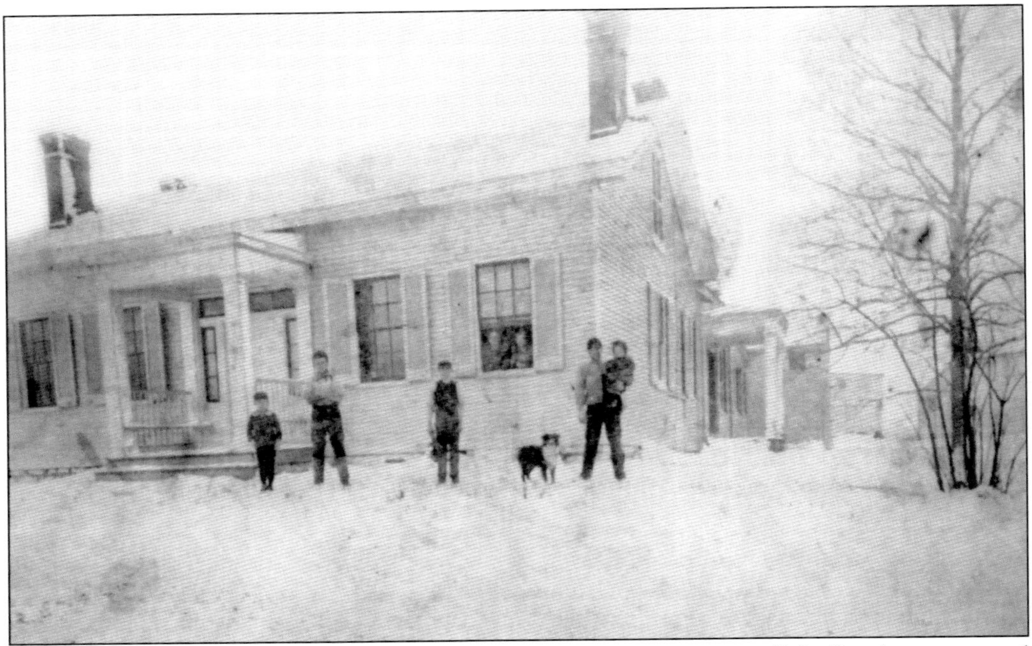

The Moeller family home was at 2471 Banning Road. Five generations of Moellers have operated Moeller Nursery and Landscaping, the longest continuous business in Colerain Township. From left to right in 1896 are William F. Moeller, son; Fred Reinking Sr., brother-in-law of Edward F. Moeller; Fred Reinking Jr., nephew of Edward F. Moeller; and Edward F. Moeller, holding daughter Emma Moeller. In the window are Caroline Moeller, wife of Edward, and Minnie Alfing, sister of Caroline. (Courtesy of the Moeller family.)

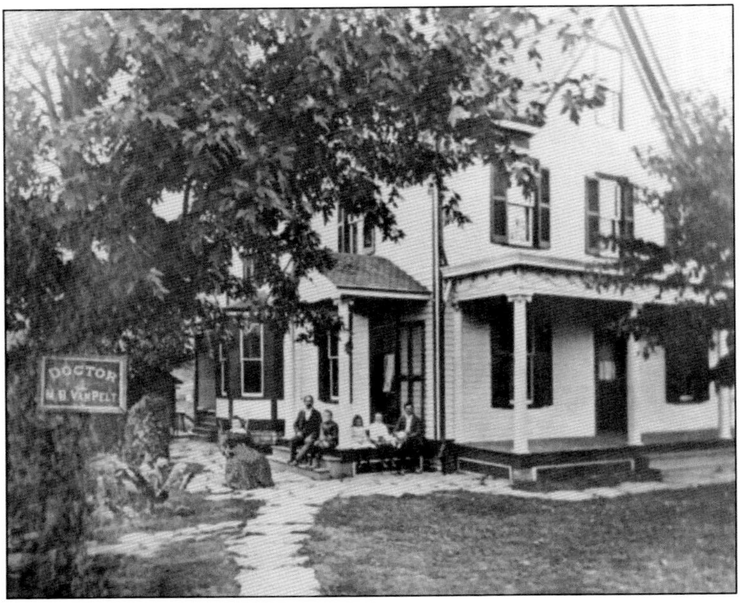

Dr. Merrel Van Pelt lived and practiced medicine from his residence in Goesbeck at the intersection of Galbraith and Blue Rock Roads. His old residence still stands. Dr. Van Pelt graduated from the Cincinnati College of Medicine and Surgery in 1889. He practiced in the Groesbeck area until the early 1900s, at which time he relocated to the College Hill area. (Courtesy of Greg Snyder.)

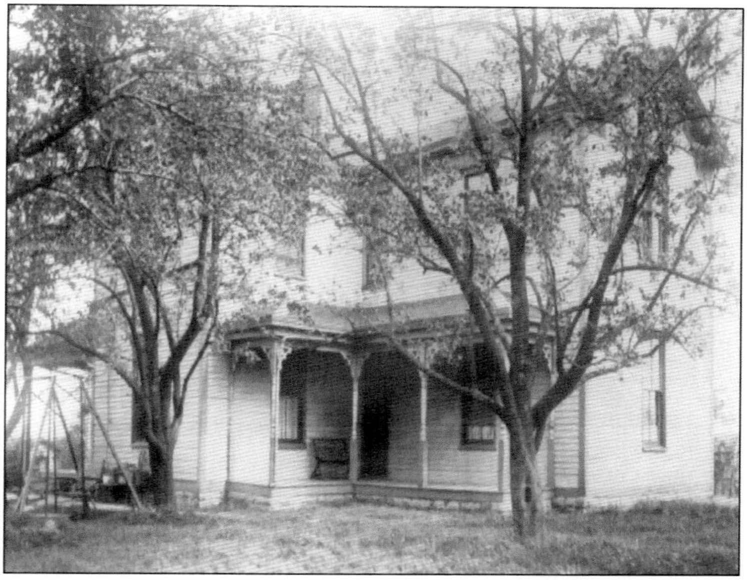

The home at 8434 Cheviot Road was built in 1870 and was part of a 35-acre farm owned by Louis and Magdalena Alfing. Here is the home as it appeared in the 1930s. The Alfings were wagon farmers and later truck farmers. They would sell their farm products at downtown markets. (Courtesy of Ed Alfing.)

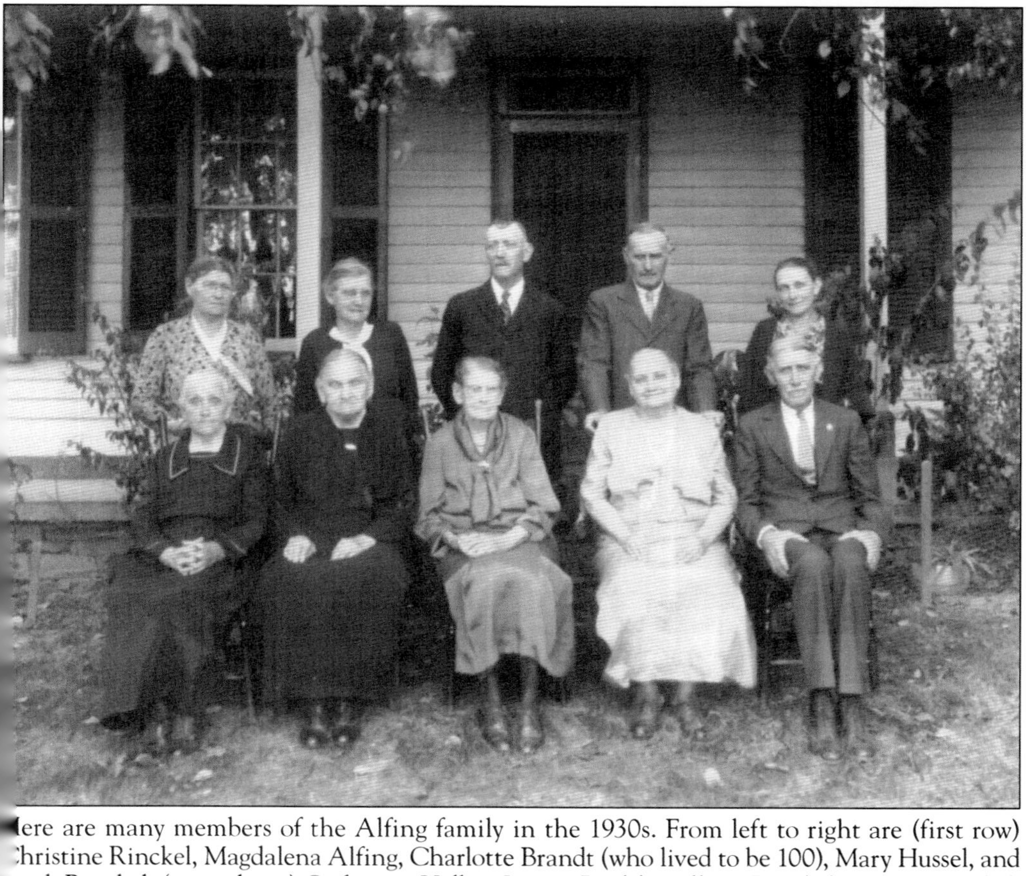

ere are many members of the Alfing family in the 1930s. From left to right are (first row) Christine Rinckel, Magdalena Alfing, Charlotte Brandt (who lived to be 100), Mary Hussel, and cob Rinckel; (second row) Catherine Helbig, Louisa Ruehl, William Rinckel, August Rinckel, nd Dorothy Zwicker. (Courtesy of Ed Alfing.)

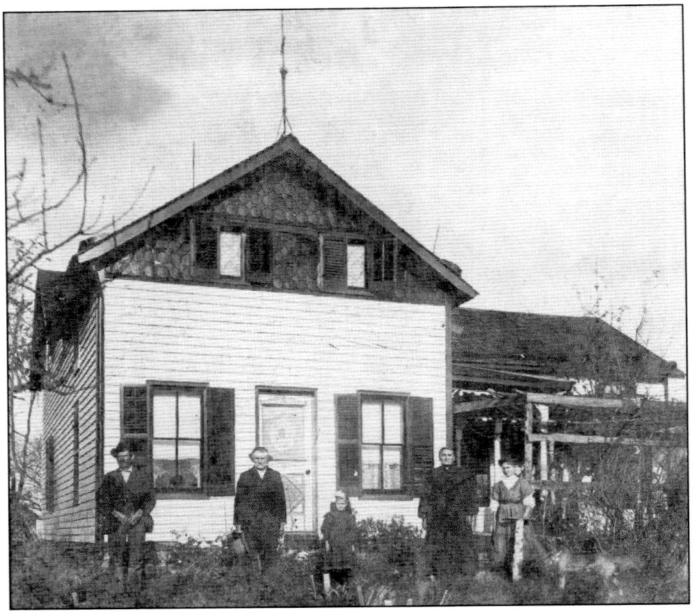

The Eschenbrenner House, at the corner of Thompson Road and Nabida Drive, was built in 1890 and is thought to be haunted. Nabida Drive was named after the three Hussel children, with the first two letters taken from their first names, Nancy, Bill and David. Pictured is the Eschenbrenner family. From left to right are Charles Eschenbrenner (son), Deboldt Eschenbrenner (father), Henrietta Eschenbrenner (granddaughter), Louisa Eschenbrenner (mother), Tillie Eschenbrenner (daughter), and Red, the dog. (Courtesy of Barb Walsh and Ann Mosier.)

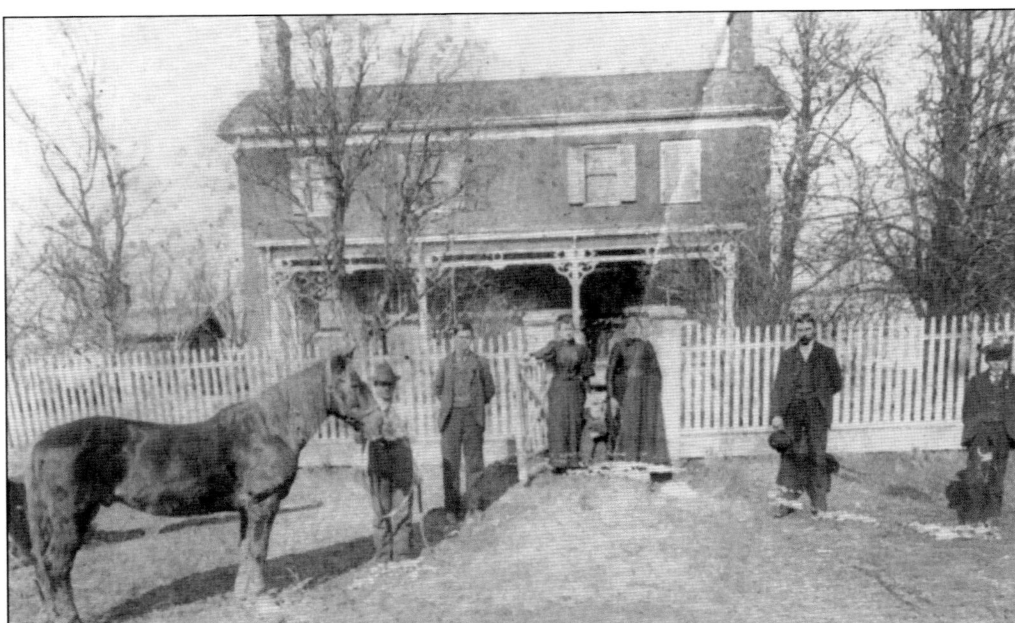

The Schwing homestead was in the northeast corner of Blue Rock and Springdale Roads This picture was taken in the early 1900s. Standing from left to right are two unidentified Clara Schwing, unidentified, John Schwing, and Elmer Schwing. (Courtesy of the Coleraine Historical Society.)

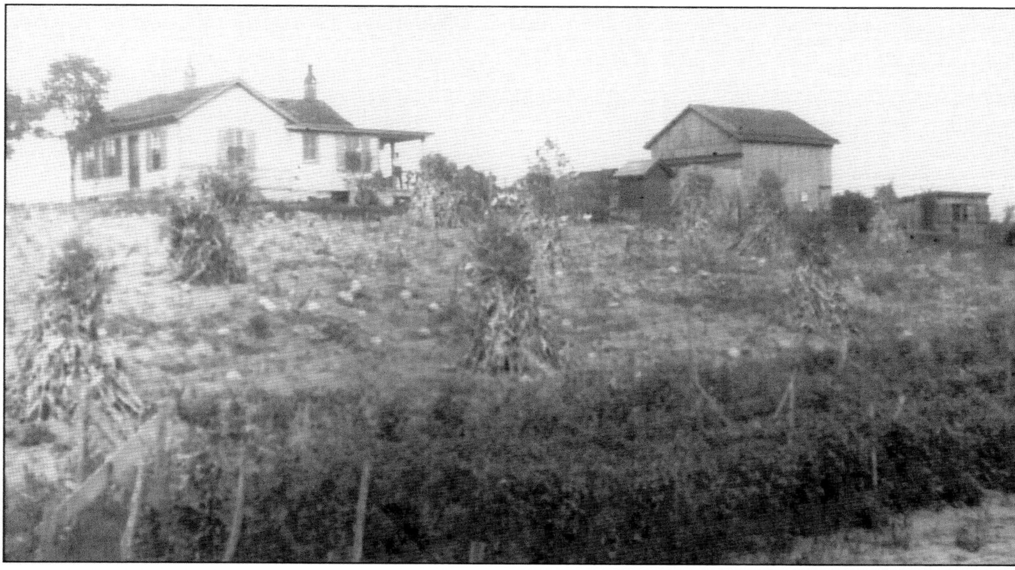

The Fred Finke Sr. farmhouse is pictured here in the early 1920s. Fred Sr. was the first fire chief of the Groesbeck Fire Department. The farmhouse was located where Arby's is today, near Shadycrest. (Courtesy of Ray Finke.)

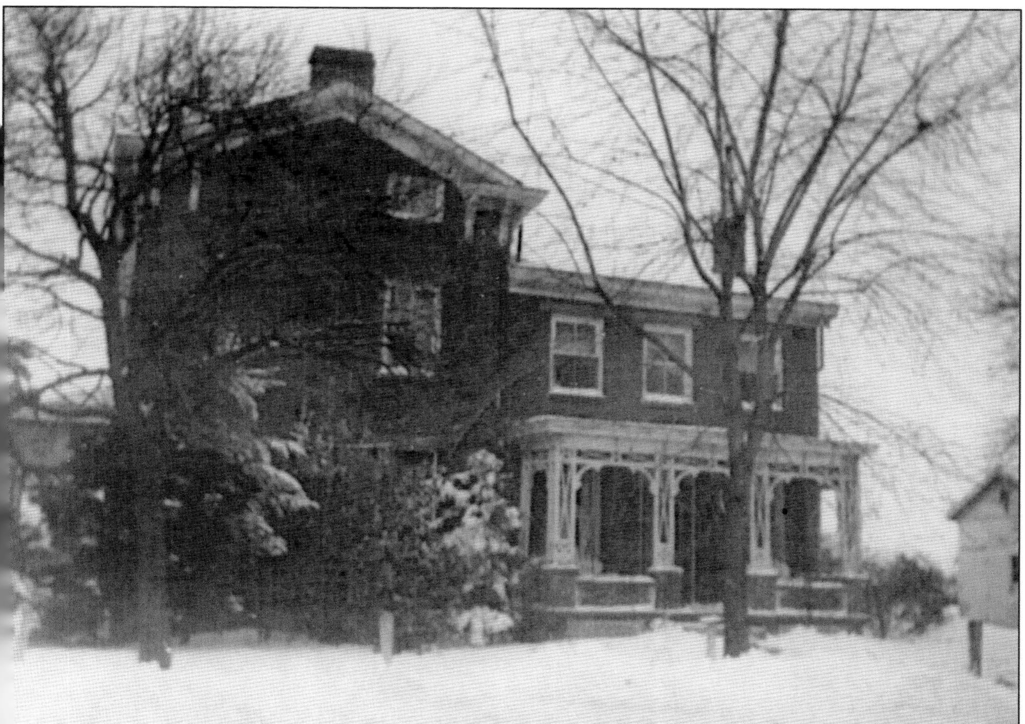

oe and Esther Hudepohl operated Hudepohl's Café on the northeast corner of Colerain Avenue nd Springdale Road. Tiny Ludwig later bought the café from the Hudepohls. This was "the" place o go to hash out flying stories if it was too windy to fly out of the old Mount Healthy Airport. he Hudepohls lived in this house just north of their café. (Courtesy of Mel Blust.)

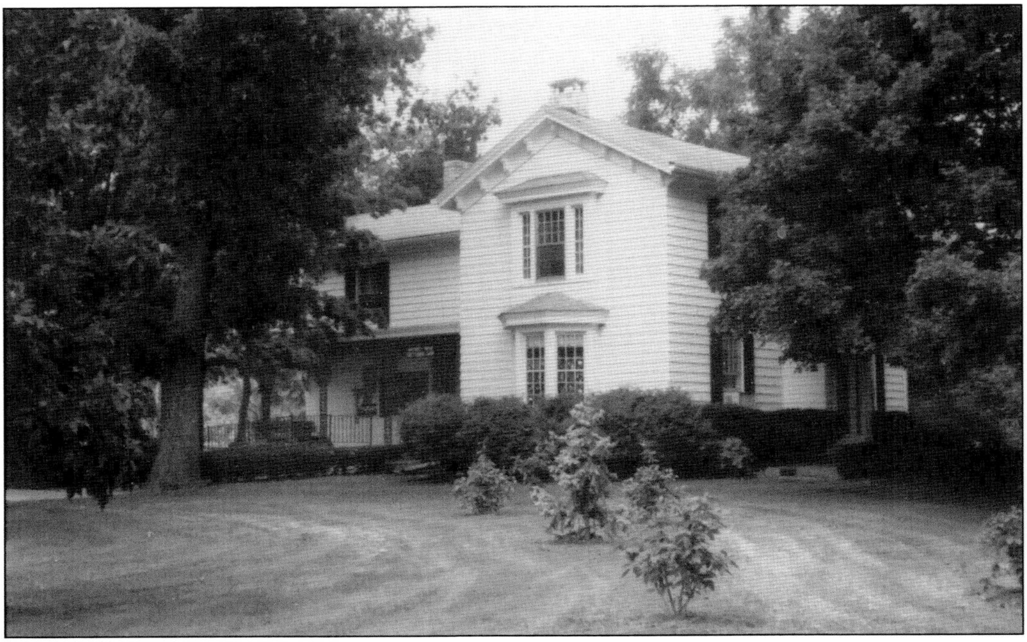

The Farbach-Werner Nature Preserve is the smallest of the regional parks owned and operated by the Hamilton County Park District. This 23-acre "oasis of green" was bequeathed to the park district in 1972. It is a living memorial to the Farbach and Werner families who once lived in this home on this beautiful property. The park is located at the southwest corner of Colerain Avenue and Poole Road. (Courtesy of Irene Light.)

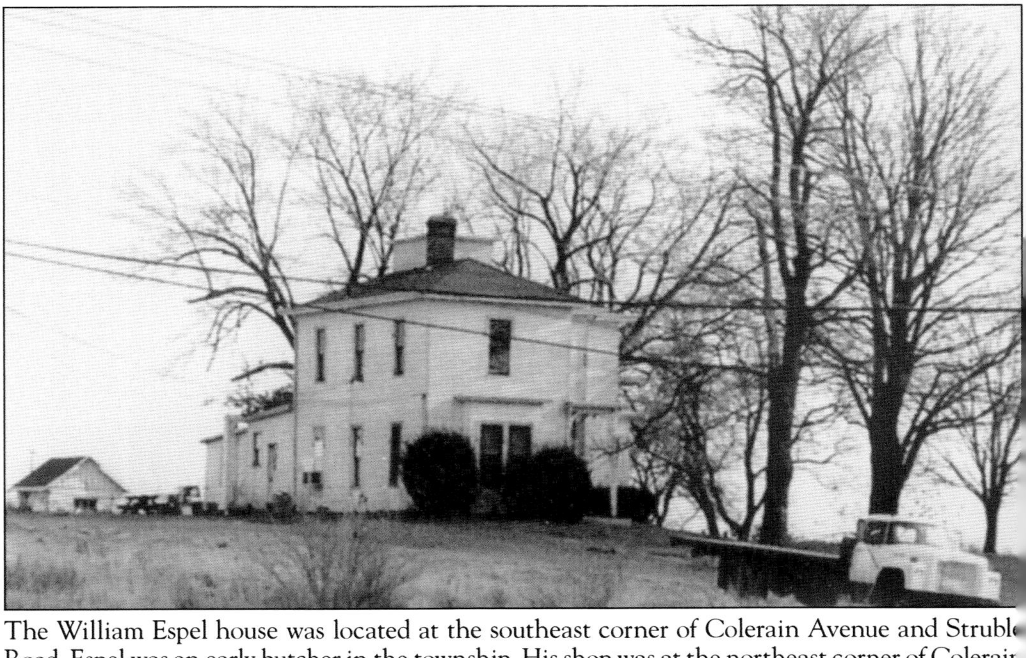

The William Espel house was located at the southeast corner of Colerain Avenue and Strubl Road. Espel was an early butcher in the township. His shop was at the northeast corner of Colerair Avenue and Springdale Road behind Hudepohl's Café. Bill and his wife raised nine children including six girls and three boys. (Courtesy of Dennis Klei.)

Five

Interesting Stops Along the Way

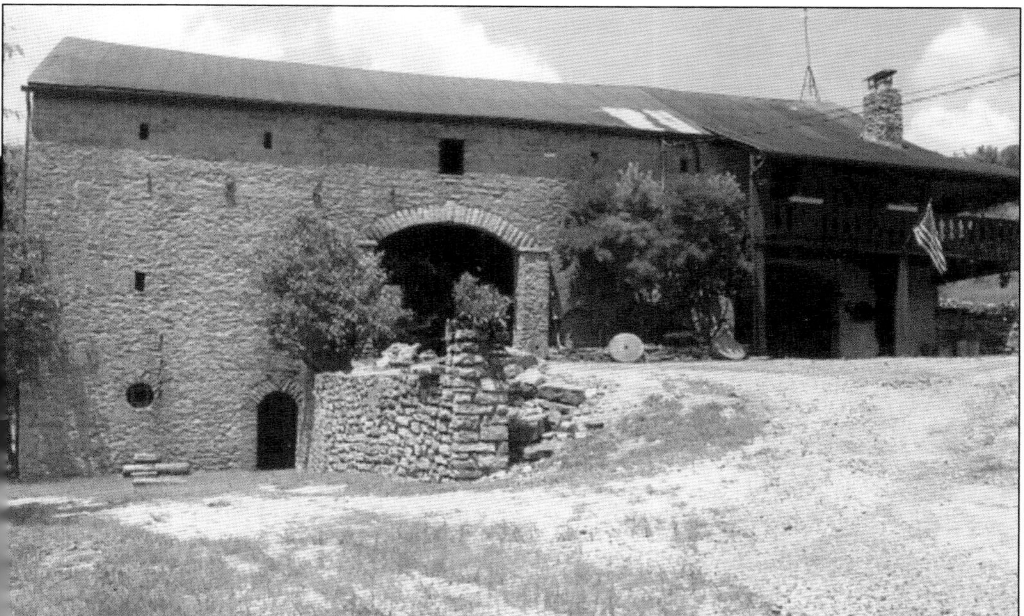

'his old stone barn at 7355 Eagle Creek Road proudly proclaims in iron numerals the year it /as built: 1861. Jacob Kleinfelter built this barn to house his winery operations. He also had a /inepress where he pressed grapes for neighboring farmers on shares. This huge stone barn has vaulted wine cellar under a concrete patio. It is well maintained and is in beautiful condition. Courtesy of Don Linz.)

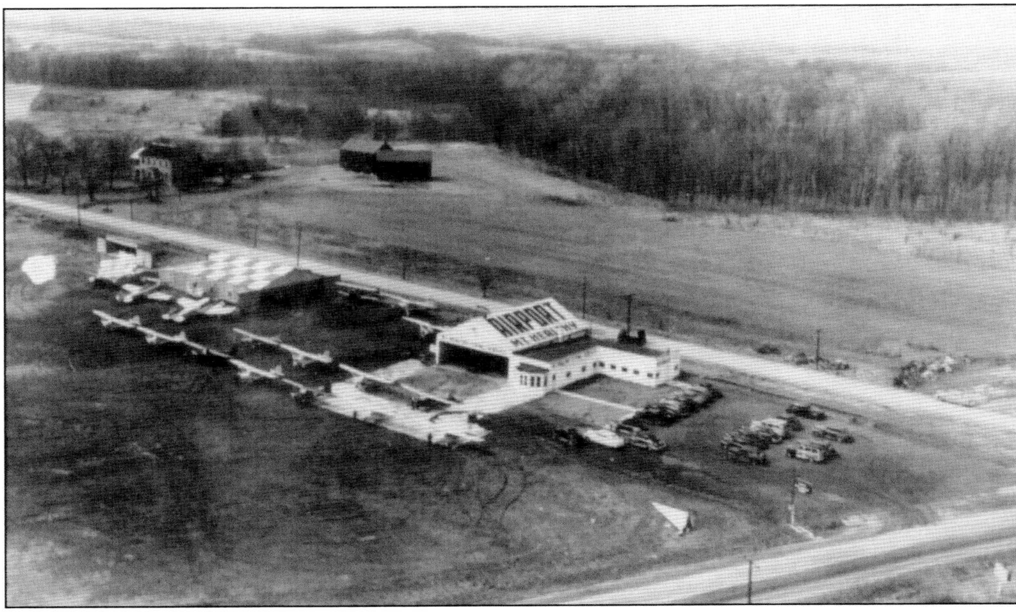

The Mount Healthy Airport was the brainchild of a group of businessmen from Mount Healthy, Ohio. This airport was in the southwest corner of Colerain Avenue and Springdale Road, where Northgate Mall is located today. That is Colerain Avenue running along the bottom and Springdale Road running across the page. The Hardin House is in the upper left. (Courtesy of Howard Hochscheid.)

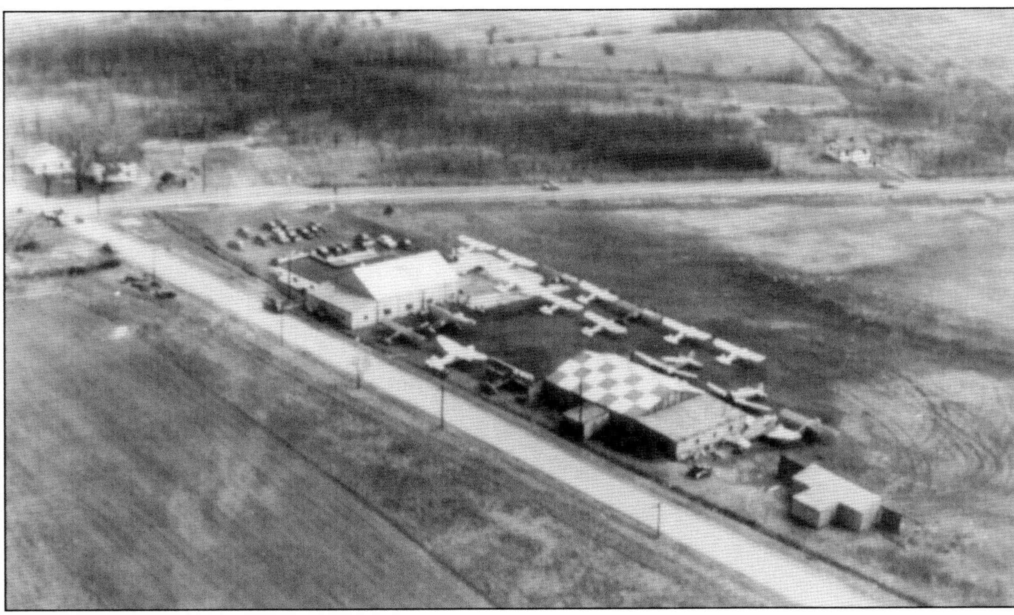

Here is the airport with the Colerain Avenue and Springdale Road intersection in the upper left There are several hangars, an administration building, various planes, and the Flying Dutchmar Restaurant that was known for its fried chicken. To land at the airport, one had to clear wires or Colerain Avenue and clear a depression at the start of the runway to land safely within its shor distance. (Courtesy of Howard Hochscheid.)

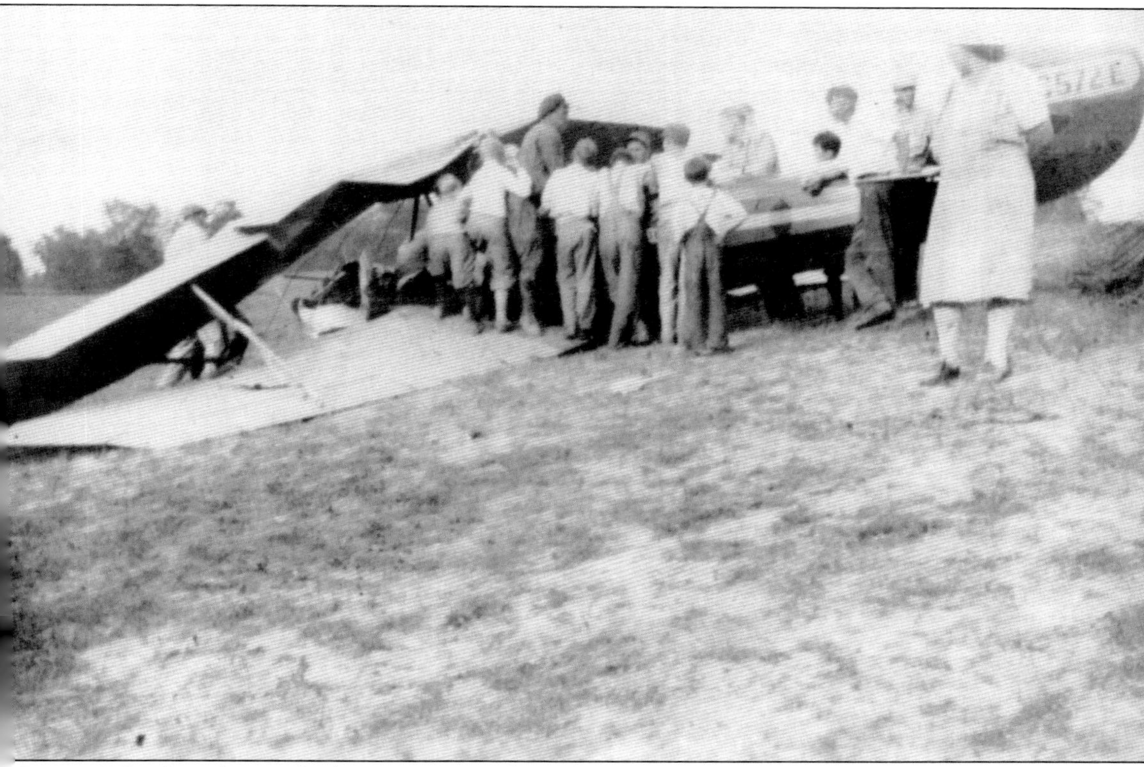

Stormy Wheeler, a licensed pilot, was giving a flying lesson in a two-seater biplane, the American Eagle. Stormy was giving instructions on a flight coming back from Hamilton when the student put the plane in a spin and froze at the controls. Stormy was in the back cockpit where the instruments were, so he took a fire extinguisher and hit the student in the front cockpit in the head. Stormy was bringing the plane out of the spin, and if he had had just 20 more feet, he would have made it. They were both killed instantly, according to the coroner. Pictured is the wreckage of the crash that occurred on William Muehlenhard's farm at 9685 Pippin Road near the Mt. Healthy airport in the late 1920s. (Courtesy of Bob Muehlenhard.)

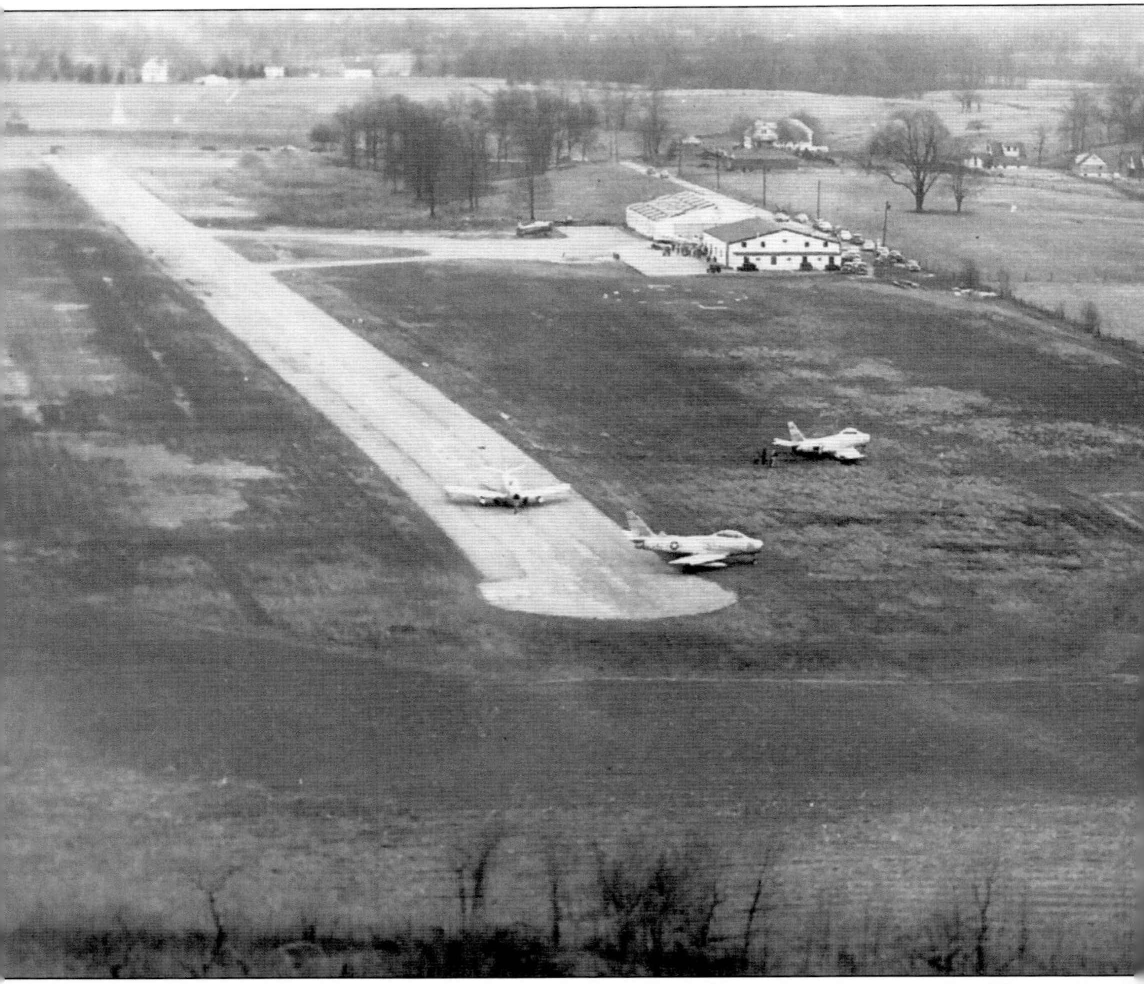

Lakewood Airpark operated from 1946 to 1956 and was located on the west side of Pippin Road near the sharp turn of Adams Road. Many returning World War II veterans attended government-approved flying schools, like Lakewood, on the G.I. Bill. One of the most significant events to occur in Colerain Township was at Lakewood Airpark. In January 1953, three F-86 Saber jets were forced to land there. The jets had run out of fuel on a flight from Scott Air Force Base in Illinois bound for Wright-Patterson Air Force Base in Dayton, Ohio. Wright-Patterson sent mechanics to Lakewood to remove all excess weight, including the wingtip fuel tanks and any armament and ammunition, to lighten the planes so they could take off on the short Lakewood runway. The mechanics strapped rockets on the plane's sides to assist with the takeoff. They carried just enough fuel to get them to the Greater Cincinnati Airport in Kentucky, where they refueled for the flight back to Wright-Patterson. Everything went according to plan, and the three planes landed safely at Wright-Patterson Air Force Base. (Courtesy of Joan Fleischaker.)

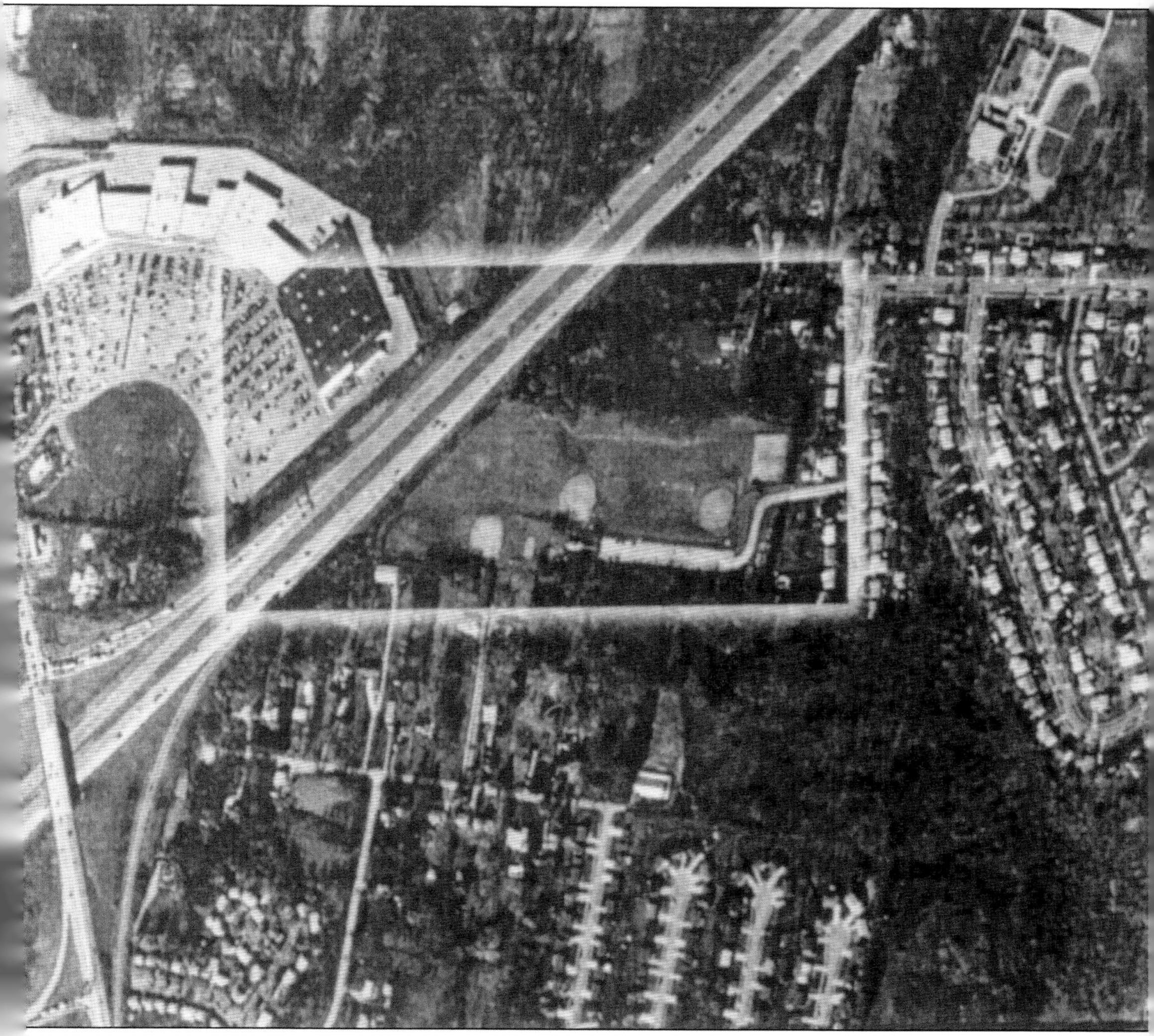

Colerain had a third airport, which was privately owned by the Clippard family. It was constructed on 33 acres that are now bisected by I-275. The south portion, bisected by I-275, is Clippard Park, which the family donated to the township. The north portion is the Colerain Towne Center, home to Walmart. A near fatal crash in 1956 involving Clippard and his son, Bill, left both with serious injuries. The outline in the picture shows the area covered by the airport. (Courtesy of Bill and Bob Clippard.)

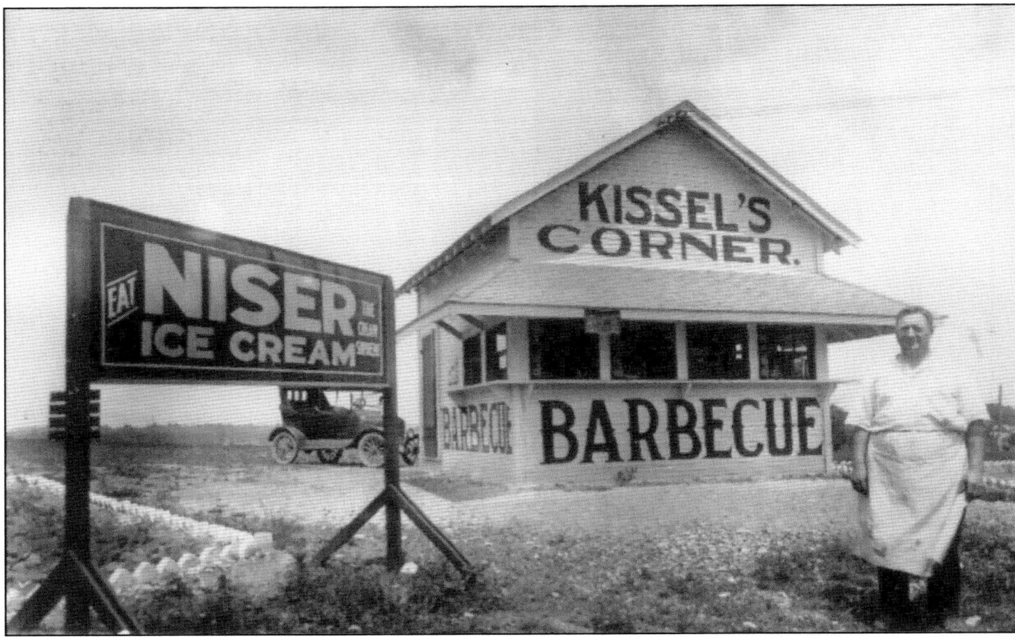

Fred Kissel moved to Colerain Township in the 1920s and opened a barbeque restaurant at the northeast corner of Colerain Avenue and Compton Road. Fred was known for his popcorn and great food. Fred's sons, Ralph and Russel, would later open Kissel's Amusement Park at 8871 Colerain Avenue. Today this site is occupied by Joseph Chevrolet. (Courtesy of Bob Kissel.)

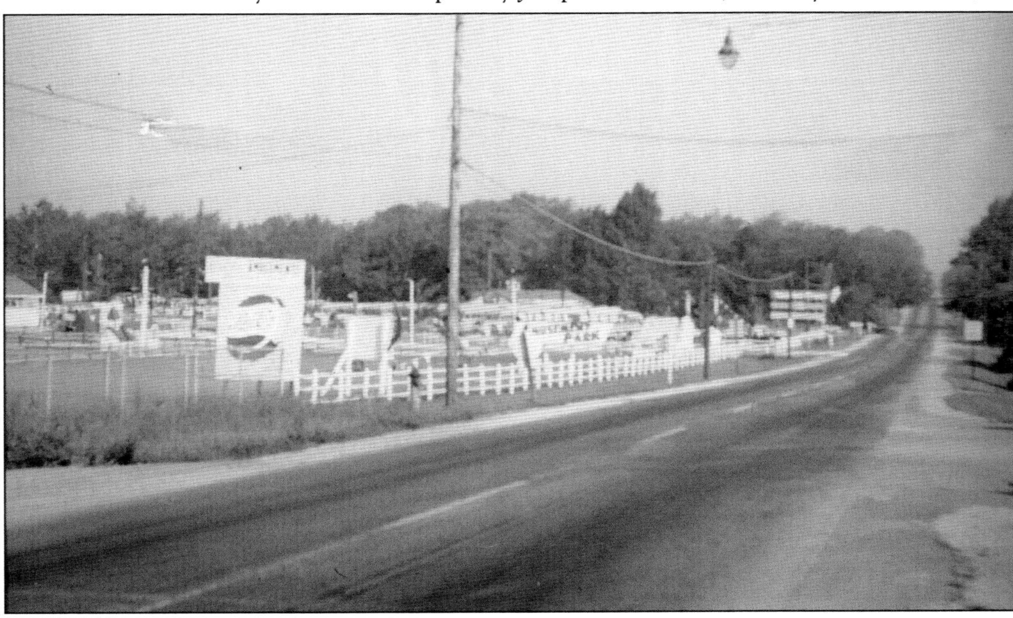

The Kissel Amusement Park included a covered picnic area, three refreshment stands, and a midway with a vast assortment of rides. It also offered a zoo with lions, deer, buffalo, llamas, horses, ponies, exotic birds, and more animals that are too numerous to mention. The widening of Colerain Avenue caused multiple traffic problems, adding to the park's difficulty competing with Kings Island. The Kissel Amusement Park closed in the early 1960s. (Courtesy of Bob Kissel.)

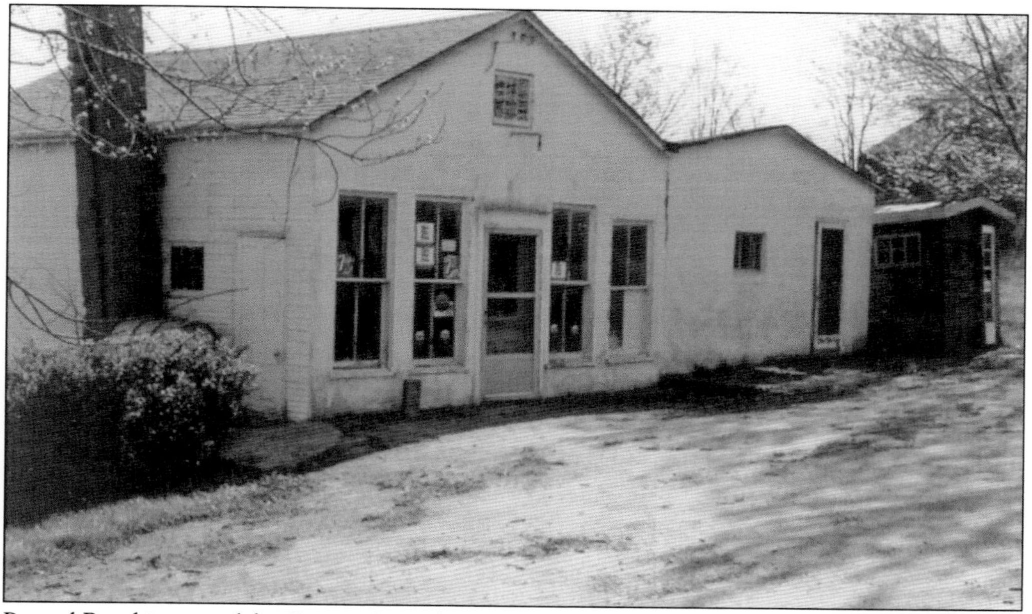

Prectel Road is named for George Prectel who, with his wife, Frieda, ran a general store on that road from 1930 until the 1970s. He was very accommodating to his customers. If the store was closed, all one had to do was ring the store's bell and George would open up. He also had one gas pump and sold Sohio products and later Phillips gasoline. This store was one of a kind. (Courtesy of Chick and Pat Haskamp.)

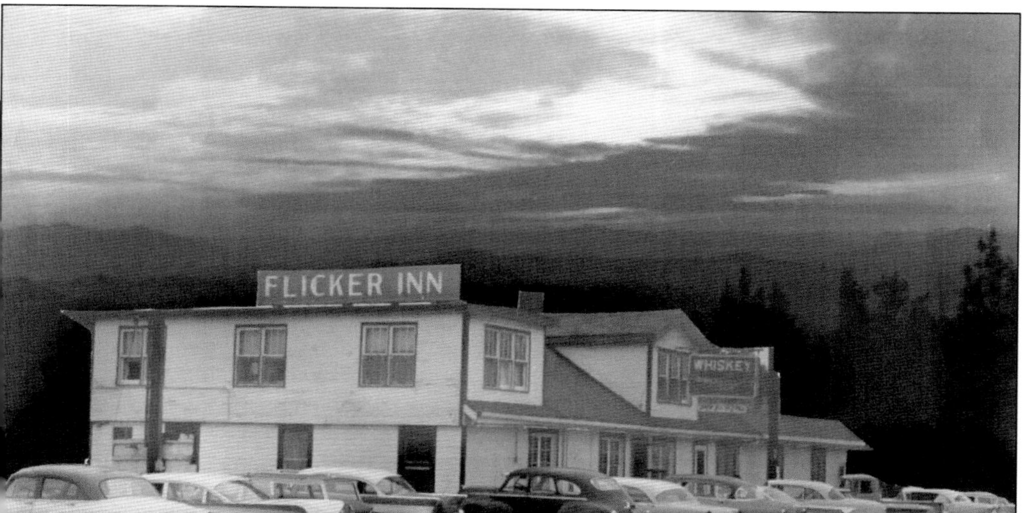

Clarence Flick opened a general store with gas pumps in 1936 at 7077 Harrison Avenue. The business evolved into a tavern that eventually added pool, shuffleboard, darts, and bowling. Dancing and a nightclub followed. On the 6-acre site, there was a baseball diamond and a football field. Baseball league games were played there from 1936 until 1961. The games and many other activities stopped when I-74 was built at the rear of the property. (Courtesy of Marlene Brookbank.)

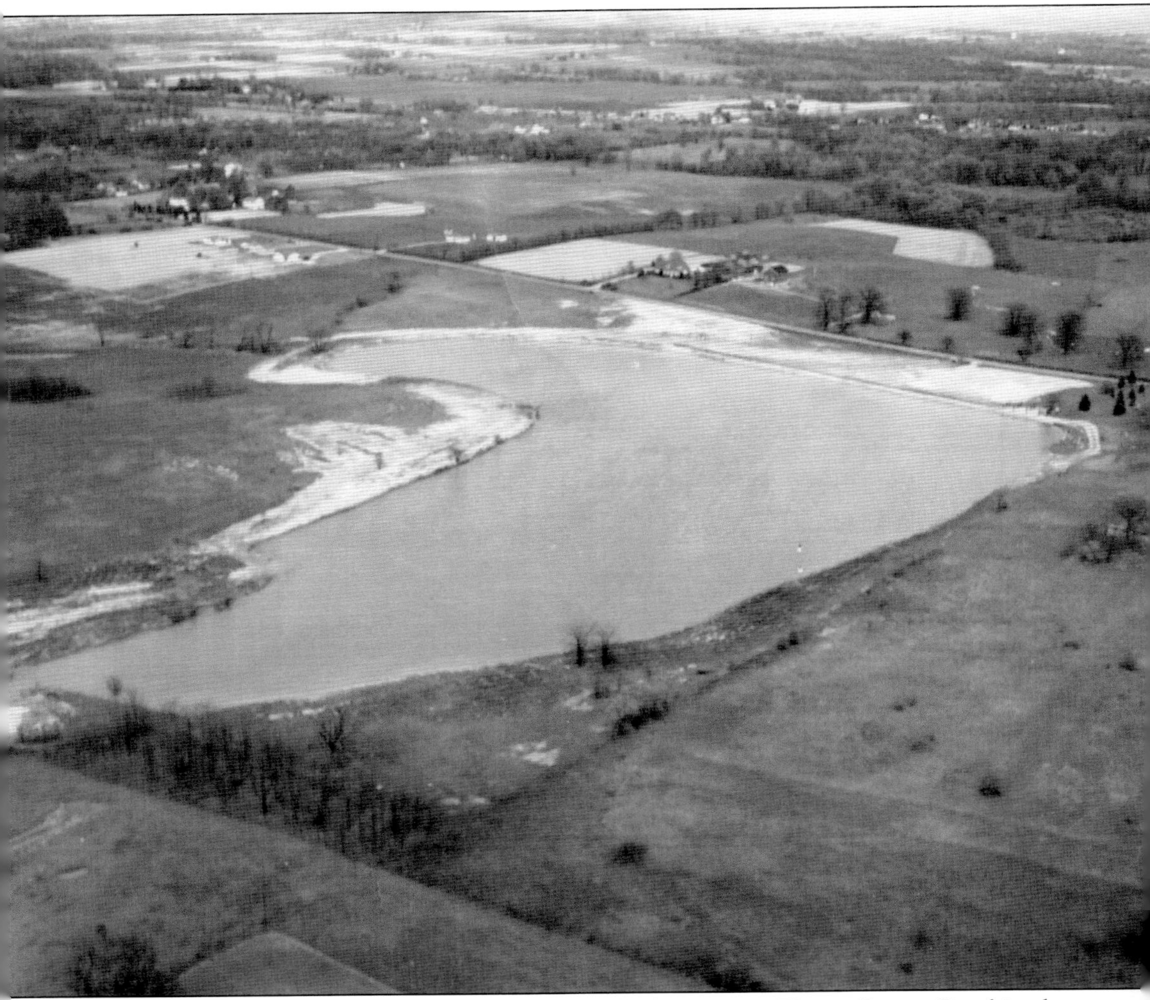

This aerial view of Lake Gloria was taken in the late 1940s. That is Pippin Road in the upper middle of the picture. The lake was man-made and was named for the original owners' daughter. Fishing, of course, was the main activity. The lake was also used by the Colerain Fire Department for their training exercises. Later the owners constructed a miniature golf course. The golf course had regulars, including an unidentified husband and wife. When the wife passed away, her wish was to be cremated and have her ashes spread over the golf course. The husband complied with her wishes. This complex was sold in the mid-2000s. (Courtesy of Chuck Easton.)

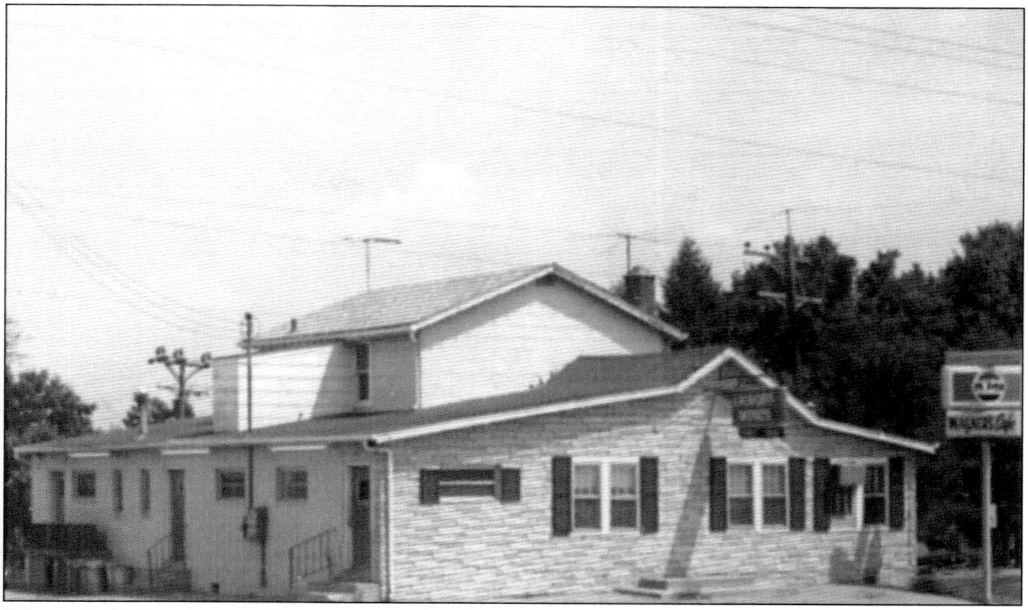

Wagner's Café at the northeast corner of Colerain Avenue and Compton Road was noted for their food. Everything was homemade and the food was delicious, especially the soups and desserts. They served breakfast, lunch, and dinner with special entrees on certain days. They served the community for 35 years. John and Vera Wagner closed their business in 1972 on the same date they had opened, September 29. (Courtesy of the Wagner family.)

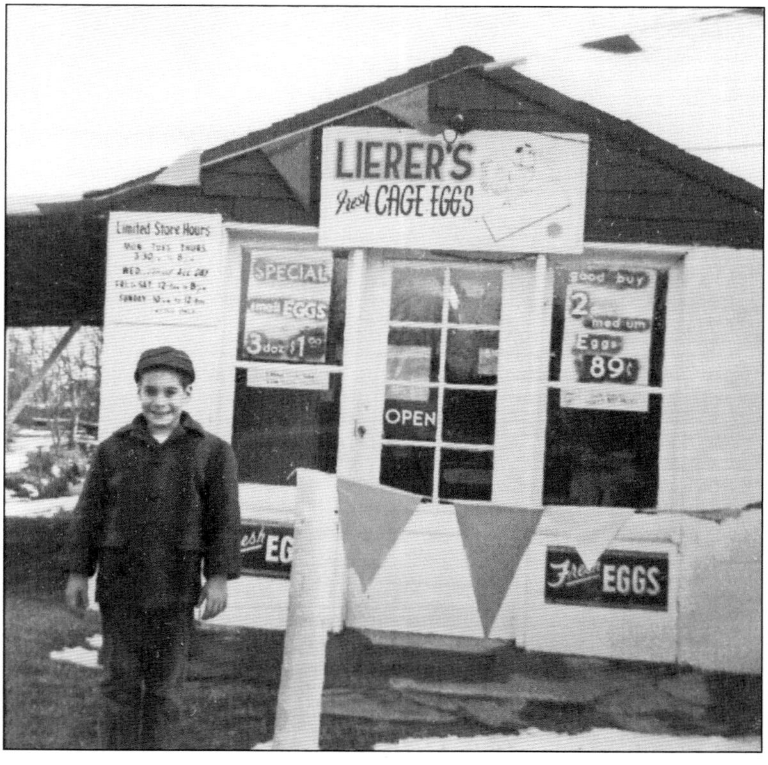

The Lierers egg business was located on the southeast corner of Colerain Avenue and Springdale Road. They were a large supplier of eggs to the local community, with over 900 laying chickens kept in a building approximately 40-feet-by-100-feet. They also sold milk, bread, soft drinks, penny candy, and other cooking items in their store. That is young John Lierer standing in front of the store. (Courtesy of John Lierer.)

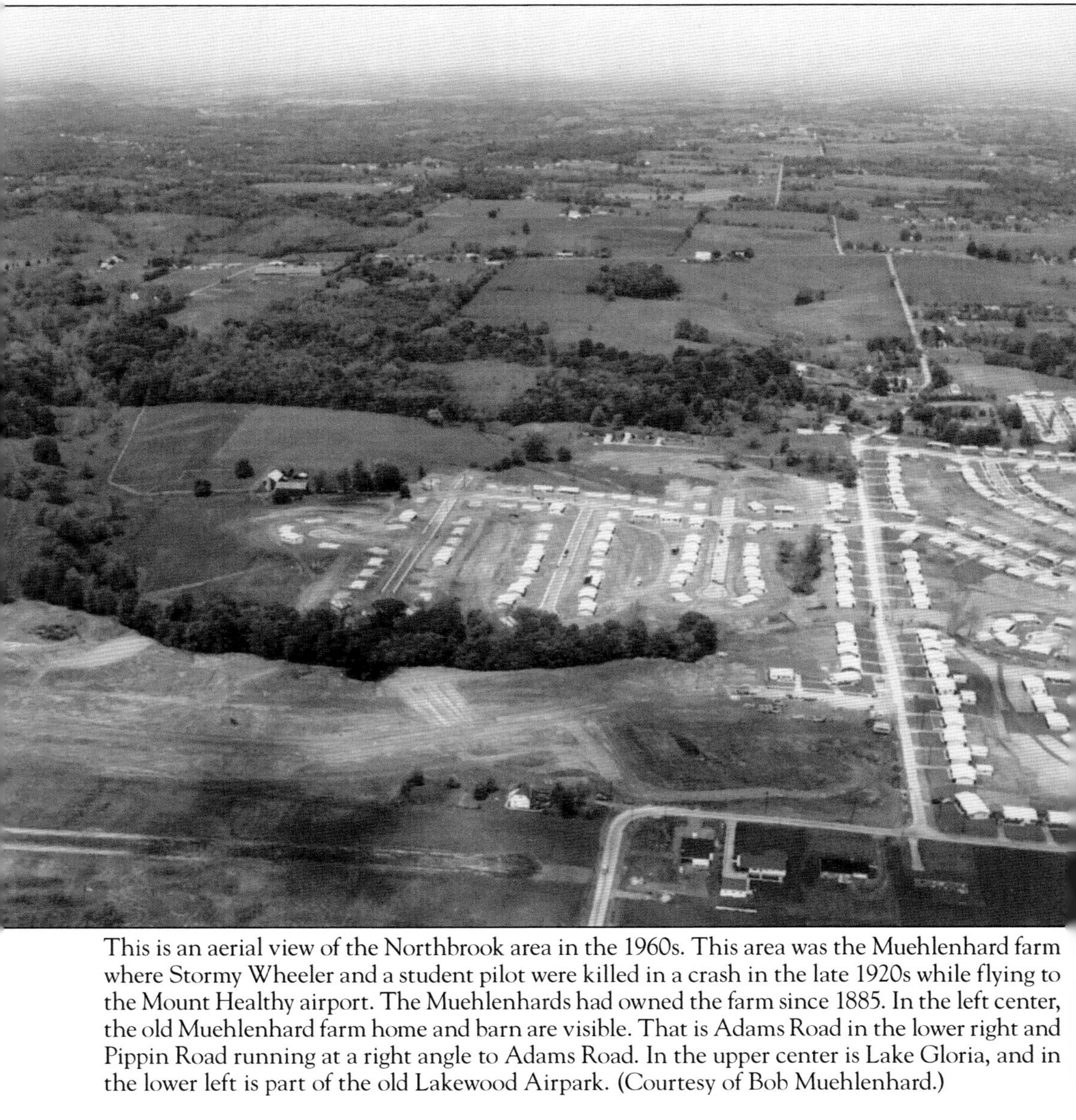

This is an aerial view of the Northbrook area in the 1960s. This area was the Muehlenhard farm where Stormy Wheeler and a student pilot were killed in a crash in the late 1920s while flying to the Mount Healthy airport. The Muehlenhards had owned the farm since 1885. In the left center, the old Muehlenhard farm home and barn are visible. That is Adams Road in the lower right and Pippin Road running at a right angle to Adams Road. In the upper center is Lake Gloria, and in the lower left is part of the old Lakewood Airpark. (Courtesy of Bob Muehlenhard.)

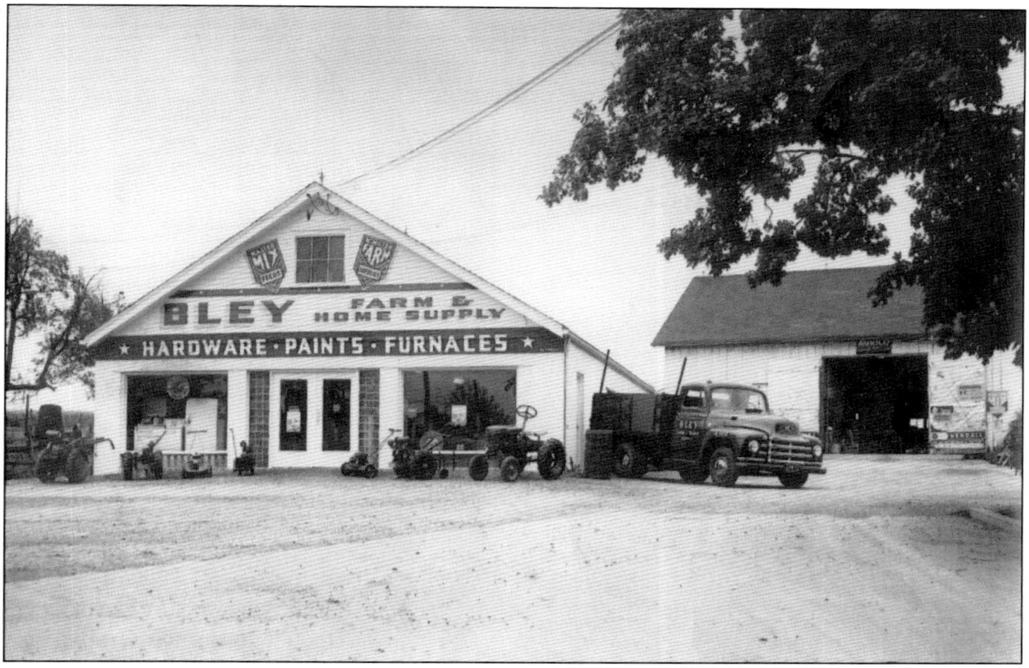

The Bley Farm and Home Supply store, located at 9337 Colerain Avenue, carried hay, seed, all kinds of hardware, shotgun shells, tractors, mowers, appliances, and more. They were in friendly competition with Lockwood Hardware. If they did not have an item, they would send the customer to Lockwood, and to reciprocate, Lockwood would do the same. They were in business from 1950 to 1964. This site is now occupied by a Big Lots store. (Courtesy of Florence Bley.)

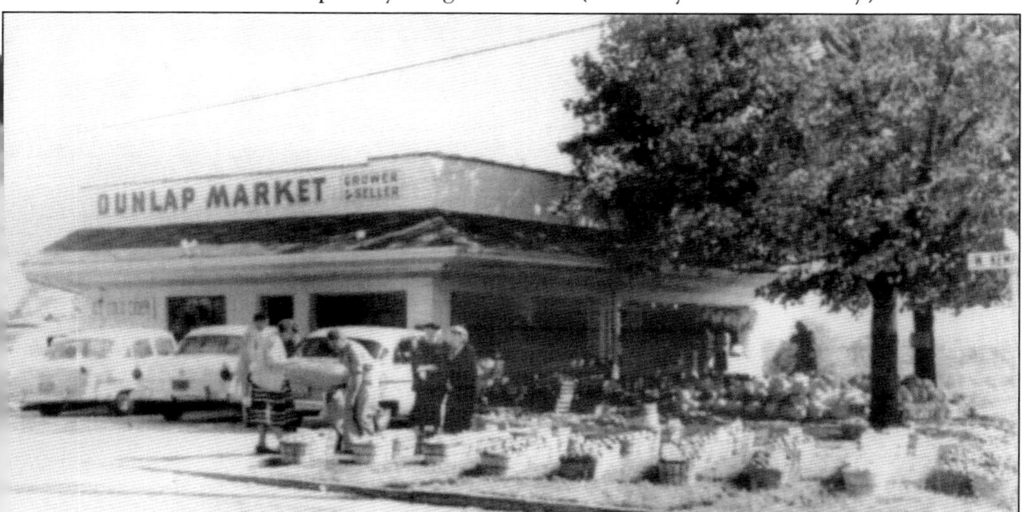

The Diefenbacher family had a produce stand on the southeast corner of Colerain Avenue and Kemper Road in Dunlap. This area generated large amounts of vehicular traffic, especially during the football season, because it was a main route to Miami University in Oxford, Ohio. They sold apples, sweet corn, cider, and many other fresh fruits and vegetables. Dale Diefenbacher was a member of the Dunlap Fire Department and, at one time, a Colerain trustee. (Courtesy of Dale Diefenbacher.)

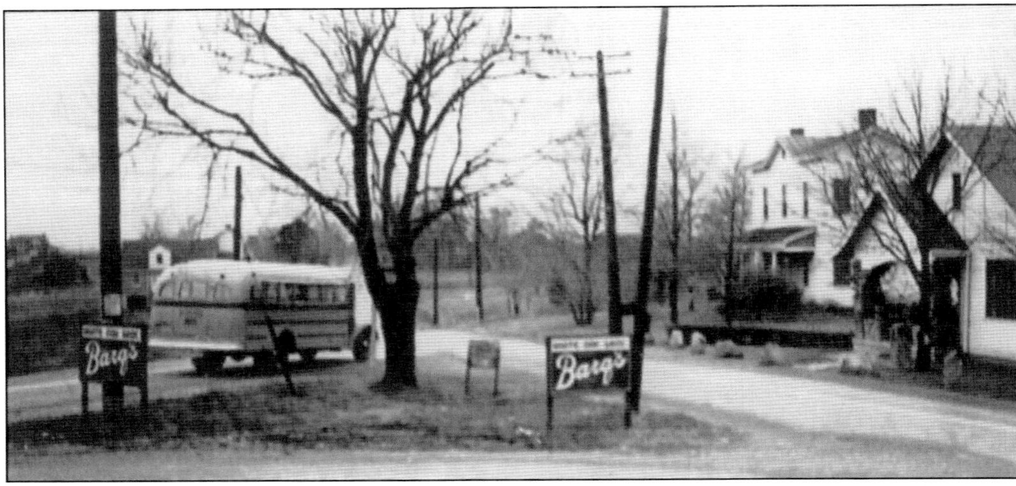

Looking north at the intersection of Cheviot and Blue Rock Roads, one can see Wissel's Corner. This picture was taken from in front of the old White Villa Grocery Store. This store operated from 1939 to 1985. It was a full-service grocery store with groceries, fruits and vegetables, a butcher shop, and other staples. Notice the wide open spaces back then compared to today. This is one of the busiest intersections in the township. Today the building is home to the Roma Italian Restaurant. (Courtesy of Howard Frey.)

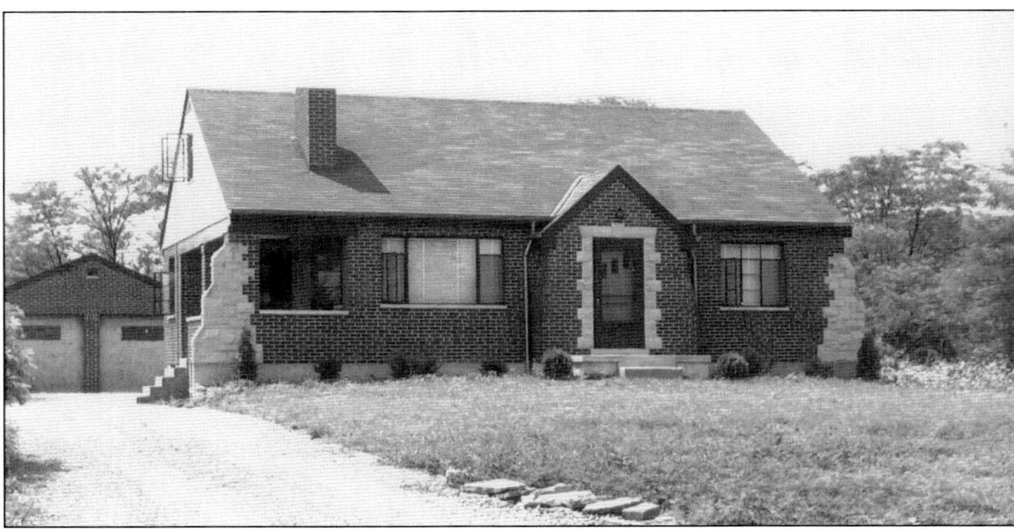

In 1954, Betty and Jim Simmermon saw a need for a child care center in Colerain Township. They started Play Time Child Care and Kindergarten in their home at 9497 Colerain Avenue (today a Burger King). Today the center continues under their daughter, Nancy, with a staff of 18 full-time and part-time teachers carrying on the tradition of first-class child care. The present site is behind the IHOP Restaurant; this is the center's third location. (Courtesy of Nancy Napier.)

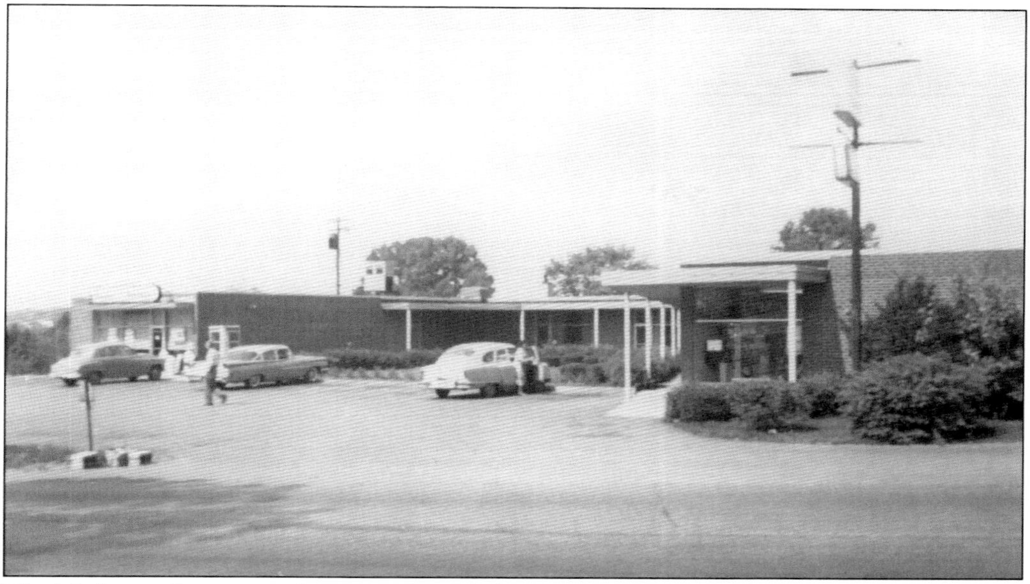

The Madonna Center, on the west side of Colerain Avenue, north of Galbraith Road, was the first planned shopping center in Colerain Township. Developed by Dr. A. H. Wilke in 1953, the Madonna Center's name was chosen by Ann Wilke, Dr. Wilke's wife, because of her devotion to Mary. The archbishop of Cincinnati, Karl J. Alter, dedicated the center. Early occupants were Duffy's Pharmacy, Alvis Appliances, Lubbe Shoes, Semona Haberdashery, Kit 'n Kris Infants' and Children's, optometrist Arthur J. Rogg, and Dr. Wilke's medical office. (Courtesy of Mel Blust.)

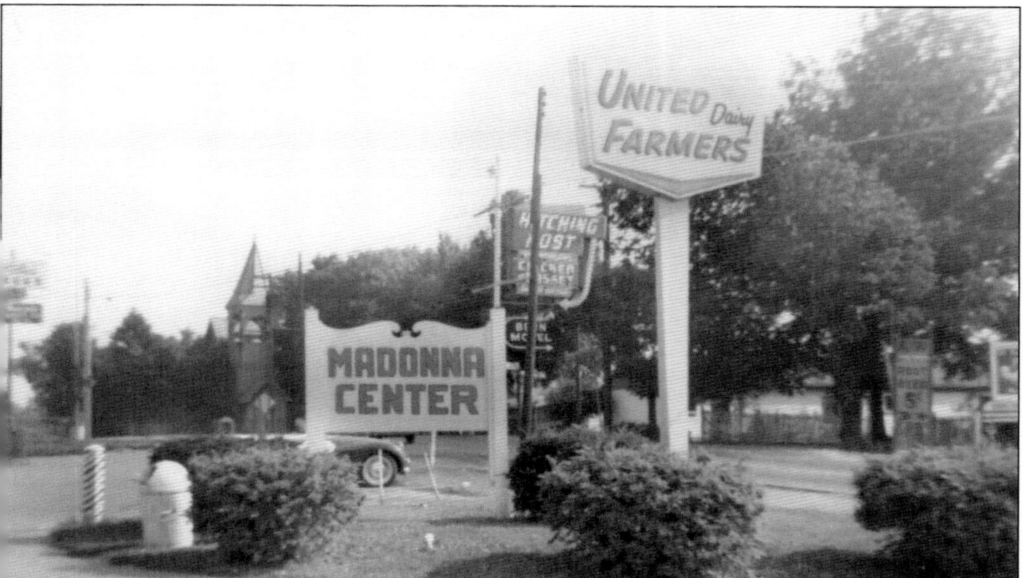

he Madonna Center on Colerain Avenue was home to a United Dairy Farmers store as well as Hitching Post Restaurant in later years. This center was across the street from the Bern Motel. ictured in the center left is the steeple of the old Groesbeck church. (Courtesy of Mel Blust.)

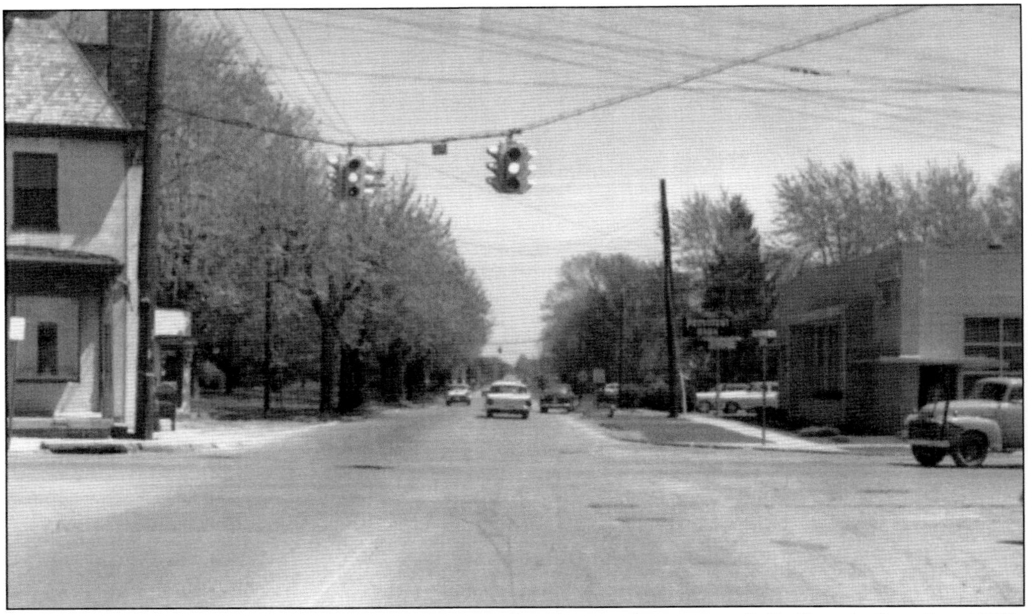

This view looks east toward the intersection of Colerain Avenue and Galbraith Road in 1953. The old Frey building is on the left, and the old Provident Bank Building is on the right. This picture was taken before both roads were widened. (Courtesy of St. Ann's Church.)

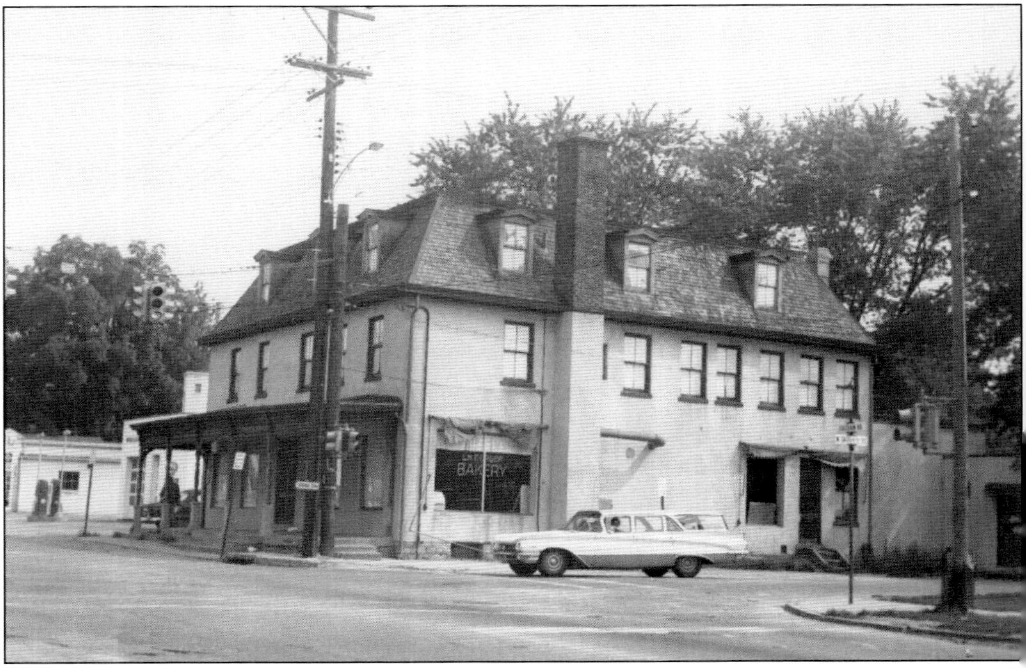

Pictured is the old Frey building, which was occupied by the L. H. Dorger Bakery. Off to the left is Armond Clawson's Mobile gas station. Further to the left is the Groesbeck Improvement Association's building, which once housed the Groesbeck Fire Department. One of the first traffic lights in the township was at Colerain Avenue and Galbraith Road. Today this is the site of a Walgreens drugstore. (Courtesy of Mel Blust.)

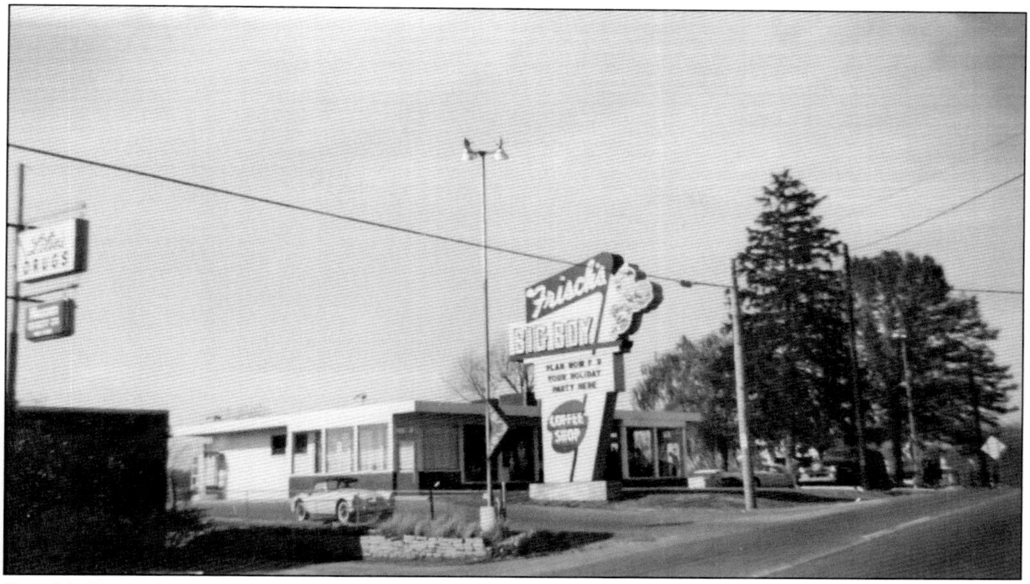

Frisch's Drive-In restaurant was located on the west side of Colerain at 8349 Colerain Avenue, next to the Madonna Center. Orders were taken from cars and delivered by a carhop so people could eat in their car. Later this site was home to Domino's Pizza, and today there is a McDonald's at this site. (Courtesy of Mel Blust.)

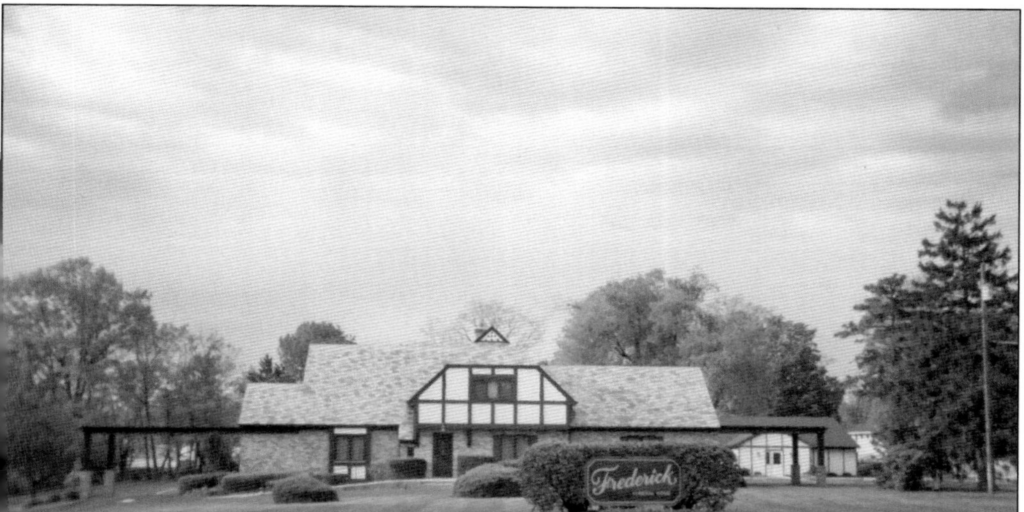

rederick Funeral Home is the only funeral home in Colerain Township. Paul Frederick Sr. started he business in the early 1930s in Corryville, within walking distance of St. George Church. The uneral home moved to Colerain Township on Banning Road near Pippin Road in 1961. It has een a family business with Paul Jr., his daughters, and now a grandson active in the business. Courtesy of Don Linz.)

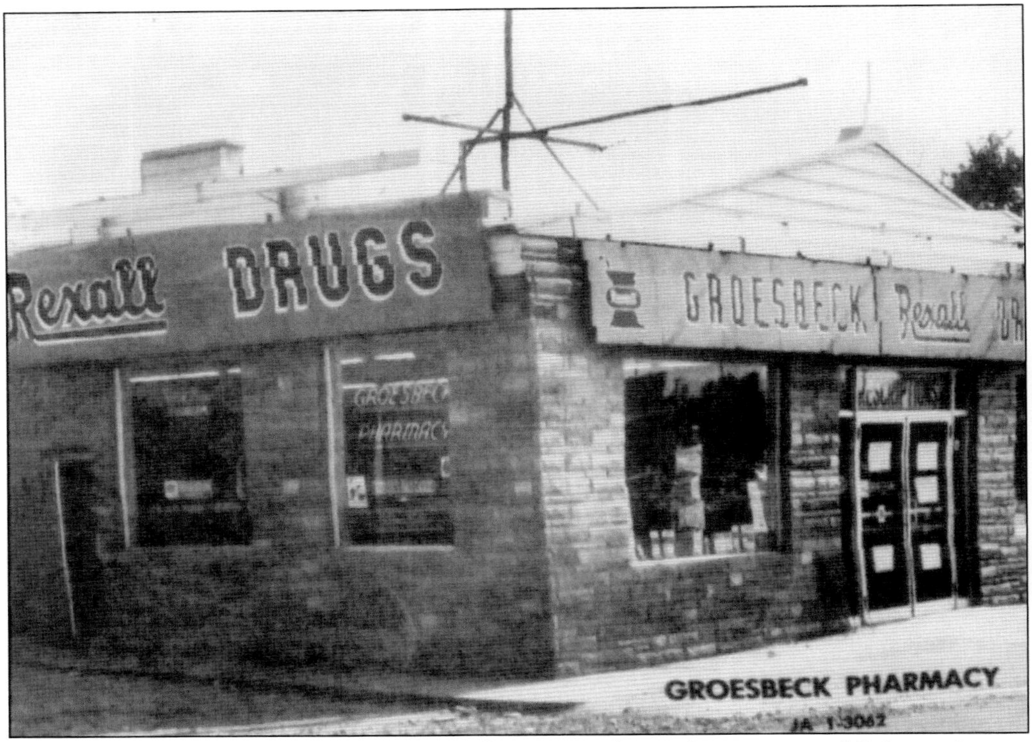

The Groesbeck Pharmacy is pictured here in the 1960s at the southwest corner of Colerain Avenue and Galbraith Road. (Courtesy of the Coleraine Historical Society.)

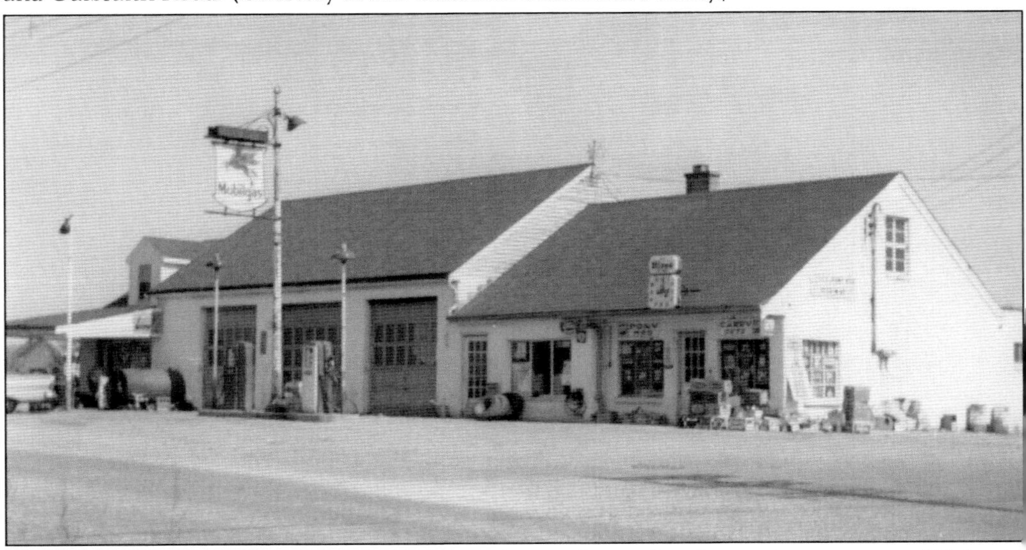

This combination garage, gas station, and pony keg was located at the northeast corner of Colerair Avenue and Struble Road. Joe Benz and his wife, Rita; her sister, Marie; and Marie's husband Bud Ferenbach, who owned the garage, opened the pony keg. This was across the street from the Benzes' home on Struble Road. The pony keg later moved to Struble Road next to the Ben: home. This was one of the first pony kegs in the area. People came from far and wide to shop there. (Courtesy of Joe and Rita Benz.)

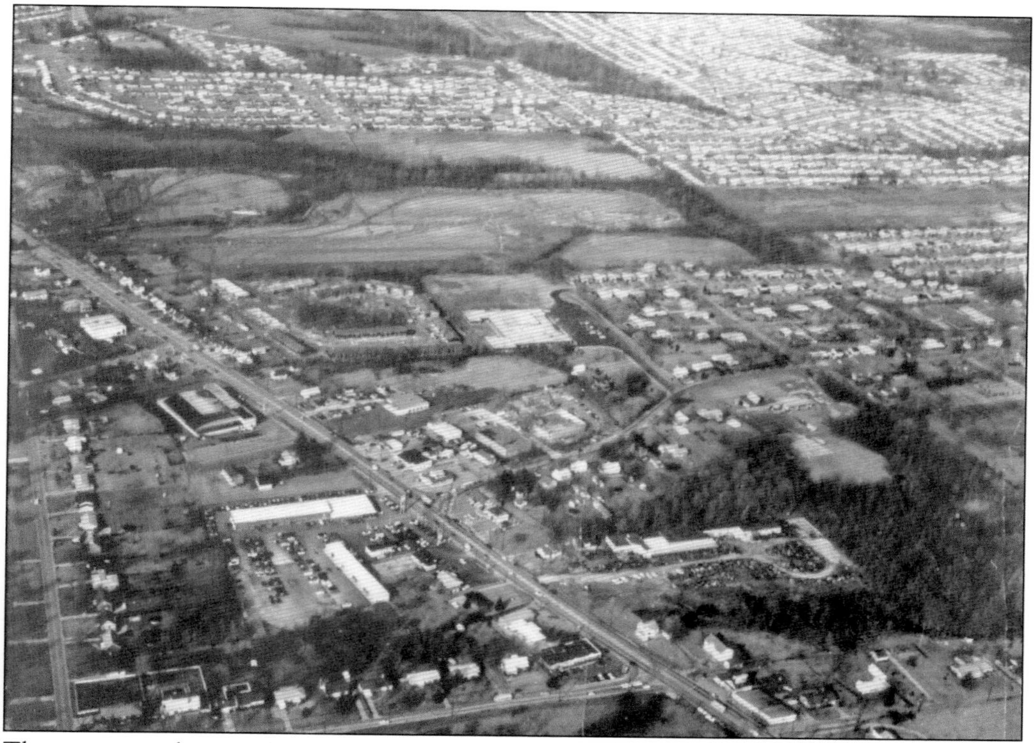

This is an aerial view of Colerain Avenue in the early 1970s entering the Bevis area. To the lower left is Poole Road. Below is the area before the Farbach-Werner site became the nature preserve. At the top, the development of the Northbook area can be seen. Times have changed. (Courtesy of Mel Blust.)

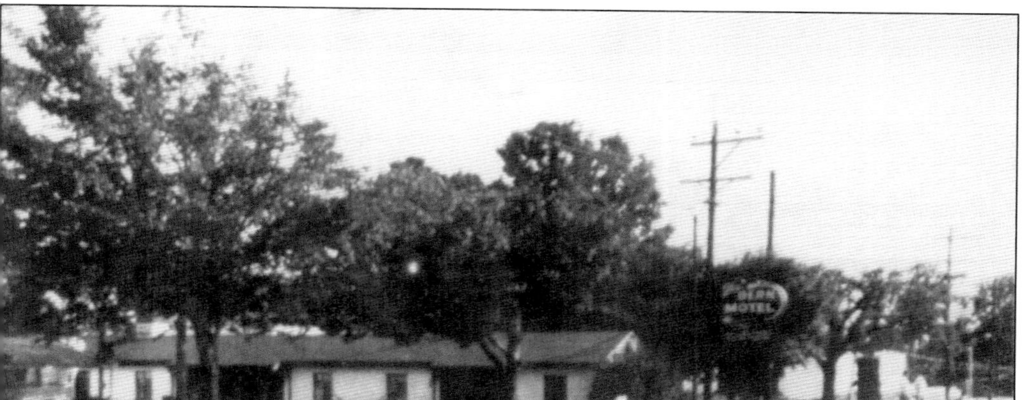

)ne of the earliest motels in Colerain was the Bern Motel, located on the east side of Colerain t 8360 Colerain Avenue. The motel was in the area of today's Bigg's store on Colerain Avenue. Courtesy of Mel Blust.)

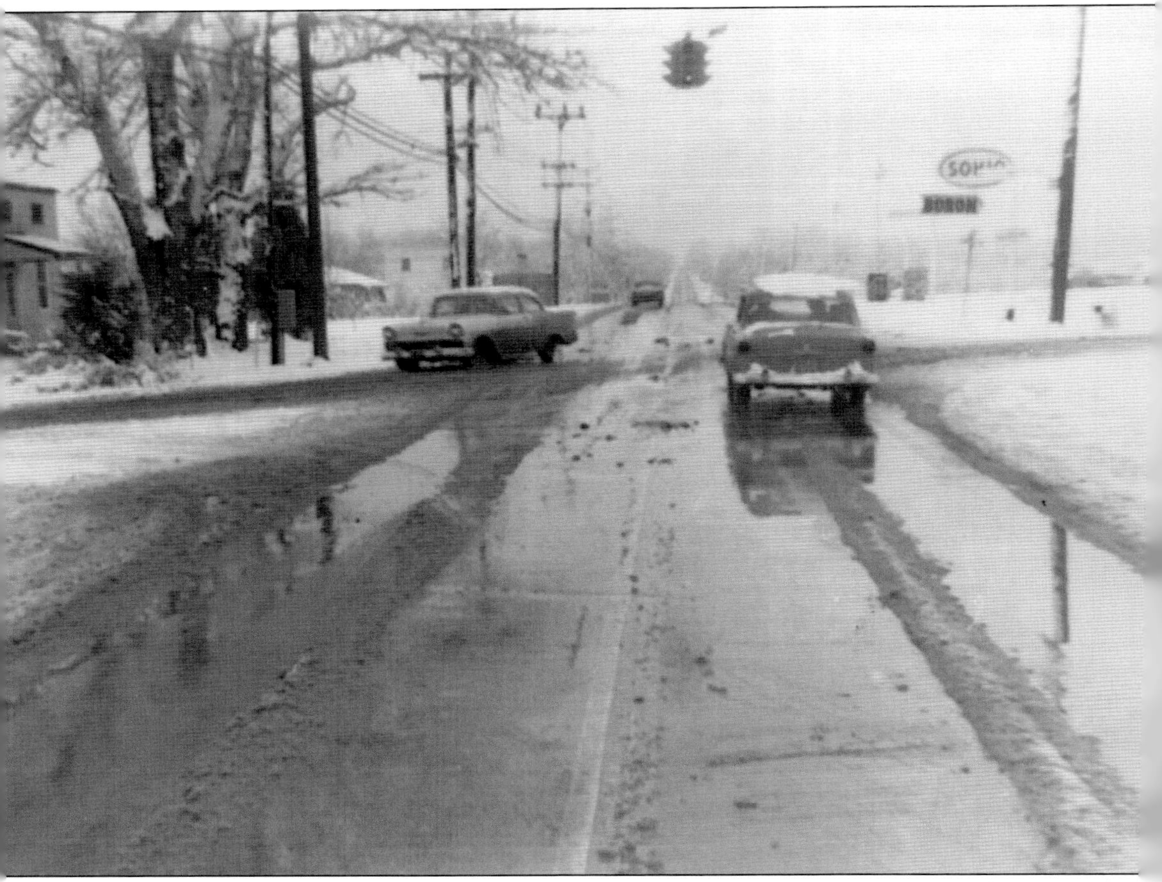

Here is a view looking south on Colerain Avenue from Springdale Road in the early 1960s. The southwest corner was the location of the Mount Healthy Airport before Northgate Mall was built in 1972. Other businesses on this corner were a Sohio service station, Bite-D-Lite, King Bee leasing, the Flying Dutchman restaurant, and various airplane hangars and administration and service buildings. For many years, the southeast corner was home to the Lierer's Egg Factory. White Castle is the present occupant. Todt's Pond was also located on this corner and is fondly remembered by the local boys as good fishing but not for swimming. (Courtesy of Marlene Bundy.)

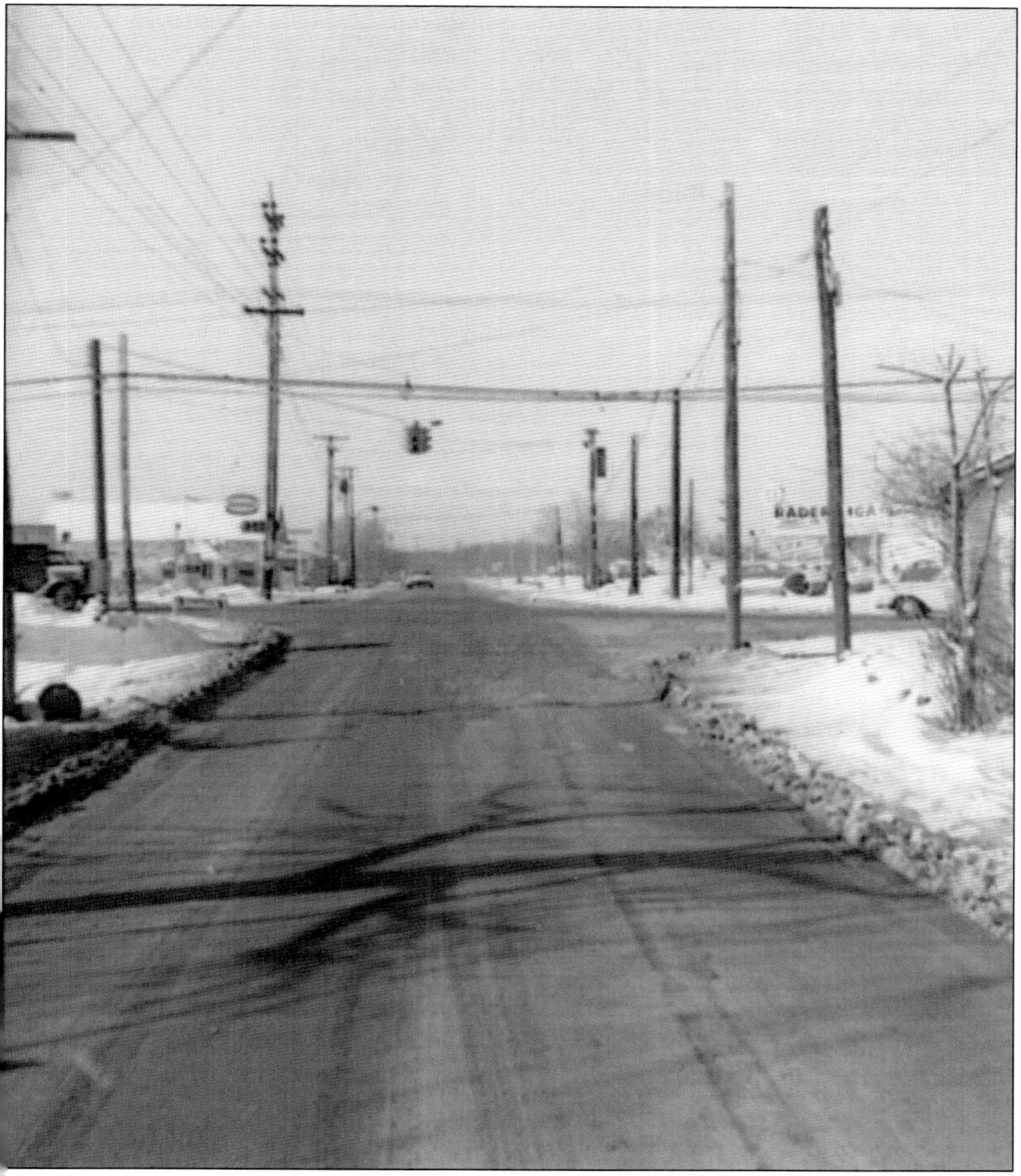

This is looking west from Springdale Road as it crosses Colerain Avenue. At one time, the northwest corner was home to an old tollhouse. Later this tollhouse received some additions and was rebuilt into a building in which airplanes from the airport were repaired and recovered. There was a large sycamore tree on this corner that took three men with their arms outstretched to reach around the tree. Paner's Auto Garage was also on this corner and later the Dent Brothers Radiator Shop. Later an IGA Grocery store could be found here. (Courtesy of Marlene Bundy.)

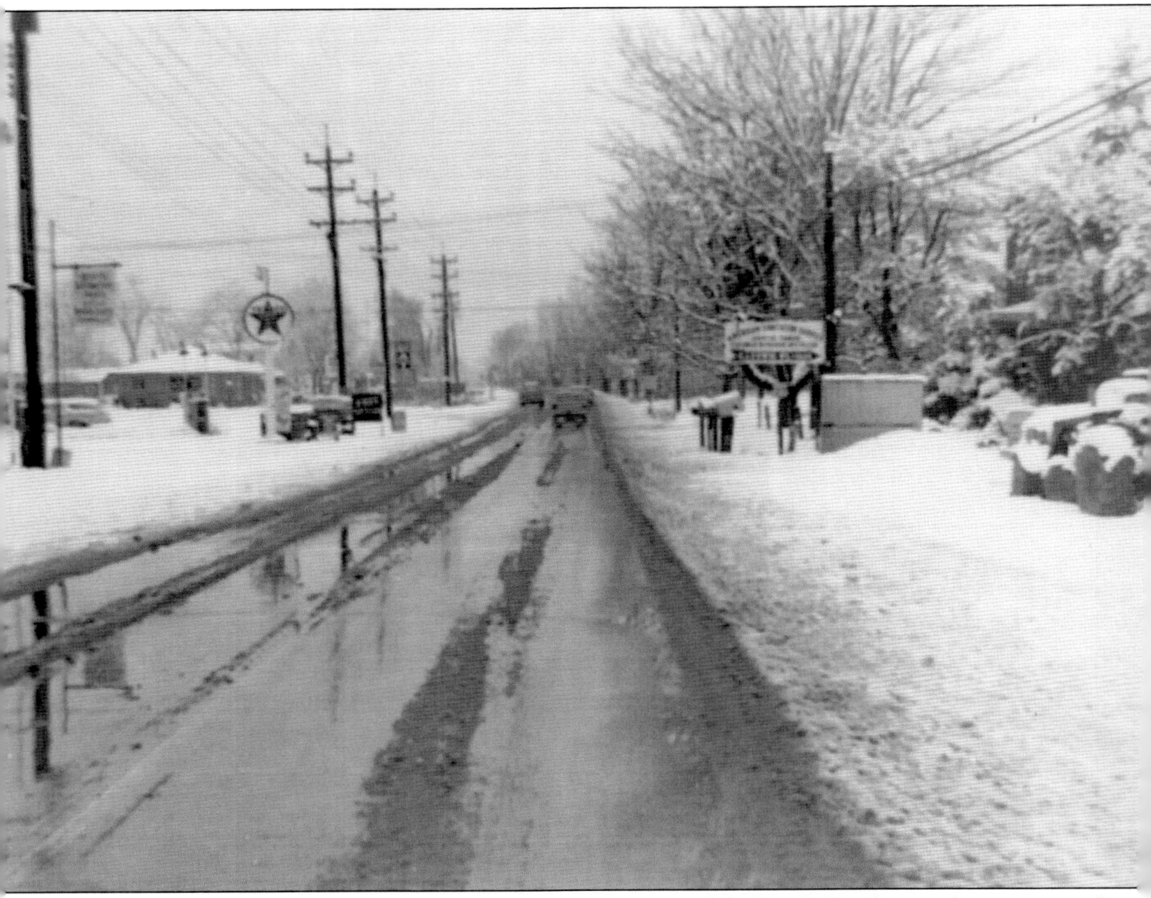

This is looking north on Colerain Avenue from Springdale Road. On the northeast corner, Joe and Esther Hudepohl operated a service station, tavern, and a dance hall. In the mid-1940s, Tiny Ludwig took over the operation. This was a favorite watering hole in this area. At one time, this corner was home to the Bevis Hotel. (Courtesy of Marlene Bundy.)

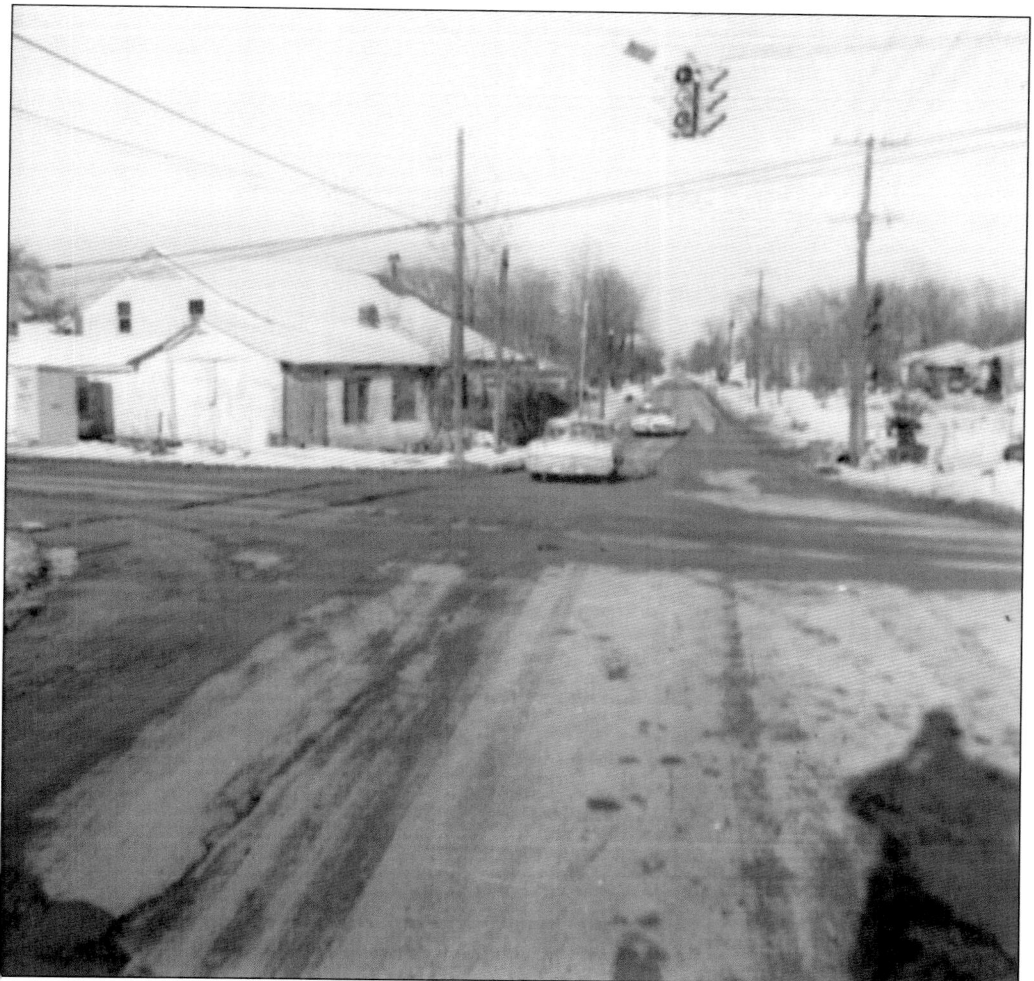

This is Springdale Road looking east as it crosses Colerain Avenue. Tiny Ludwig's Tavern is on the left, and the Lierer Egg Factory is on the right. (Courtesy of Marlene Bundy.)

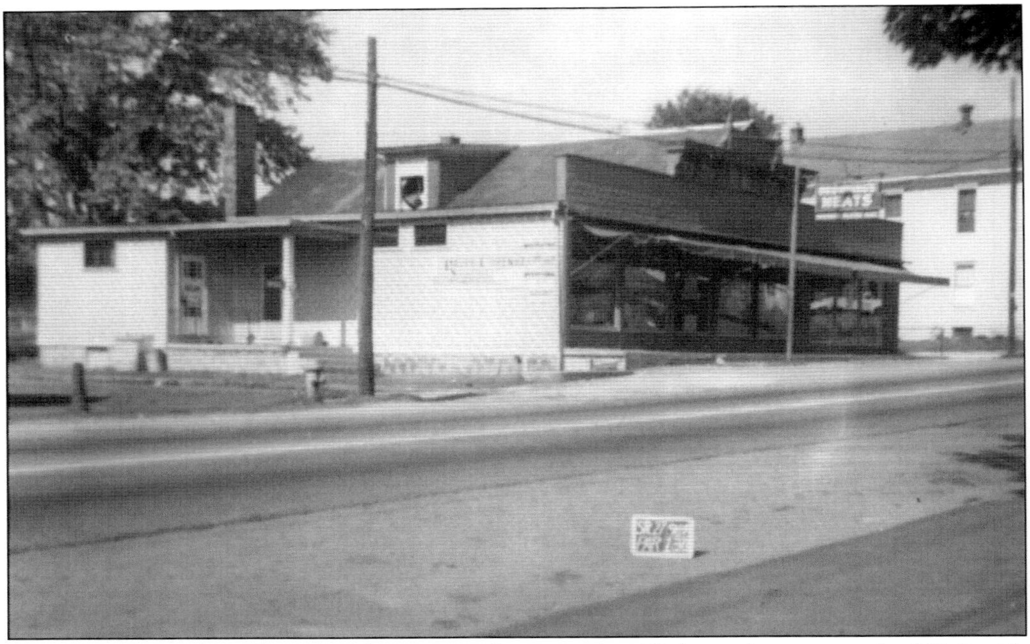

The old Lockwood Hardware building was on the west side of ColerainAvenue, north of Galbraith Road, at 8251 Colerain Avenue. When this picture was taken in 1962, this building was home to Browning's Meats. (Courtesy of Mel Blust.)

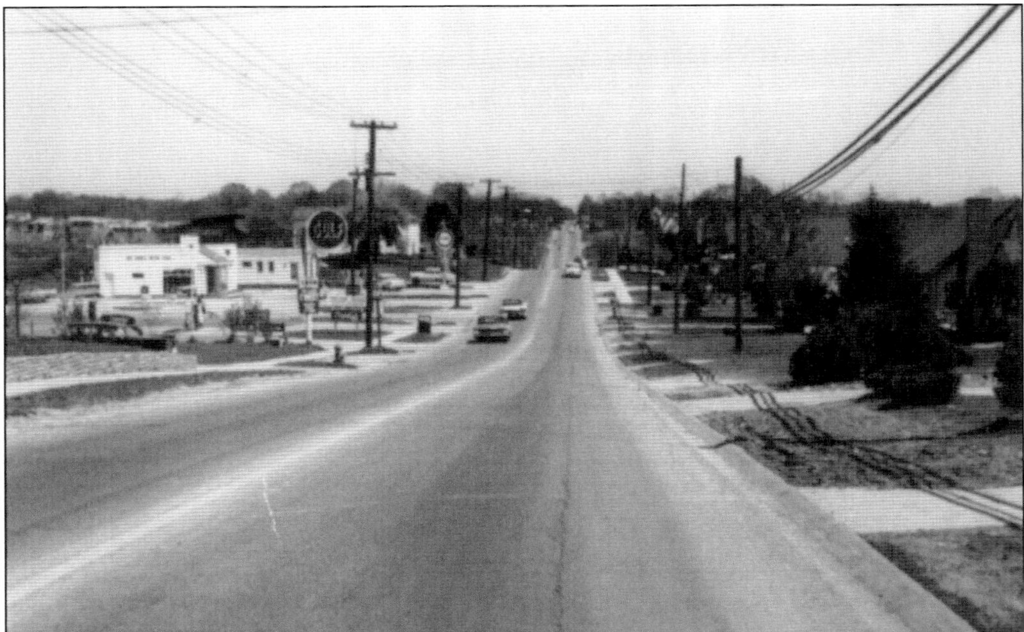

In this view looking east on Galbraith Road in the early 1950s, much of the area is still undevelopec compared to today. Notice the service stations on the left that are now long gone. (Courtesy o St. Ann's Church.)

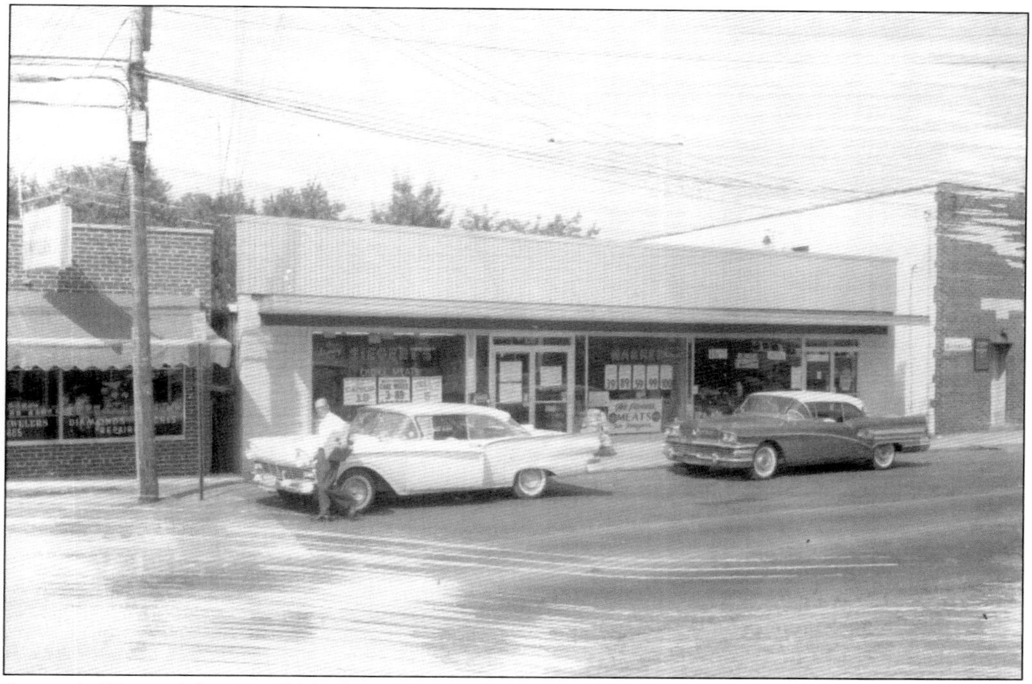

Siegert's Choice Meats and Market is pictured in the 1960s on the west side of Colerain Avenue, south of Galbraith Road, at 8149 Colerain Avenue. (Courtesy of Mel Blust.)

This is the strip center on the east side of Colerain Avenue, south of Galbraith Road, in the early 1960s. The center still stands, but most of the businesses shown in this photograph have either gone out of business or have moved to other locations. On the right is Sam's Grill, a favorite restaurant. (Courtesy of Mel Blust.)

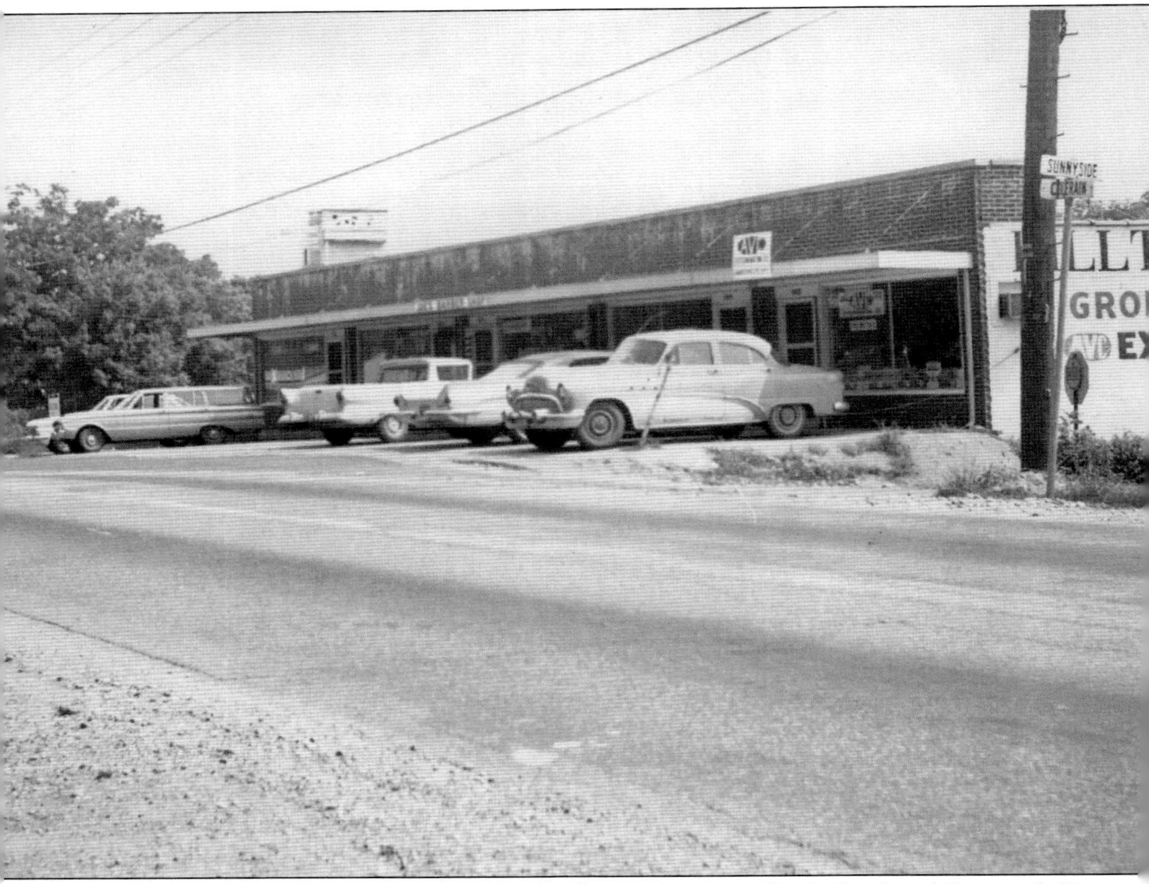

This strip center was on the east side of Colerain Avenue at Poole Road and Sunnyside Drive. This center was demolished, and today this site is near the entrance to the Target Store. (Courtesy of Mel Blust.)

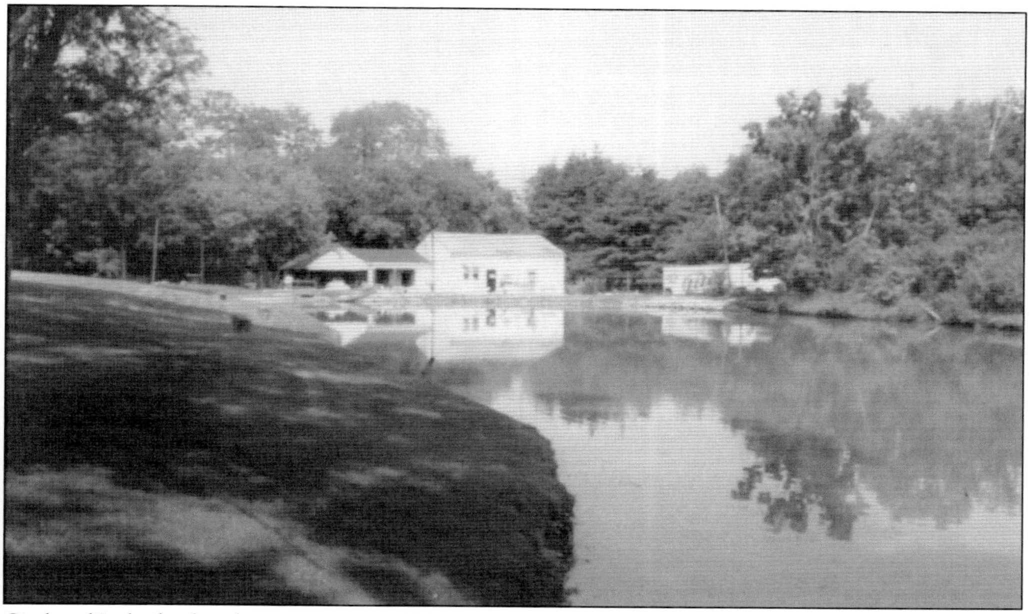

Orchard Lake had its beginnings in 1892 on property originally owned by Jesse Bevis. Today the fishing lake and tavern are located at 3611 Bevis Lane. It is rumored that the area was once home to an apple orchard, hence the name Orchard Lake. A small bait shop was constructed in 1935, and in 1951, the tavern was constructed. Until that time, it was strictly used for fishing. Another rumor is that two slot machines and a motorcycle are in the lake. (Courtesy of Don Linz.)

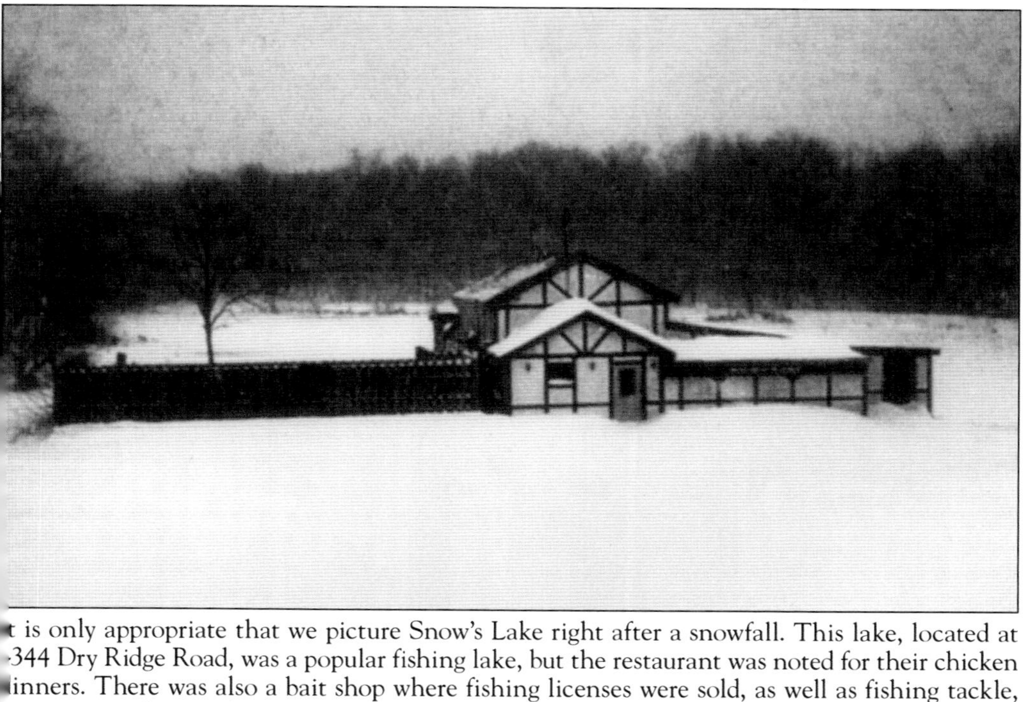

t is only appropriate that we picture Snow's Lake right after a snowfall. This lake, located at 344 Dry Ridge Road, was a popular fishing lake, but the restaurant was noted for their chicken linners. There was also a bait shop where fishing licenses were sold, as well as fishing tackle, ninnows, night crawlers, and other types of bait. The lake had no lights, so fishermen had to ring their own lanterns to fish at night. (Courtesy of the *Northwest Press.*)

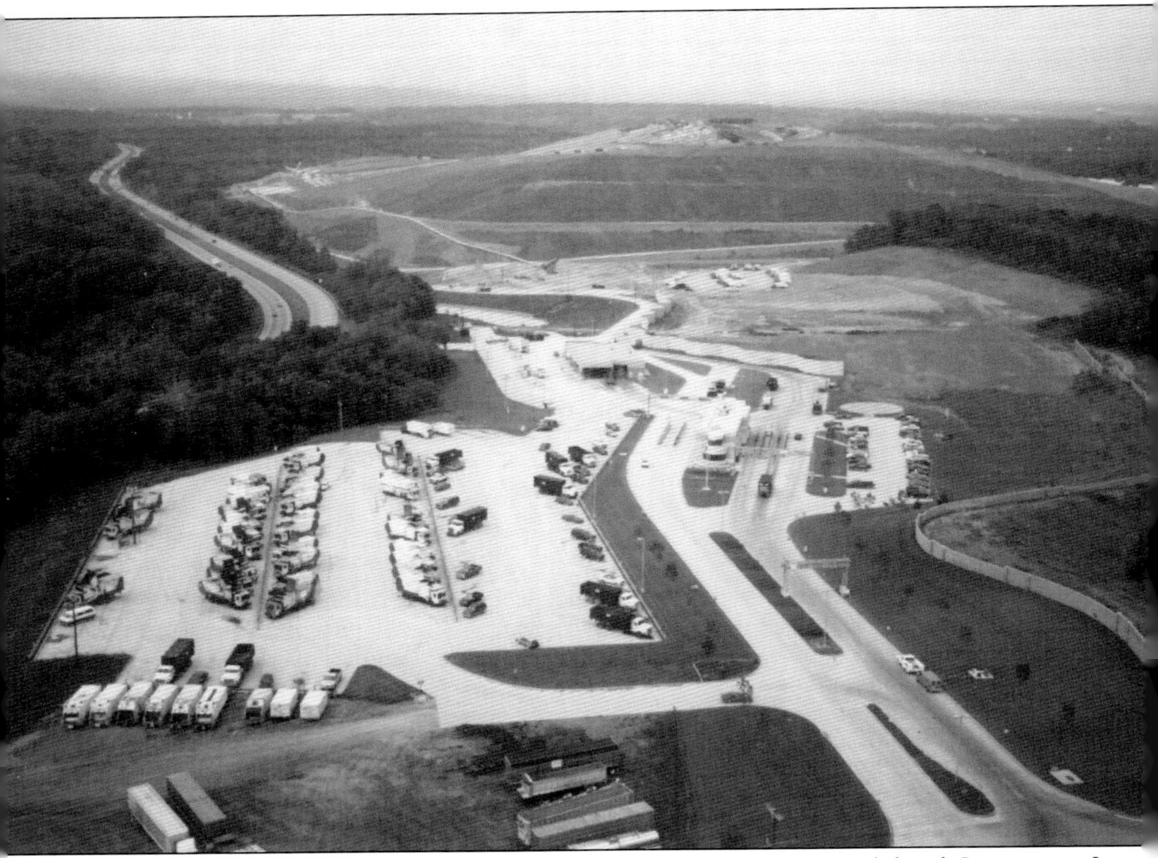

One of the major businesses in Colerain Township is Rumpke Consolidated Companies, Inc. The company owns the largest landfill in the State of Ohio. The business started in the early 1930s by collecting garbage and trash from residents and restaurants to feed William Rumpke's hogs. When the hogs were large enough to sell, at about 300 pounds, he would buy about 40 new shoats (young hogs that have already received shots and weigh about 50 pounds). The process was then started over again. It took about 3 months for the shoats to reach full size. (Courtesy of Rumpke Consolidated Companies, Inc.)

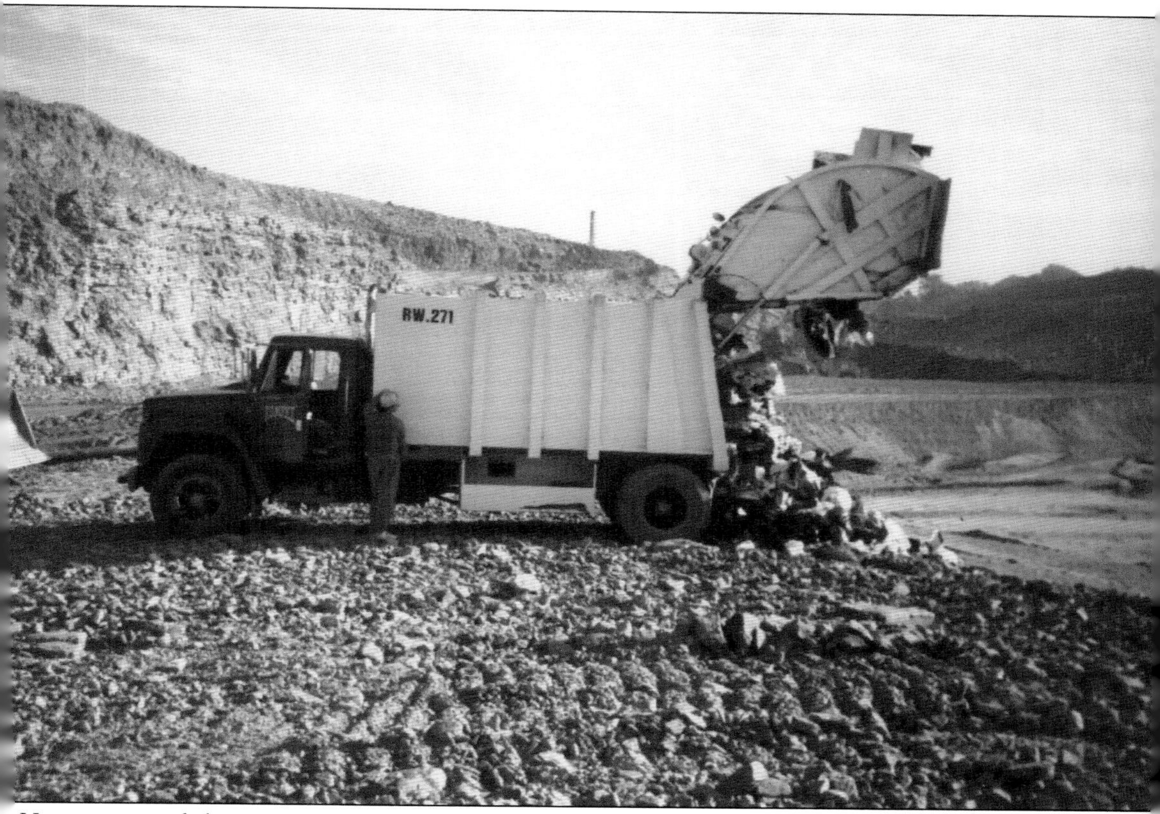

Here is one of the 900 trucks that collects up to 10,000 tons of trash a day, a rate that means the landfill has 13 years left before it reaches its current limit. (Courtesy of Rumpke Consolidated Companies, Inc.)

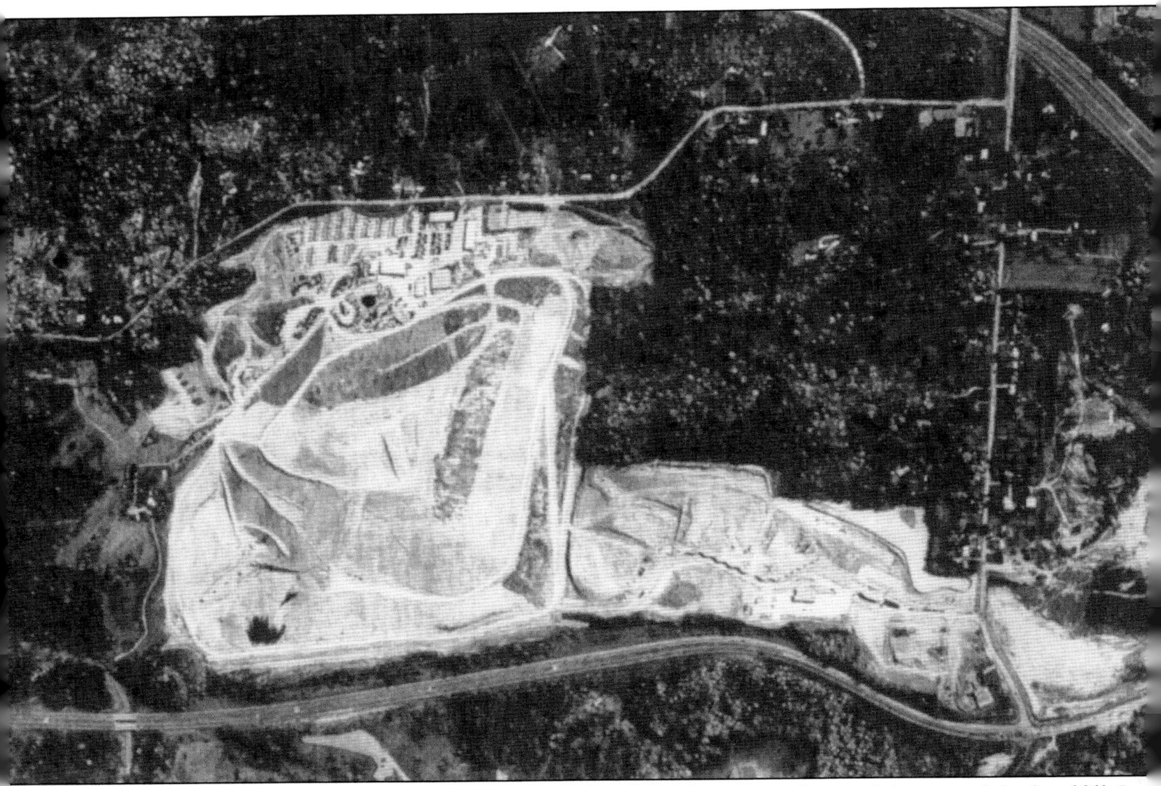

Mount Rumpke rises 1,000 feet above sea level with an American flag sticking out of the landfill. It is not only the highest point in Colerain Township; it also covers the most acreage of any business in the township. Among the items buried here are a 14-year-old circus elephant and the world's largest Hershey's bar. Rumpke is still very much a family operation, employing over 70 Rumpke kin. This aerial view is from 1994. (Courtesy of Rumpke Consolidated Companies, Inc.)

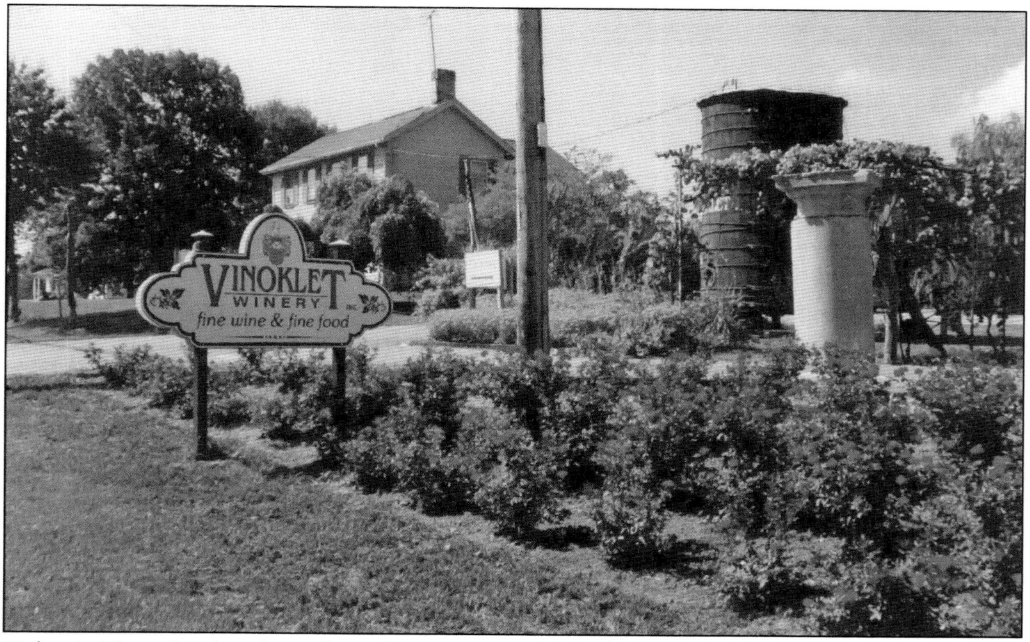

Colerain Township has the only working winery in Hamilton County. Kreso Mikulic, a Croatian native, had a dream come true. For Kreso it was a long, hard struggle, but he could not be deterred from his vision. His goal was to have this winery and a multitude of grape arbors. He called it Vinoklet, which is Croatian for "small house and vineyard." (Courtesy of Don Linz.)

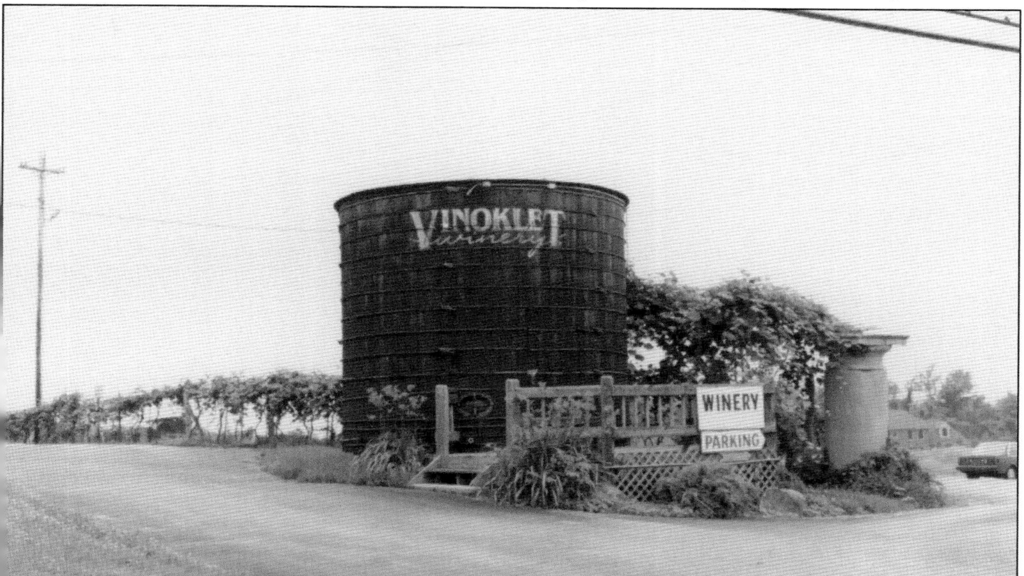

The Vinoklet Winery on old Colerain Avenue in Dunlap is a registered state tourist attraction. When entering the winery parking lot, there is a 15-foot, 25,000-gallon barrel nearby. This barrel is a first in North America, and there is no other like it. The barrel has been converted into a tasting room with a bar and a fireplace. It can accommodate 12 to 15 people. (Courtesy of Kreso Mikulic.)

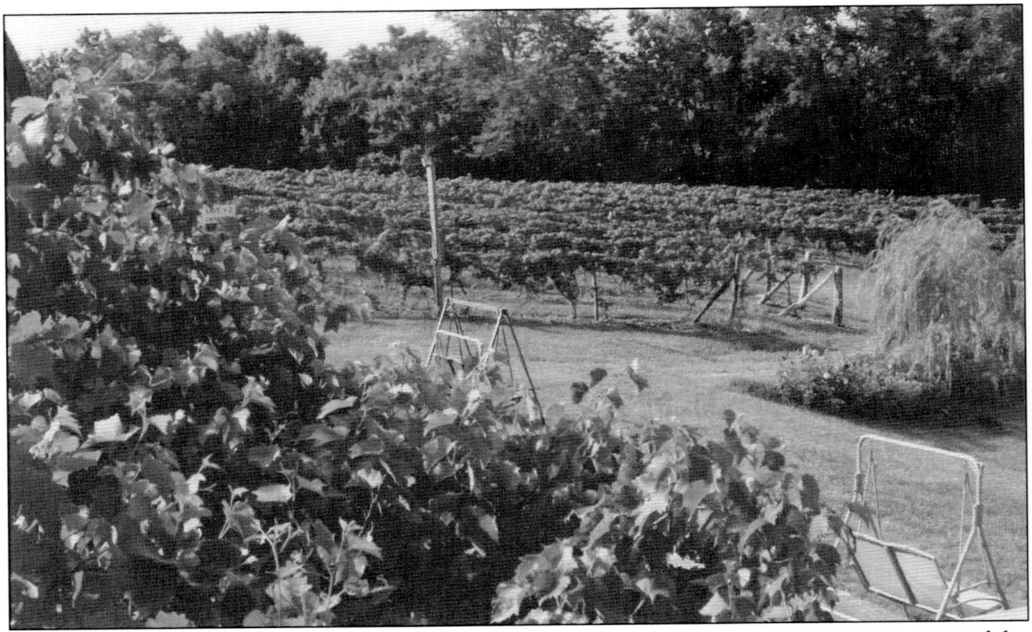

Perched on top of picturesque rolling hills, the Vinoklet Winery provides a panoramic view of the surrounding vineyards and lakes. This charming location provides an atmosphere for a different kind of dinner. Here visitors can sample different wines, walk the fields, relax with a glass of wine by the lake, and grill their own dinner to perfection along with the dinner buffet that is offered. (Courtesy of Don Linz.)

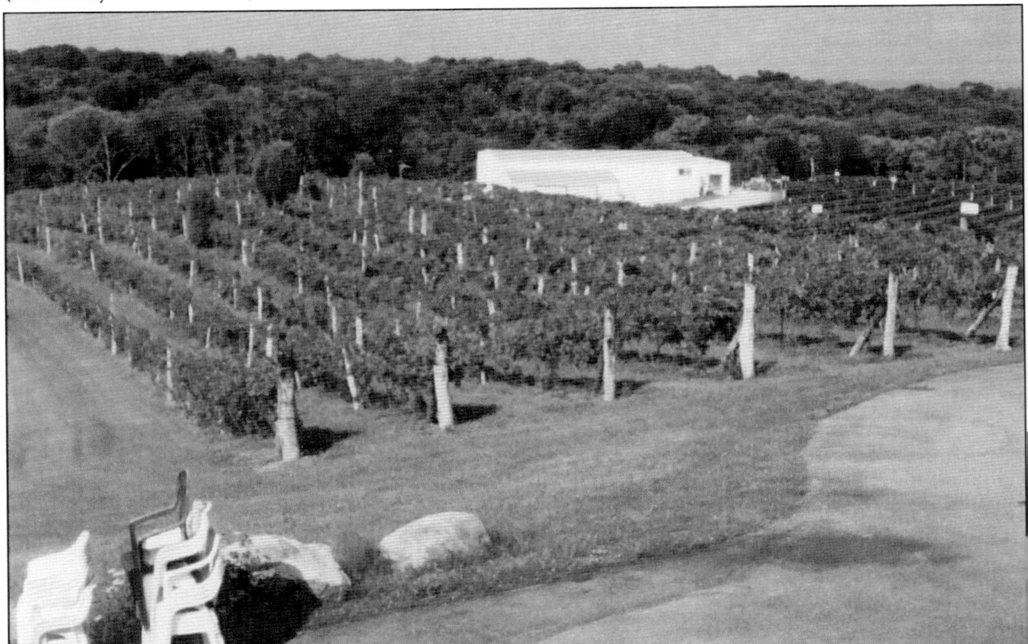

This is another view of Vinoklet's grape arbors and the rolling hills. The building in the upper center is a major part of the winery operation and houses most of the equipment used at the vineyard. (Courtesy of Don Linz.)

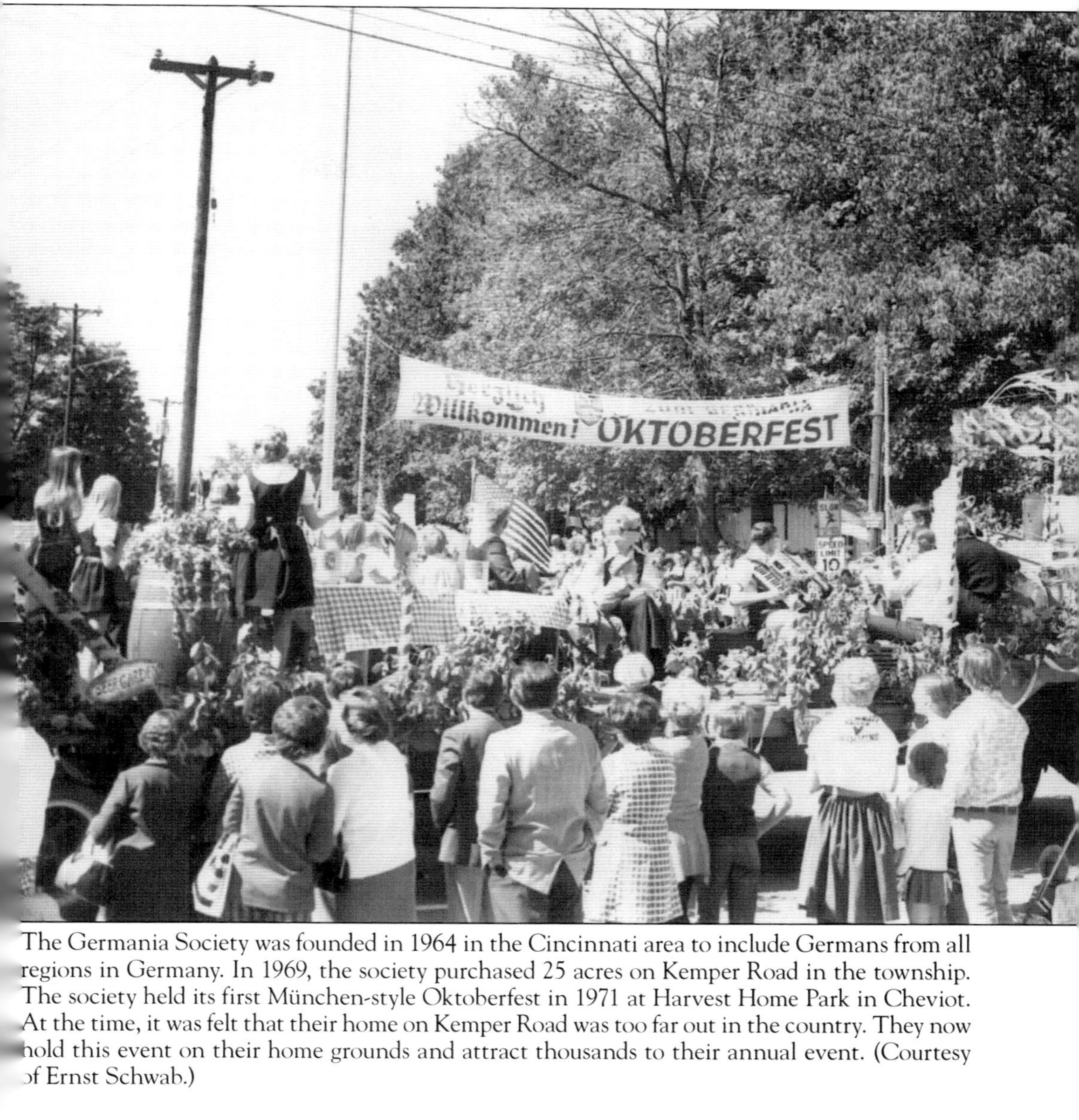

The Germania Society was founded in 1964 in the Cincinnati area to include Germans from all regions in Germany. In 1969, the society purchased 25 acres on Kemper Road in the township. The society held its first München-style Oktoberfest in 1971 at Harvest Home Park in Cheviot. At the time, it was felt that their home on Kemper Road was too far out in the country. They now hold this event on their home grounds and attract thousands to their annual event. (Courtesy of Ernst Schwab.)

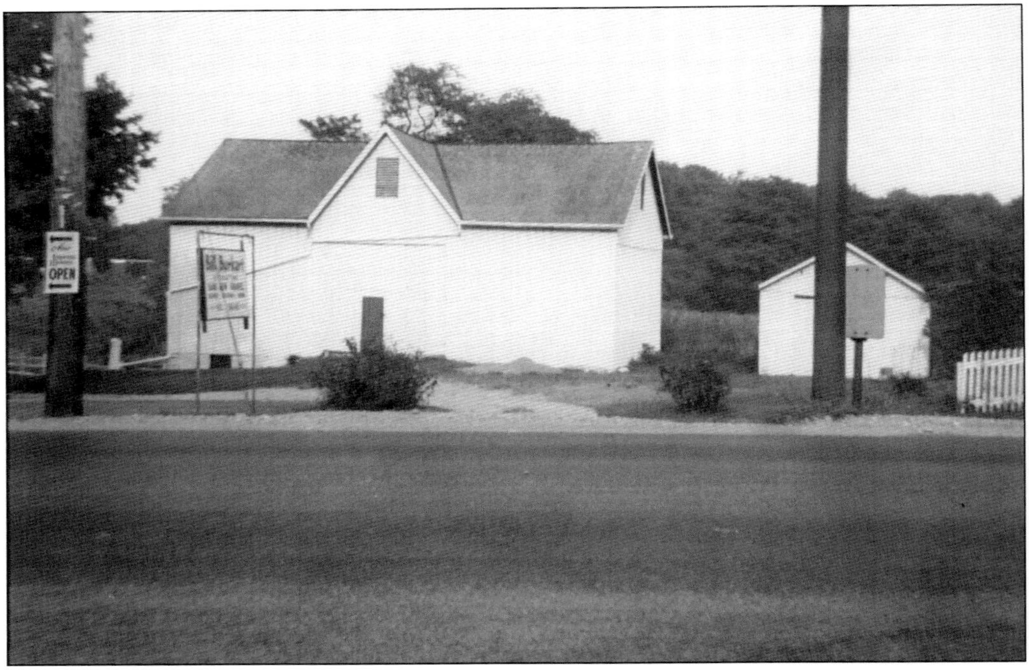

These old barns show the township when it was primarily a farming community. The barns were located on the east side of Colerain Avenue and Poole Road. They have since been demolished. This site is now home to a Midas Muffler Shop. (Courtesy of Mel Blust.)

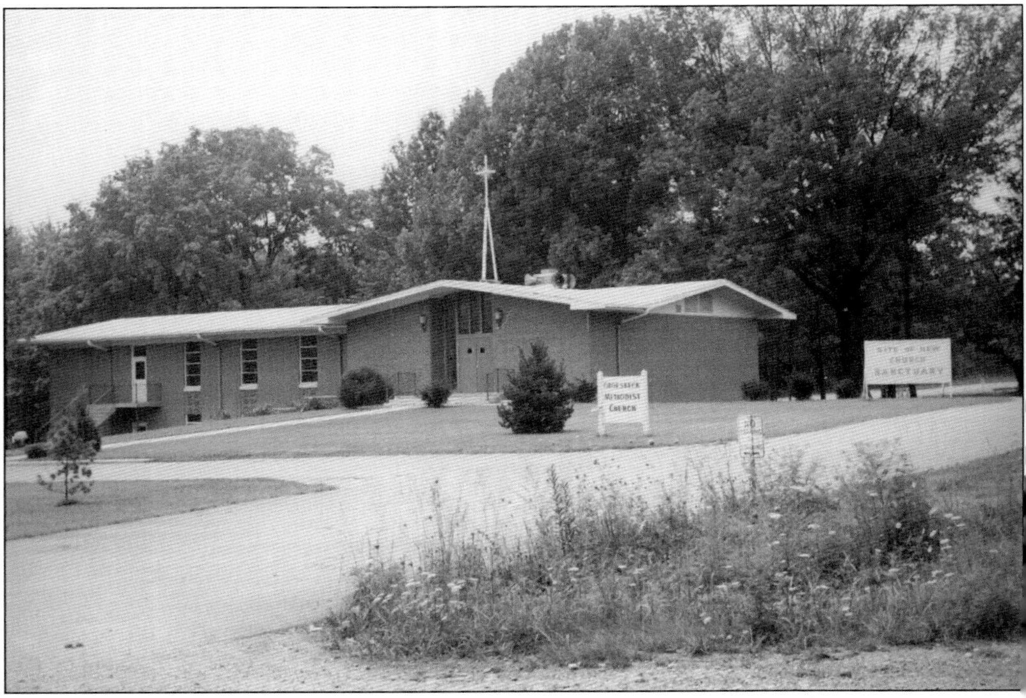

The Groesbeck Methodist Church announces the site of their new church sanctuary at 8871 Colerain Avenue. (Courtesy of Mel Blust.)

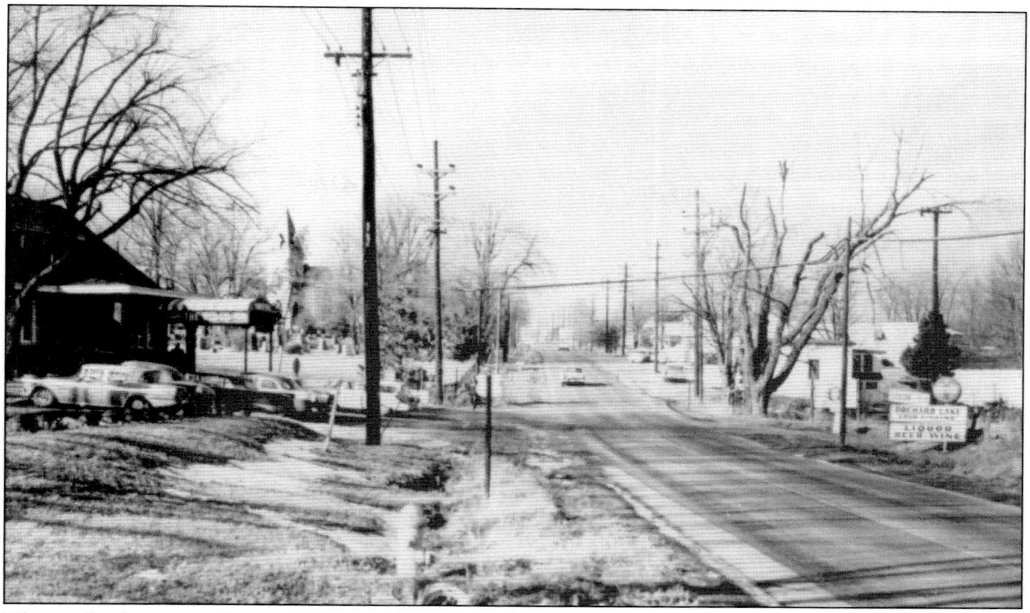

This is looking north on Colerain Avenue at Dry Ridge Road. The Ridge Café is on the left with the old Methodist church (currently the Masonic Lodge) and cemetery in the background. Orchard Lake fishing and tavern are off to the right. With the widening of Colerain Avenue and the construction of I-275, Dry Ridge Road moved north of the old Methodist church. Many of these buildings were removed during construction. (Courtesy of the Coleraine Historical Society.)

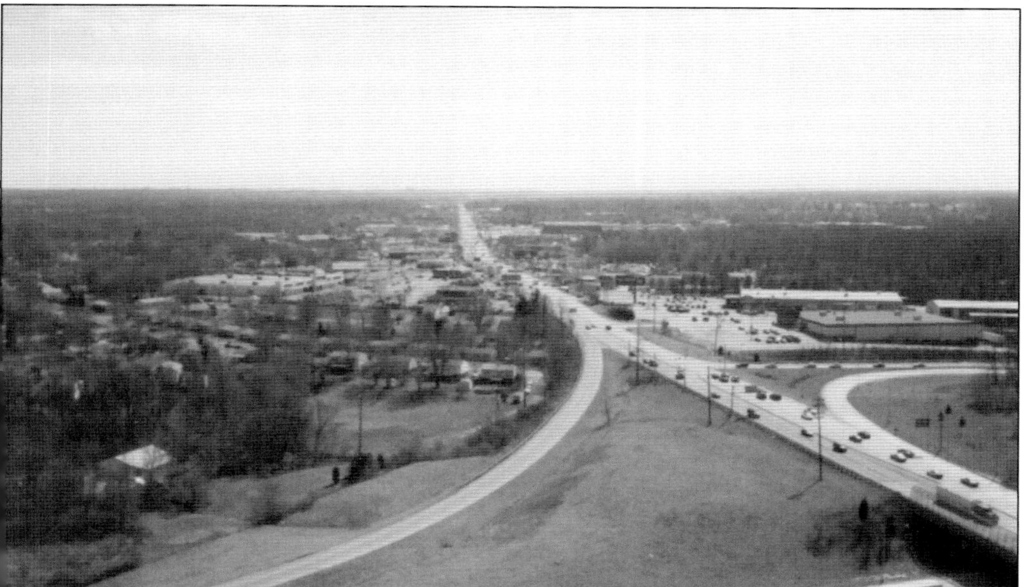

'his is looking south on Colerain Avenue from I-275 in 2000. This picture was taken from the top f the telephone transmission tower at Stehlin's Meat Market. In the center right is the old Furrow's uilding. This area is now the site of the Stone Creek Town Center. (Courtesy of Ed Mohr.)

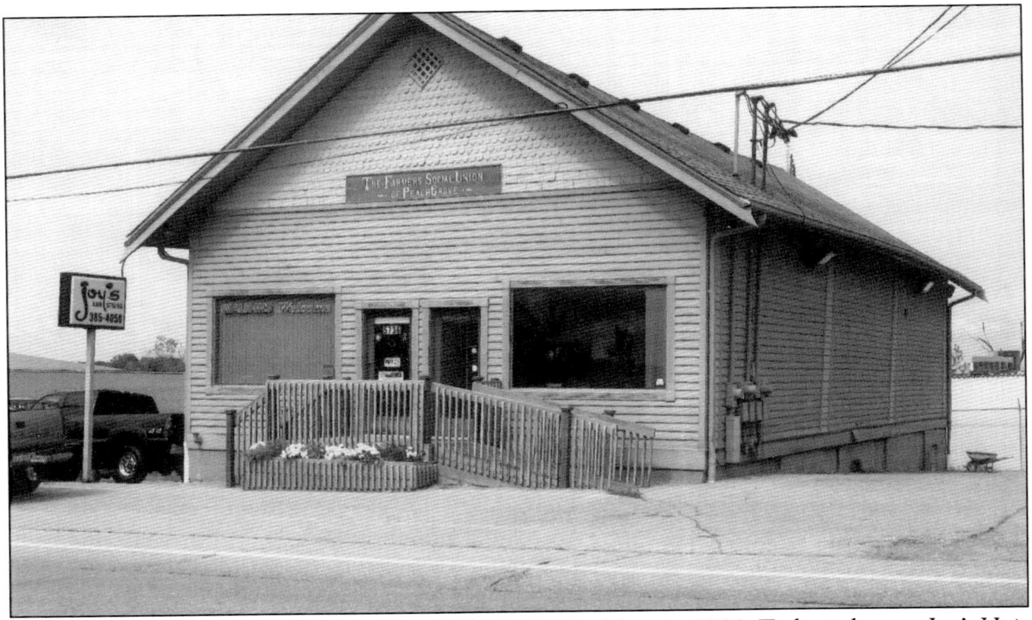

The Farmers Social Union of Peach Grove built this building in 1900. Today it houses Joy's Hair Styling and Ruehl's Plumbing Shop. Earlier it was a gathering place for all kinds of activities. After the nearby Peach Grove School outgrew its facilities, many of the larger entertainments were held at this hall. In the 1920s, St. Paul's Church on Blue Rock Road held its services there while the church was being remodeled. (Courtesy of Don Linz.)

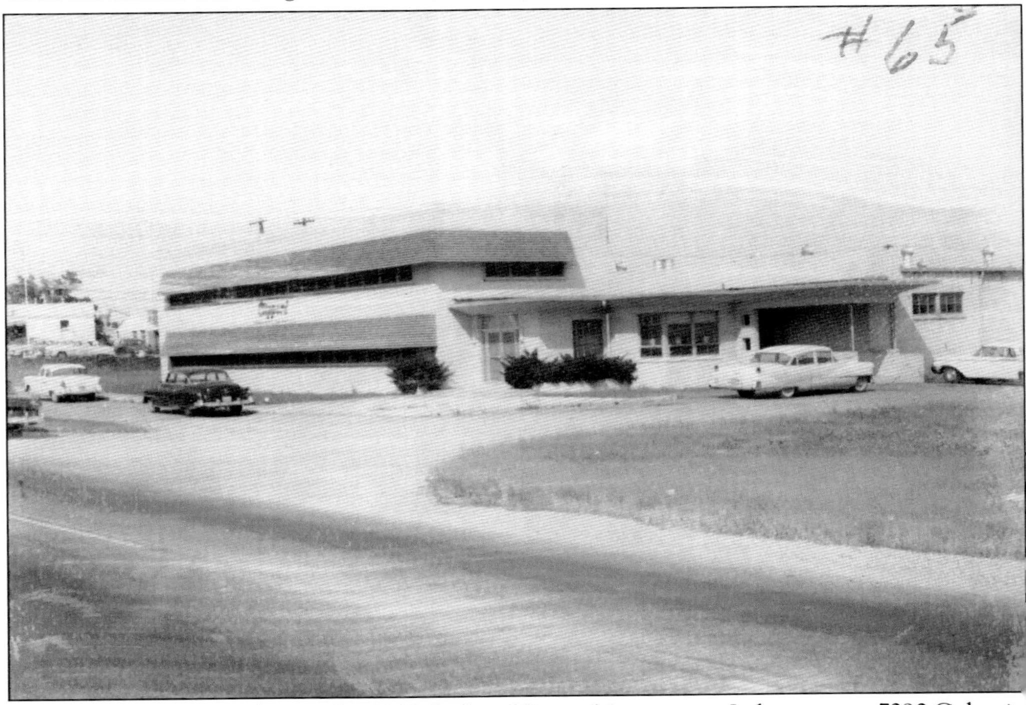

This photograph was taken in the 1960s before Clippard Instrument Laboratory at 7390 Colerain Avenue (pictured) built a major addition to its plant. (Courtesy of Mel Blust.)

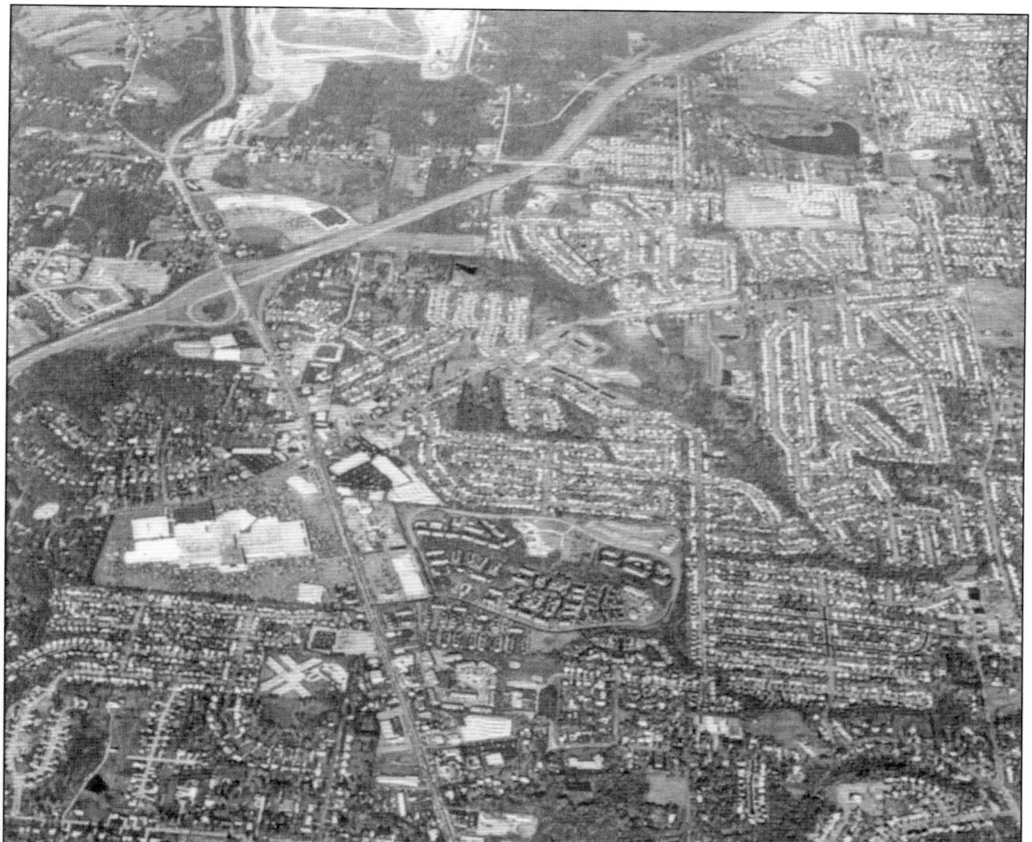

This aerial view shows Colerain Avenue with Ronald Reagan Highway at the bottom and the Rumpke landfill at the top. Notice that the Reagan Highway ended at Colerain Avenue when this picture was taken. That is Northgate Mall in the upper middle left, and I-275 runs across the upper portion of the picture. This portion of Colerain Township was very densely populated. (Courtesy of Mel Blust.)

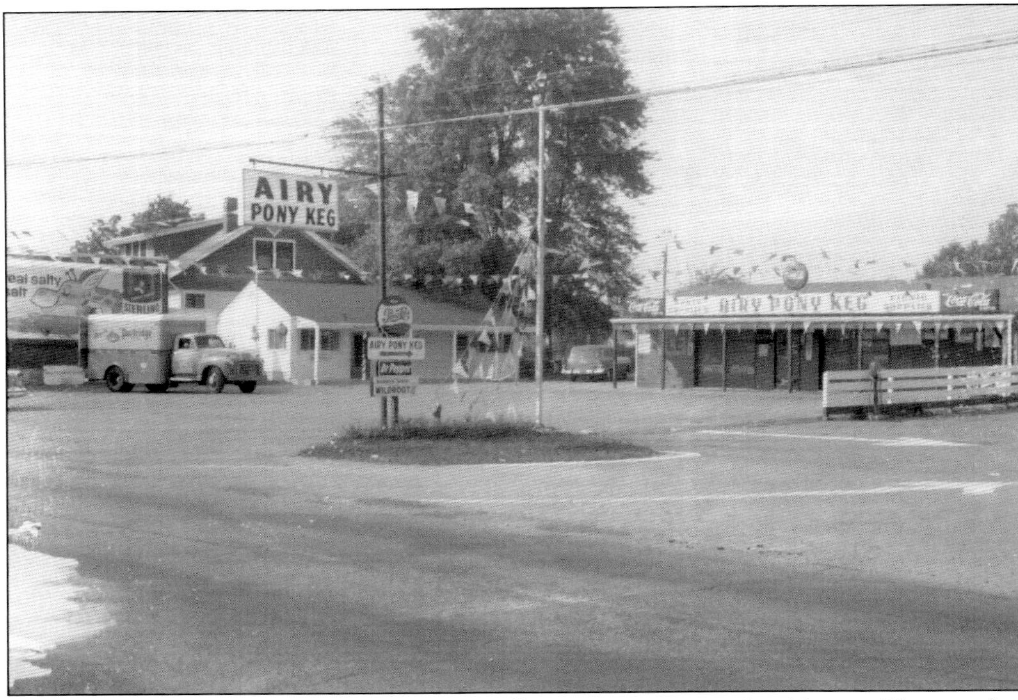

The Airy Pony Keg, pictured in the 1960s, is still serving customers after 46 years. The pony keg was a forerunner of today's convenience stores. It is located at 7549 Colerain Avenue. (Courtesy of Mel Blust.)

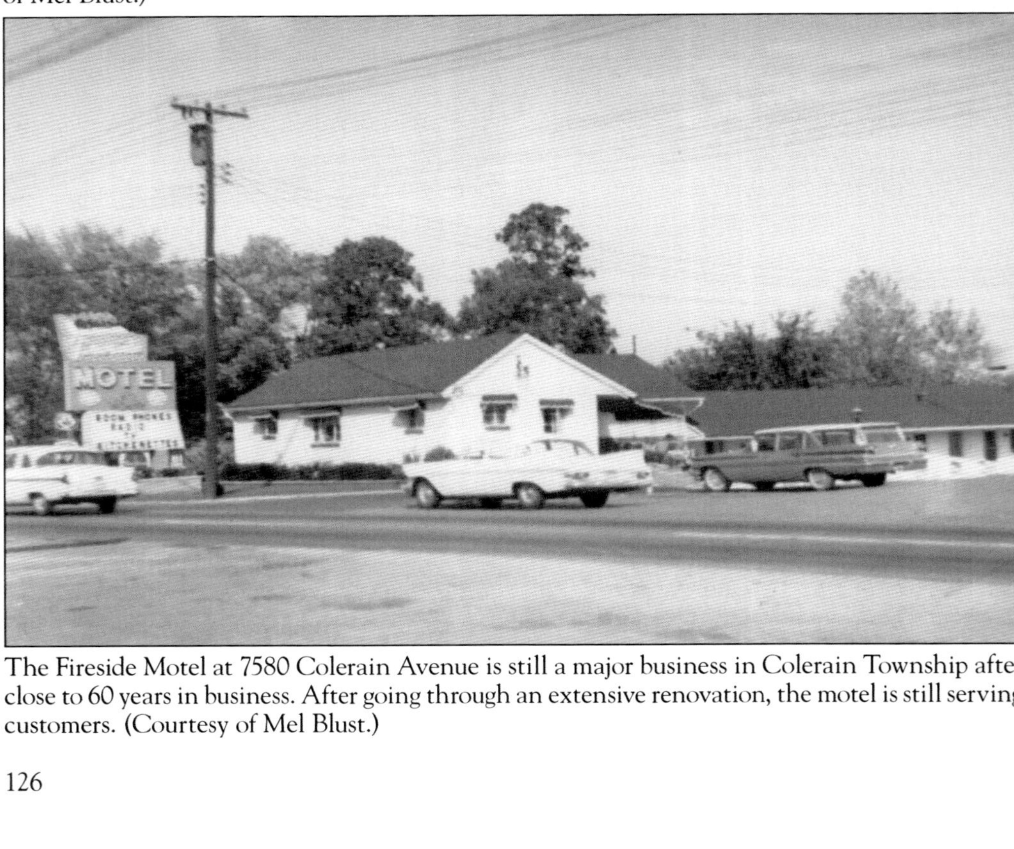

The Fireside Motel at 7580 Colerain Avenue is still a major business in Colerain Township after close to 60 years in business. After going through an extensive renovation, the motel is still serving customers. (Courtesy of Mel Blust.)

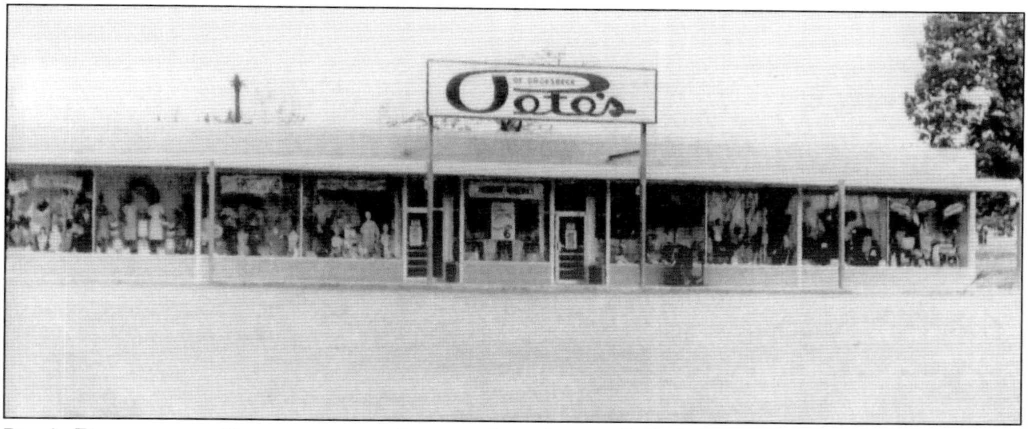

Pete's Department Store was a major retail outlet in Colerain Township for many years, starting in the 1960s. The township was growing rapidly, and Pete's opened a 10,000-square-foot store at the northwest corner of Colerain Avenue and Galbraith Road. (Courtesy of the Coleraine Historical Society.)

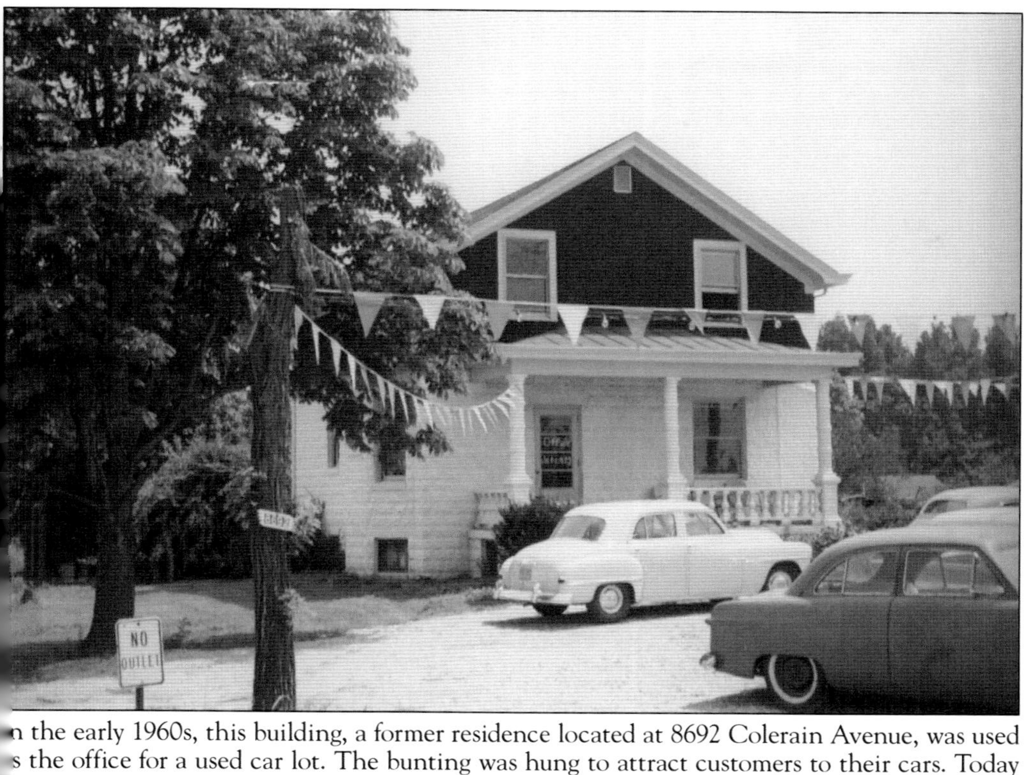

n the early 1960s, this building, a former residence located at 8692 Colerain Avenue, was used s the office for a used car lot. The bunting was hung to attract customers to their cars. Today his site is occupied by Joseph's Car Dealerships, Body Shop. Colerain Avenue has many new and sed car lots. (Courtesy of Mel Blust.)

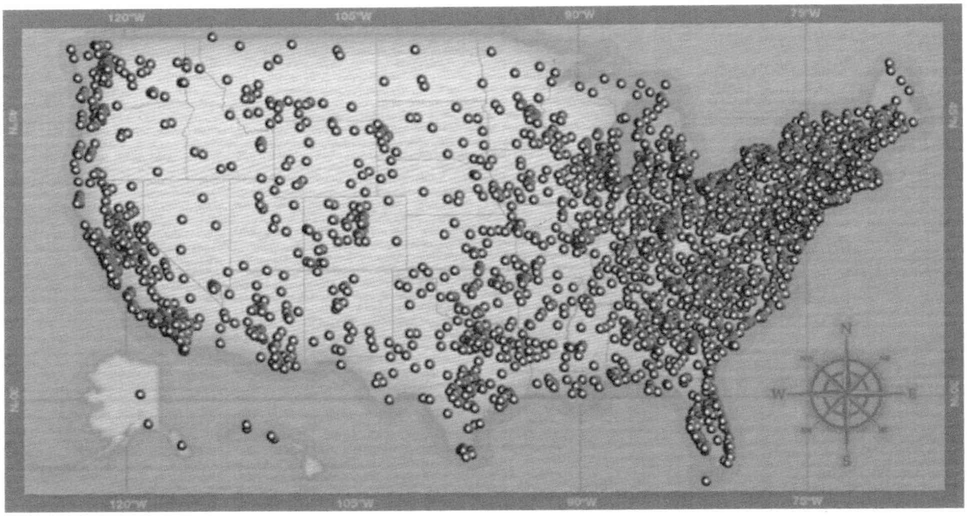

Consistent with our mission to preserve history on a local level, this book was printed in South Carolina on American-made paper and manufactured entirely in the United States. Products carrying the accredited Forest Stewardship Council (FSC) label are printed on 100 percent FSC-certified paper.

MADE IN THE USA